Toyo Nishi

L

Landscape
Architecture

Landscape Architecture

THE SHAPING OF MAN'S NATURAL ENVIRONMENT

John Ormsbee Simonds

McGraw-HILL BOOK COMPANY, INC.

New York   Toronto   London

Book and jacket design by Laurence Lustig

*This text is gratefully
dedicated*

To my professors, whose gifts to all who would accept them were the open mind, the discerning eye, the awakened curiosity, and the compelling vision of that which is higher, wider, deeper, and greater — and worth the striving for . . .

To my colleagues at Carnegie Tech, whose search for truth and whose free and constant interchange of ideas have provided a stimulating climate for discussion and research . . .

To my students, who in thoughtful agreement or in lively dissent have proved a reverberating sounding board and constant source of inspiration . . .

To my associates in practice, for whom each project is a fresh opportunity to achieve that which is more meaningful and to whom the planning of a better environment for living is a strong and vital compulsion . . .

To the late John Knox Shear — architect, philosopher, scholar, and friend — who suggested and encouraged the writing of this work . . .

To my lovely wife, Marjorie . . .

And to my four delightful children, in spite of whom this book was somehow written.

CONTENTS

With especial thanks to:

Miss Katherine McNamara, Librarian,
Harvard University, Graduate School of Design

Miss Nancy Chalfant, Librarian,
Fine Arts Library, Carnegie Institute of Technology

Mr. Wilder Green, Assistant Director, and
Mr. Willard Tangen, Librarian,
Department of Architecture and Design,
The Museum of Modern Art, New York

Robert S. Taylor, Associate Professor,
School of Architecture,
Princeton University

Miss Emily Stenhouse of the Traveling Exhibition Service,
Smithsonian Institution,
Washington, D.C.

Mr. K. Yonezawa, Managing Director,
Kokusai Bunka Shinkokai (Japanese Cultural Institute),
Tokyo, Japan

Margaret Stewart Weaver, secretary
par excellence

Philip Douglas Simonds, brother and partner,
for his generous encouragement and for
his helpful observations and ideas.

FOREWORD

THIS IS A BOOK for architects, landscape architects, and planners, although not exclusively, for it is addressed to anyone (and everyone) whose task it may be to plan a structure, a garden, a park, a city, or any other project in the all-embracing landscape.

But to start at the beginning. . . .

Some years ago the late John Knox Shear, then Head of the Department of Architecture at Carnegie Tech, proposed that the author develop and teach a new course for student architects. This course should, as Shear explained it, "extract from the field of landscape architecture those facts, concepts, and principles of most value to architects, both in their studies and, later, in their professional work."

The course, happily, was well received, and was soon expanded by a second semester that enlarged upon the landscape architectural aspects to include those of most interest to urban and regional planners.

As the years went by the lecture notes were amplified. Hundreds of drawings and diagrams were sketched in the margins, and illustrative photographs were inserted like plums in a pudding. Without intention a book had almost grown into being — but not quite. For a book, so the editors tell us, must be more concise and better interrelated than a series of lecture notes. And so the material has been carefully reworked — pruned, grafted, and trained to a more attractive and useful form. As a proper book, at last, it contains less foliage and more fruit.

Landscape Architecture was intended to meet the demand for a book that would outline the landscape planning process — from the selection of a site to the completed project — in simple, clear, and practical terms.

It introduces us to the *forms, forces, and features* of the natural and man-made landscape;

Discusses *site selection, site analysis,* and the principles of *site planning;*

Deals with the planning of workable and well-related *use-areas;*

Considers the creation of meaningful *spaces,* in terms of use, form, materials, and color;

Examines the planning of optimum *site-structure relationships;*

Explores at length the design of structures and spaces in relation to *pedestrian and automobile traffic;*

Searches out and reviews the lessons of history and contemporary thought on the *composition of structures;*

Describes the design of a *planned community;* and

Reappraises *the city and the region* in terms of planning a more efficient, productive, and pleasant environment for man.

As one might expect, this book on landscape architecture borrows much from the architects and urban planners for whom, among others, it is intended, and deals with an area of the planning process that is in many ways common to all three fields.

It is not intended that the reader of this text will become, per se, a landscape architect. As with training in other fields, proficiency in landscape architecture comes with long years of study, travel, observation, and professional practice. The reader should, however, gain through this book a more keen and telling awareness of the landscape that surrounds him. And he should gain much useful knowledge that will enable him to work and plan in the landscape with greater assurance — and with better results. This, at least, has been our express intent.

PROLOGUE:

*The hunter and
the philosopher*

ONCE THERE WAS a hunter who spent his days tracking the wide prairies of North Dakota with his gun and dog and sometimes with a small boy who would beg to trot along. On this particular morning hunter and boy, far out on the prairie, sat watching intently a rise of ground ahead of them. It was pocked with gopher holes. From time to time a small striped gopher would nervously whisk from the mouth of his den to the cover of the matted prairie grass and soon reappear to dive back into his den with cheek food pouches bulging.

"Smart little outfits, the gophers," the hunter observed. "I mean the way they have things figured out. Whenever you come upon a gopher village you can be sure it will be near a patch of grain where they can get their food, and close by a creek or slough for water. They'll not build their towns near willow clumps or alders for there's where the owls or hawks will be roosting. And you'll not be finding them near a pile of rocks or stony ledges where their enemies the snakes will be hiding ready to snatch them. When these wise little fellows build their towns, they search out the southeast slope of a knoll that will catch the full sweep of the sun each day to keep their dens warm and cozy. The winter blizzards that pound out of the north and west and leave the windward slopes of the rises frozen solid will only drift loose powder snow on top of their homes.

"When they dig their dens," continued the hunter, "do you know what they do? They slant the runway steeply down for two or three feet and then double back up near the surface again where they level off a nice dry shelf. That's where they lie — on their ledges, close under the sod roots, out of the wind, warmed by the sun, close to their food and water, as far as they can get from their enemies, and surrounded by all their gopher friends. Yes sir, they sure have it all planned out!"

"Is our town built on a southeast slope?" the small boy asked thoughtfully.

"No," said the hunter, "our town slopes down to the north, in the teeth of the bitter winter winds and cold as a frosty gun barrel." He frowned. "Even in summer the breezes work against us. When we built the new flax mill, the only mill for forty miles, where do you think we put it? We built it right smack on the only spot where every breeze in the summertime can catch the smoke from its chimney and pour it across our houses and into our open windows!"

"At least our town is near the river and water," said the boy defensively.

"Yes," replied the hunter. "But where near the river did we build our homes? On the low flat land inside the river bend, that's where. And each spring when the snows melt on the prairies and the river swells, it floods out every cellar in our town."

"Gophers would plan things better than that," the small boy decided.

"Yes," said the hunter, "a gopher would be smarter."

"When gophers plan their homes and towns," the boy philosophized, "they seem to do it better than men do."

"Yes," mused the hunter, "and so do most of the animals I know. Sometimes I wonder why."

1

FUNDAMENTALS 1

Man, too, is an animal. He still retains and is largely motivated by his natural animal instincts. If we are to plan* for man intelligently, we must acknowledge and accommodate these instincts; the failure of many an important planning project can be traced to the failure of the planner to recognize this simple fact.

MAN

One characteristic of animal behavior is that it is dominated by the physical presence of what the animal wants or fears. . . . Man has freed himself from this dominance in two steps. First, he can remember what is out of sight. The apparatus of speech allows him to recall what is absent, and to put it beside what is present; his field of action is larger because his mind holds more choices side by side. And second, the practice of speech allows man to become familiar with the absent situation, to handle and to explore it, and so at last to become agile in it and control it.

J. BRONOWSKI

Spiral nebula in Ursa Major

Man, then, is an animal (a *superior* animal, we commonly assume, although neither history nor close observation altogether support this assumption).

If we should stand a bare man in the forest, with his pale skin, weak teeth, thin arms, and knobby knees, he would not look very impressive among the other animals. As an *animal*, the bear with his powerful jaws and sharp claws would clearly seem superior. Even the turtle, as an animal, seems more cunningly contrived, both for protection and attack, as do the dog, the skunk, and the porcupine. All creatures of nature, upon reflection, seem superbly equipped for living their lives in their natural habitat and for meeting normal situations. All except the humans.

Man, lacking speed, strength, and other apparent natural attributes, has long since learned that he can best attack a situation with his mind. Truth to tell, he has little other choice.

Man alone of all creatures has the ability to weigh the factors of a problem and reason out a course of action. He is able, moreover, to learn not only from his own experiences but also from the disasters, the triumphs, and the lesser experiences of untold thousands of his fellows. He can borrow from, and apply to the solution of any problem, the accumulated wisdom of all mankind.

Man's essential strength — the very reason for his survival and the key to all future achievement — is his unique power of perception and

---

* The terms *plan, planning,* and *planner* as used in this text will refer to the planning of man's physical environment — by architect, landscape architect, engineer, and urban or regional planner, working separately, or more ideally, in close collaboration.

3

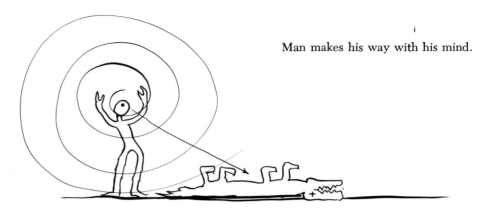

Man makes his way with his mind.

deduction. Perception (making oneself aware of all conditions and applicable factors) and deduction (deriving, through reason, an appropriate course of action) are the very essence of planning.

Down through the dim chaotic ages, the force of man's mind has met and mastered situation after situation, has raised him (through this planning process) to a position of supremacy over all the other creatures of the earth.

Man has in fact inherited the earth. This vast globe on which he dwells is his, his to develop further, to master and control. Surely, man with his twinkling mind should by now have created for himself a paradise upon this earth.

Has he? Have we? What have we done with our natural heritage?

We have plundered our forests.

We have ripped at our hills and laid them open to erosion.

We have befouled our rivers until even the fish and wildlife have been killed or driven off by the stench and fumes.

Our roads and passageways are narrow, tight, and dirty, and crisscrossed to form senseless friction points.

A consequence of the violation of nature

Man is trapped in the arid, fuming workings of his own machinery.

We have built our homes, our schools, our factories tight row on dreary row, with little thought for trees, or clean air, or sunlight.

Looking about us with a clear and critical eye we find much to disturb and shock us. Our cluttered highways, sprawling suburbs, and straining cities offend more often than they inspire or please.

Man, the animal, *Homo sapiens* (the wise one), is a victim of his own planning. He is trapped, body and soul, in the artificial mechanistic environment he has created about himself. Somewhere in the complex process of evolving his living spaces, cities, and traffic ways, modern man has become so absorbed in the power of his machines, so absorbed in the pursuit of his new techniques of building, so absorbed with his new materials of construction, that he has neglected man himself. His own deepest instincts are violated. His basic human desires remain unsatisfied. Divorced from his natural habitat, he has almost forgotten the glow and exuberance of being a healthy animal and feeling fully alive.

Many of contemporary man's ailments — his hypertensions and his neuroses — are clearly no more than the physical evidence of his rebellion against his physical environment and his frustration at the widening gap between the environment he yearns for and the stifling, artificial one we planners have so far provided for him.

Life itself is dictated by our moment-by-moment adjustment to our environment. Science has shown that the life habits of all organisms vary with their environment. Just as the bacterial culture in the petri dish must have its proper and scientifically designed medium for optimum development, and the potted geranium cutting its proper and controlled conditions of growth to produce a thriving plant, so man — complicated, hypersensitive man — must have for his optimum development a highly specialized environment. It is baffling that the nature of this environment has been so little explored. Volumes have been written on the conditions under which rare types of orchids may best

5

be grown; numerous manuals can be found on the proper raising and care of guinea pigs, white rats, goldfish, and parakeets; but little has been written on the nature of the physical environment best suited to the fullest development of man. Here is a challenging field of research, a field that must stem from much further investigation into the nature of man himself.

The naturalist tells us that if a fox or rabbit is snared in a field and then kept in a cage, the animal's clear eyes will soon become dull, his coat will lose its luster, and his spirit will flag. So it is with man too long or too far removed from nature. For man is first of all an animal. He is a creature of the meadow, the forest, the sea, and the plain. He is born with the love of fresh air in his lungs, dry paths under his feet, and the penetrating heat of the sun on his skin. He is born with a love for the feel and smell of rich warm earth, the taste and sparkle of clear water, the refreshing coolness of foliage overhead, and the spacious blue dome of the sky. Deep down inside the soul of animal-man is a longing for these things, a desire sometimes compelling, sometimes quiescent, but always there.

It has been said by many men and in many ways that, other things being equal, the happiest man is the man who lives in closest, fullest harmony with nature. One might then reason: Why not restore man to the woods? Let him have his water and earth and sky, and plenty of it. But is the primeval forest — preserved, untouched, or simulated — the ideal environment for man? Hardly, for the story of man is the story of his unending struggle to ameliorate the forces of nature. Gradually, painfully, he has improved his shelters, secured a more sustained and varied supply of food, and extended control over his environment to improve his way of living.

What alternatives, then, are left? Is it possible that man the inventor, the master planner, can devise a wholly artificial environment in which he can better fulfill his potential and more happily work out his destiny? This prospect seems extremely doubtful. A perceptive analysis of man's most successful ventures in planning would reveal that he has effected the greatest improvements in his environment not by striving to subjugate nature wholly, nor by restoring nature insofar as possible to its original state (as if to make amends), nor by rejecting nature, but rather by harmoniously integrating his works with nature's. He can achieve this integration by modulating structural forms with natural ones, by bringing nature — hills, ravines, sunlight, water, plants, and air — into his areas of planning concentration, and by thoughtfully and sympathetically spacing his structures among the hills, along the rivers and valleys, and out into the landscape.

Man is perhaps unique among the animals in his yearning for order and beauty. It is doubtful whether any other animal enjoys a "view," contemplates the magnificence of a venerable oak, or delights in tracing the undulations of a shoreline. Man instinctively seeks harmony; he is repelled by disorder, friction, ugliness, and the illogical. Can he be content while our towns and cities are still oriented to crowded streets rather than to open parks? While railroads pierce and slice through our communities? While freight trucks rumble past our churches and our homes? Can he be satisfied while our children on their way to school

---

Everything we have to do to live, nature makes us do with lust and pleasure.

SENECA

To be wholly alive a man must know storms, he must feel the ocean as his home or the air as his habitation. He must smell the things of earth, hear the sounds of living things and taste the rich abundance of the soil and sea.

JAMES MICHENER

*. . . and when he looked
At sky or sea, it was with
    the testing eyes
Of the man who knows the
    weather under his skin,
The man who smells the weather
    in the changed breeze
And has tried himself against it
    and lived by it.
It is a taut look but there is
    a freedom in it.*

STEPHEN VINCENT BENET

*These are the Four that are never content, that have never been filled since the Dews began. . . .
Jacola's ° mouth, and the glut of the Kite, and the hands of the Ape, and the Eyes of Man.*

RUDYARD KIPLING

° Jacola is the hyena.

With our mammal lungs we might dive deep into water and survive for some minutes. It is true that man can expose himself to anomalous and unfavorable conditions and endure hours, weeks, years under strain of maladjustment. But the effects of improper adjustment are cumulative, and we pay a penalty for spending long periods of our lives enmeshed and entangled in unnatural, abnormal surroundings, such as we now have to face every day.

. . .

In spite of technological progress, or perhaps because of its spottiness, our man-made environment has shown an ominous tendency to slip more and more out of control. The farther man has moved away from the balanced integration of nature, the more his physical environment has become harmful.

. . .

No doubt the constructed environment as we actually have it is generally full of such visual collision, of turmoil to the eye, and of neglected optical litter. Nervously wholesome surroundings, spaces in which nervous balance can be found and organic life can thus be served and preserved, undoubtedly have their own laws, tuned to a common human physiology. There is that stupendous whole of a constructed environment, which, like fate, envelops civilized life. It must not be allowed to conflict seriously with . . . natural laws.

. . .

We are convinced that patient research, starting from the elementary and progressing to the complex, can indeed gradually remodel the constructed world about us, to reach new levels of organic wholesomeness.

. . .

The ancient idea of a world wisely ordered to function affords an emotional gratification that has shown eminent and long-tested survival value. It is the inspiration for all planning and designing.

RICHARD NEUTRA

must cross and recross murderous traffic ways? While traffic itself must jam in and out of the city, morning and evening, through clogged and noisy valley floors, although these valley floors should, by all right, be green, free-flowing parkways leading into spacious suburbs and the open countryside beyond?

Planners, we must face this disturbing fact — our basic urban, suburban, and rural pattern is ill-conceived, disjointed, and askew. Our community and highway patterns bear little logical relationship to one another and to our topographical, climatological, physiological, and ecological patterns. We have grown, and often continue to grow, piecemeal, haphazardly, without logic. We are dissatisfied. We are puzzled. We are frustrated. Somewhere in the planning process we have failed.

Sound planning, we can learn from observation, is not achieved problem by problem or site by site. Masterly planning examines each project in the light of an inspired and inspiring vision, solves each problem as a part of a total and compelling concept, which, upon consideration, should be self-evident to the planner. Stated simply, <u>the aim of the planner is to create for mankind a better environment, a better way of life</u>. Clearly, if man is a product of environment as well as of heredity, the nature of this environment must be a major concern. This ideal environment would be a world of order and of beauty — a world where tensions and frictions had been in the main dissolved; where man could achieve his optimum development; and where, as the planners of old Peking envisioned, man could live and grow and develop "in harmony with nature, God, and his fellow man."

Such an environment can never be created whole; once created it could never be maintained in static form. By its very definition it must be dynamic and expanding, changing as man's requirements change. It will never, in all probability, be achieved. But planning toward the creation of this ideal environment must be, for all physical planners, at once their major problem, their science, and their goal.

All planning for man must of course meet the measure of his physical dimensions. It must also meet the test and measure of his senses — sight, taste, hearing, scent, and touch. And it must meet the measure of his habits, responses, and impulses. Yet it is not enough to satisfy the instincts of the physical, animal man alone. One must also satisfy the complete human being.

As planners, we deal not only with areas, spaces, and materials, not only with instincts and feelings, but also with concepts and ideas, the stuff of man's mind. Our plans must appeal to man's intellect. They must fulfill his hopes and satisfy his yearnings. Through use of the proper planning concept, we may bring a man to his knees in an attitude of prayer, or urge him to march, or even elevate him to a high plane of idealism. It is not enough to accommodate man. Good planning must satisfy him, delight him, exalt him, and inspire him.

Aristotle in teaching his pupils the art and science of persuasion, held that to appeal to man an orator must first understand and *know* man. And he described to them in detail the characteristics of men and women of various ages and stations. A planner must also know man. Planning in all ages has been for man alone, and has not only mirrored but actively shaped man's culture and philosophy.

7

Fundamentals

Each species produces its own forms which provide for its specific requirements in the struggle for existence. In lower organisms, the process of adaptation is so intimately related to the life cycle that it is hardly distinguishable; in vigorously motile and highly socialized organisms, the central forms are no longer individual, but are produced by the community to provide a wider adaptation to satisfy specific needs. The honeycomb of the bees and the beaver's dam are very advanced examples of such forms. Unlike the insects, however, the environmental adaptation of man is infinitely complicated by his own half-social, half-individual makeup, his uneven evolutionary development, and his distribution over every variety of geographic, topographic, and climatic conditions.

GARRETT ECKBO
DANIEL U. KILEY
JAMES C. ROSE

Our planning professions have a common goal in their aim to determine, to create, and then keep current, optimum relations between people and their environments.

. . .

Like the modern medical practitioner, we seek to bring about in humans a psycho-somatic balance, an all-over health in the whole man. This involves psychological factors as well as physical and physiological ones.

. . .

The success of a work of design may be soundly evaluated only by its over-all long-term effect on the healthy, happy survival of humans. Any other evaluation of architecture, landscape architecture, or city planning makes little if any sense.

NORMAN NEWTON

Our five senses together give us an organ of acquaintance, with which we perceive and experience the outer world.

HANS VETTER

The life of the mind is traditionally divided into three aspects: thinking, willing, and feeling.

BERTRAND RUSSELL

The Greeks and Romans had never bothered about the future but had tried to establish their paradise right here upon the earth.

. . .

Then came the other extreme of the Middle Ages when man built himself a paradise beyond the highest clouds and turned this world into a vale of tears for high and low.

. . .

The Renaissance was not a political or a religious movement. It was a state of mind. In the Renaissance men no longer concentrated all of their thoughts and their efforts upon the blessed existence that awaited them in Heaven. They tried to establish their paradise upon this planet, and truth to tell, they succeeded in a remarkable degree.

HENDRIK VAN LOON

The occupied landscape may be richer by far in all the subtle amenities of the original land if only the designs we apply are . . . becoming to the form as well as to the complexion of the meadows, woods and slopes we presume to compliment. . . . Landscape character should be intensified, not obliterated; and the ultimate harmony should emerge as a blend in which the native quality of the region and the spot still prevails after the inevitable mutilation of the construction undertaken to produce needed roads, buildings and other works of civility and comfort. These "humanized" landscapes are to us the most inviting and beloved, and we are pleased and inspired largely insofar as the whole structure and sentiment of the landscape can be preserved.

. . .

There can be no deviation from the rule that the newly prepared landscape must be . . . a distillate or sublimation of the original myriad forms if it is to be a work of art in the sense of a high art form, timeless and historical.

STANLEY WHITE

Civilizations have risen and fallen without apparently perceiving the full import of their relations with the earth.

LEWIS MUMFORD

From the dawn of China's primitive folk religion, the relationship between man and nature has been conceived as a deep, reciprocal involvement in which each can affect the other. As the forces of nature can bring prosperity or disaster to man, so can man disrupt the delicate balance of nature by his misdeeds, for Heaven, Earth and man constitute a single, indivisible unity, which is governed by cosmic law (tao).

. . .

No boundaries may be drawn between the supernatural world, the domain of nature, and that of man. Hence, if this sensitive organism is to function easily, man must do his part; when he conforms to natural law, society enjoys peace and tranquility; when he transgresses it, both Heaven and nature are disturbed, the intricate machinery of the cosmos breaks down, and calamities ensue.

. . .

Characteristically Chinese, this attitude toward nature pervades all of China's poetry, art and religion, and underlies the thinking of its great Sages whose philosophy is dominated by the notion of Heaven and man functioning in unison. It shines through Confucian ethics where the rules for preserving harmonious relations between man and man are seen as measures to attain deeper harmonies between man and universe. And it is epitomized in the precepts of Lao Tzu who taught that only by subordinating himself to nature's ways could man lead a meaningful life.

THE WORLD'S GREAT RELIGIONS

Rape by the carryall

Modern man with his great knowledge has it within his power to create on this earth a paradise beyond his fondest dreaming. But he is failing. And he *will* fail so long as his plans are conceived in obvious and heavy-handed violation of nature and nature's principles. The most significant feature of our modern planning is not the scale of our structures, nor the scope of our developments, but rather our utter disdain of nature and our seeming contempt for topography, topsoil, air currents, watersheds, and our forests and vegetal mantle. Modern man thinks with his bulldozer, plans with his thirty-yard carryall. Millions upon millions of acres of well-watered, wooded, rolling ground have been blithely plowed under and leveled for home sites, factories, and schools. Small wonder so many of our cities and highways are (climatologically speaking) barren deserts of steel and masonry, and our subdivisions so often hardbaked stretches of treeless sand and shale.

For the moment, it seems, we have lost our touch. Perhaps, before our planning can progress, we must look back. We must regain the old instincts, relearn the old truths. We must return to the fundamental planning wisdom of the gopher building his home and village and the beaver engineering his dam. We must return to the planning approach of the farmer working from day to day — fully aware of nature's forces, forms, and features; respecting and responding to them; adapting them to his purposes. We must rediscover nature.

9

The early rationalists having rediscovered nature, found there were, after all, fixed standards beneath her apparent diversities. They concluded that history might advance through progressive discoveries and clarification of these standards.

JOSEPH HUDNUT

Improbable as it may sound, it is a fact that the contemporary architect or engineer faces few problems in structural design which nature has not already met and solved. By our own standards, her designs are structurally more efficient and esthetically more satisfactory than ours. We should — to paraphrase that forthright pre-Civil War critic, Horatio Greenough — learn from nature like men and not copy her like apes. But the truth of the matter is that we have only recently perfected the means whereby her structures can really be understood.

FRED M. SEVERUD

In Spengler's most moving passage, where he identifies the "landscape" as the base of the "culture", he says that . . . man . . . is so held to it by myriad fibres, that without it life, soul, and thought are inconceivable.

STANLEY WHITE

Roots

10

NATURE

Nature reveals herself to each man according to his interests. To the naturalist, nature unfolds a breathtaking wonderland of spider web, egg mass, and fern frond. To the miner, nature is the tenacious yet prodigious source of minerals — coal, copper, tungsten, lead, silver. To the hydroelectric engineer, nature is a limitless reservoir of power. To the structural engineer, nature in her every guise is an eloquent demonstration of the universal principles of form creation that he seeks to understand and apply to his work.

To the physical planner, nature reveals herself as the eternal, living, formidable, yet beneficent background and base for his every project

*Every process in nature has
its necessary form. These
processes always result in
functional forms. They follow
the law of the shortest distance
between points: cooling occurs
only on surfaces exposed to
cooling, pressure only on points
of pressure, tension on lines
of tension; motion creates for
itself forms of movement —
for each energy there is a form
of energy.
All technical forms can be
deduced from forms in na-
ture. The laws of least resistance
and of economy of effort
make it inevitable that similar
activities shall always lead to
similar forms. So man can
master the powers of nature in
another and quite different
way from what he has done
hitherto.
If he but applied all the
principles that the organism has
adopted in its striving toward
useful ends, he will find there
enough employment for all
his capital, strength and talent
for centuries to come. Every
bush, every tree can instruct
him, advise him, and show him
inventions, apparatuses, technical appliances without number.*

RAOUL FRANCE

*Nature is the basis, but man
is the goal.*

GEORGE SANTAYANA

A plant

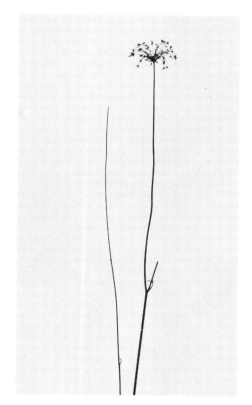

Weeds in snow

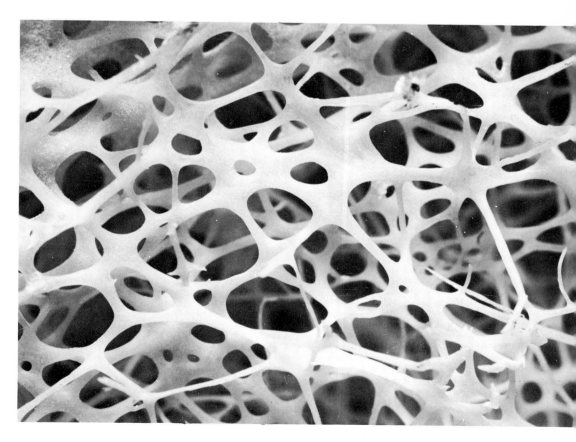

Bone cell structure

and plan. It is fundamental to the success of his planning that he come to know and understand nature. Just as a hunter is at home with nature — drinks of her springs, uses her cover, hunts into the prevailing winds, knows when the game will be feeding on the beechnuts and acorns of the ridges and when on the berries in the hollows, and senses the coming of a storm and instinctively seeks out shelter. Just as a sailor is at home on the sea — reads the shoal, senses the sandbar, interprets the sky, and observes the changing conformation of the ocean bottom. Just so must a planner be conversant with nature, with all her features, forces, and forms. Until, for any major tract of land, local building site, or landscape area, he can instinctively recognize the natural characteristics, limitations, and fullest planning possibilities. And being thus aware, his planning may achieve the conscious development of a system of harmonious relationships.

History shows us inspiring examples of man in control of, yet in harmony with, nature. One such example is the city of Kyoto, Japan.

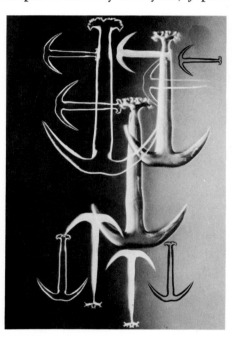

Sea anchors

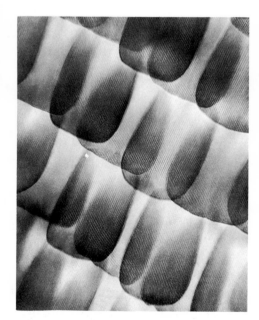

Crystal structure

Overlapping scales of a butterfly

Diatoms

Nature's ingenious process of pollination. As the honey bee lands and presses into the blossom after nectar, it triggers the flower stamen, forcing it down in an arc to make contact with and deposit pollen on the bee's body. Bee, flower, mechanism — what has man made that is comparable?

Interaction between man and environment in the West is abstract, an I – It relationship; in the East it is concrete, immediate, and based on an I – Thou relationship. Western man fights nature; Eastern man adapts himself to Nature and nature to himself. These are broad generalizations and, like all generalizations, should be taken with a grain of salt. But I believe that they may help to explain some of the essential differences out of which the different attitudes of East and West to life and environment develop and which are each in its own right destined to play its part in the transformation of the present and the future.

E. A. GUTKIND

For centuries European art has turned its back on the fundamental conception of nature in art, and Western man has imagined himself and nature as being in antithesis. In reality, his much-vaunted individuality is an illusion, and the truth which the Orient now reveals to him is that his identity is not separate from nature and his fellow-beings, but is at one with her and them.

CHRISTOPHER TUNNARD

Kyoto,
Mountain green,
And water clean.

RAI SANYO

Set amidst a national forest of pine and maple trees, Kyoto overlooks a broad river valley in which clear mountain water slides and splashes between great mossy boulders. Here in ordered arrangement are terraced the stone, timber, and paper buildings of the city, each structure planned to the total site and fitted with great artistry to the ground on which it stands. In this beautiful city each owner considers his land a trust. Each tree, rock, and spring is considered a special blessing from his gods, to be preserved and developed, to the best of his ability, for the benefit of city, neighbors, and friends. Here, as one overlooks the wooded city or moves through its pleasant streets, one realizes the fullest meaning of the phrase, "the stewardship of land." Kyoto is a city of great harmonies, great order, and great beauty, because from broadest concept to smallest detail *it was planned that way.*

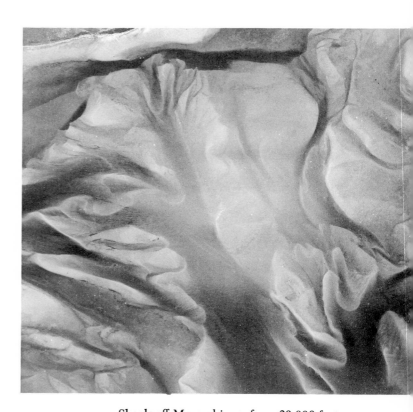

Shoals off Mozambique, from 20,000 feet

Pond lilies

LANDSCAPE CHARACTER

Looking down at the surface of our globe or moving in any direction across it, we find areas where there is an apparent harmony or unity among all the natural elements — ground forms, rock formations, vegetation, and even animal life. We may say of these areas that they possess a naturally produced *landscape character*. The more complete and obvious this unity, the stronger the landscape character.

Let us imagine that we have been dropped into a corner of Utah's great spruce forest. All about us steeply rise wild and rugged slopes of rock bristling with tall spires of green spruce trees that tower against the sky. The deep shadowy ravines are choked with great boulders

Seascape

and fallen trees. Melting snow drips or trickles from the crevices or gurgles underneath the tangled forest duff. White water rushes and foams from high ledge to chasm, cascading toward the stillness of a mountain lake that lies below, deep blue at its center, shading to pale green along its gravelly edges. Here all is harmony, all is complete. Even the brown bear lumbering close to shore is clearly native to this place. The leaping trout, the wading tern, the "caw-caw" of the flapping crow is part of this scene, part of its *landscape character*.

The blazing Arizona desert, the fetid, dripping Georgia swamp, the bleak and desolate arctic tundra, the flat sedge island waterland off Barnegat Bay, each has its own distinctive landscape character, and

15

Dunes

each evokes in the observer a strong and distinctive emotional response. No matter what the natural landscape character of an area, and no matter what the mood it produces in us — exhilaration, sadness, eeriness, or awe — we experience a very real pleasure in sensing the unity and harmony of the total scene. The more complete this unity and harmony, the more complete the pleasure of the observer. The degree of evident harmony or unity of the various elements of a landscape area is a measure not only of the pleasure induced in us, but also of the quality we call "beauty." For beauty by definition is "the evident harmonious relationship of all parts of a thing observed."

Natural landscape beauty is of many varying qualities, which include:

The picturesque	The graceful
The ethereal	The stark
The bizarre	The serene
The idyllic	The majestic
The delicate	The bold

Natural landscape character, too, is of many categories or types, including:

Mountain	Plain	Prairie
Sea	Canyon	Hill
River	Desert	Glen
Lake	Swamp	Stream
Forest	Pond	Valley

Each of these and other types may be subdivided infinitely. A "forest" landscape character, for instance, might be one of the following subtypes:

Oak	White pine	Timberline	Windswept
Beech	Red pine	Swamp	New Jersey river
Cedar	Yellow pine	Rain	New Jersey coastal
Maple	Loblolly pine	Jungle	New Jersey bog
Hemlock	Pinon pine	Tropic	New Jersey dune
Palm	Pitch pine	Arctic	New Jersey ridge
Cypress	Himalayan pine	Alaskan	New Jersey plain
Fir	Scotch pine	Burmese	Rocky Mountain
Cottonwood	Austrian pine	Bornean	Adirondack
Teak	Norway pine	Lebanese	Alpine

Each of the myriad examples that come to mind is itself a distinctive landscape type. For each landscape type, the more closely the object or area approaches the ideal (or has the most of those qualities that we associate with perfection in a given type), the more intense is our pleasure.

The absence of beauty we call "ugliness." Ugliness results from a sensed lack of unity among elements, or the presence of one or more incongruous elements. Since that which is beautiful tends to please and

Cactus forest

Tropic coast

The intensification of the natural landscape character through sympathetic handling of man-made spaces and forms.

17

that which is ugly tends to disturb, it follows that a visual harmony of all parts of a landscape (or any other object or thing in the landscape) is desirable.

With only the visual aspects of site character in mind, it would seem that in developing a natural landscape area we should do all that we could to preserve and intensify its native landscape character. We would therefore eliminate objects that were out of character, and might even introduce objects to increase or accentuate this character.

Elimination of incongruous elements   In all planning, as in life, the elimination of an incongruous element usually effects an improvement.

For example, let us suppose that we have wandered into a giant sequoia forest and stand in silent awe of the tremendous upward thrust of the redwood boles and their imposing, timeless grandeur. And then suppose that on the forest floor we should happen to notice a neatly cultivated bed of pink petunias. These same petunias in a suburban garden bed might make quite a pleasant splash. But to find them here in the redwood forest would first shock and then annoy us. They would annoy us because our experience would tell us that in this natural redwood grove petunias are out of place. They would set up unpleasant visual and mental tensions, and should we come often enough to this place it is possible, even probable, that we would ultimately root them out with the toe of our boot. We would be eliminating an element that was in conflict with the natural landscape character.

An incident from the author's own experience further illustrates this point. As a small boy his summers were spent in a camp on Lake George, a backwoods Michigan lake nestled among the cedars. At the lower end of this lake he found a spot that he came to think of as his private bullfrog pond. It was a clearing in the cattails, jammed with mossy logs and stumps and closed almost tight with the pads of waterlilies. When he waded quietly through the cattails, he would spy huge green-black bullfrogs floating among the pads or squatting dreamily on the logs. These he hunted for their saddles, which were most welcome at the family table. Every day he visited his pond, lying hour after hour on a log, motionless, with a club poised ready for a frog to surface. It was an idyllic world of cedar smell, sunlight, patrolling dragonflies, lapping water, and contentment.

One morning he found that a battered yellow oil drum had been washed into his frog pond by a storm. He pushed it outside the cattails. Next morning it was back. Again he pushed it from the pond, farther this time, but not far enough. Finding it once again floating jauntily among the lily pads, he shoved it out and went for a rowboat. With the anchor rope he towed the drum to the deepest part of the lake, bashed a jagged hole in its top with a broken axehead, and determinedly scuttled it. As he watched it slowly founder he wondered why he had felt such anger at an old, rusty, metal barrel. Years later, when in retrospect the author considered the pond in terms of its landscape character, he realized at last why the drum had had to go — it was a disturbing, inharmonious element in the landscape and had to be eliminated.

Introduction of accentuating elements   If it is true that the elimination of some elements from an area can improve its landscape character, it follows that other elements might be introduced with the same result. To accentuate the landscape quality of one corner of a cactus desert, for instance, we might remove an old tire that had been tossed there and replace it with a clump of fine native cactus plants gathered from the surrounding sandy draws. Or we might plant a single picturesque Joshua tree that would reflect and articulate the area's mood or landscape expression.

The elimination of an incongruous element will usually effect an improvement.

To sum up then, the landscape character of any area may be developed or intensified by eliminating any negative elements and by accentuating its positive qualities.

To improve a landscape or land area intelligently we must not only recognize its essential natural character but also possess knowledge that will enable us to achieve the optimum development of that character.

During the Ming dynasty in China this art was so highly refined that within a single garden of a few acres one might experience lofty mountain scenery, a misty lake shore, a bamboo grove at the edge of a quiet pond, a pine-sheltered forest overlook, and a cascading waterfall. And, through the skill of the planner, the transition areas between viewing points were so masterfully contrived as to be fully as pleasant and dramatic as the major views themselves.

Use as a landscape factor   Up to this point we have considered the natural landscape as something to be *observed,* in some of our larger parks for example, or along scenic railways or parkways, or at the better resort hotels. In such cases man becomes a micro-visitor, permitted only to enter an area inconspicuously, observe respectfully, and leave unobtrusively. But there are relatively few areas that can be reserved in their pristine state or developed solely to display the most of their natural beauty.

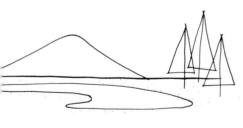

In the natural landscape man is an intruder.

Man generally considers land in terms of use. At this point he is quite likely to ask: "What's all this talk about beauty? Let's not go off the deep end here, we have to be practical. Let's forget this hocus-pocus about landscape character. What I want to know is, how can this piece of land be *used?*"

But the hard, cold fact of the matter is that the most important factor in considering the use of land is a thorough understanding of its landscape character in the broadest sense. For the planner must first of all comprehend the physical characteristics and nature of the site and its extensional environment, before he can accomplish any of the following:

1. Determine those projects or uses which are clearly unsuitable and which would be incongruous not only on the immediate site but also in the surrounding landscape area, and thus appear to be misplaced, misfit, and (by definition) ugly. Such an improper use would be disturbing not only esthetically, but practically, for an unsuitable use senselessly forced upon a landscape generates frictions that may not

These Japanese homes of hewn timber and thatch seem strangely at home here and "in character" with the ancient cedar grove that is their site.

Esthetic values are inherent in things. Things emanate from them, somewhat as odors do from food or from flowers. And like tangible perfumes they determine our sensitive or emotional reaction. Esthetic impacts influence us at all moments. Consciously, or in most cases subconsciously, they provoke friendly or hostile reactions. They escape from our rationalistic strongholds, directly back to our emotions and therefore out of our control. This means esthetic values are no simple trimmings but indeed have their roots in the depth of the soul. Their impact on man's decisions reach even into the most practical problems, into the shaping of things of daily use — cars, bridges — and above all, of our human environment.

SIEGFRIED GIEDION

20

only destroy the most desirable qualities of the landscape area but may preclude proper function as well.

2. Recognize those uses for which the site is best suited and which will exploit its full potential.

3. Introduce into the area only those uses which are appropriate.

4. Apply and develop these uses intelligently in studied relationship to the landscape features.

5. Ensure that the planned project comprises a complex of functions ideally related to the best features of the site.

6. Ensure that these applied uses are integrated to produce a modified landscape that is visually and functionally beautiful. Since man instinctively turns to that which is beautiful, and since a normal function of a project is to attract and please man, beauty is often considered an element of function.

It is visually beautiful, there is a visual harmony among all its parts — *it looks good.* It is functionally beautiful, there is a functional harmony among all its parts — *it works well.* It has unity, it is beautiful — *I like it.*

Anything planned in the landscape affects the landscape. Each new plan application sets up a series of reactions and counterreactions not only about the immediate site but upon its extensional environment as well. This environment may extend for many miles in a given direction and include hundreds of square miles.

Chicago, for example, was long known to many mainly in terms of its arduous, straining highway approach from the east. A new freeway leading to its eastern city limits has, for these people, converted Chicago into a seeming wonder city.

A single malodorous tannery on the shore of Lake Charlevoix in Michigan has destroyed the valuable resort potential of Boyne City and a large area of one of Michigan's most beautiful lakes. Although suited to its immediate site, this ill-considered enterprise has desecrated its extensional landscape environment with tragic consequences.

A new park plaza in Pittsburgh has changed the city's center of gravity and created a refreshing oasis in the typical urban desert of asphalt and masonry.

Mellon Square, Pittsburgh, Pa.

In considering the development of any area of the earth's surface we must realize that this surface is a continuous plane. Any project applied to this plane affects not only the specific area but all flow past the project site. Each new addition or change, however minute, imposes upon the land certain new physical properties and visual qualities. It can thus be seen that the planner is engaged in a continuing process of creating or modifying landscape character.

Landscape organization   The natural landscape is in repose, a repose of equilibrium. It has its own cohesive, harmonious order in which all forms are an expression of topography, climate, natural growth, and the forces of nature. In the primeval forest or upon the open plain, man is an intruder. If he penetrates the wilderness by trail or road, he may either "roll with" the topography and the natural features of the site and develop expressive harmonies, or he may "buck" the landscape and generate destructive frictions and tensions. As man's activity in an area increases, the landscape becomes more and more organized; *well* organized if the organization is one of fitting relationships, *poorly* if the organization is chaotic or illogical. The organization of any area may entail a concentration of its natural landscape character, an integration of natural and man-made elements, or the creation of a wholly man-made complex of spaces and forms. In any case, the commendable plans are those that develop systems of unity, that effect a resolution of all man-made and natural forces and thus create a new landscape of order and repose.

The planned landscape   We are all familiar with landscape areas in which there is a man-made or artificially produced harmony of all the parts. There come to mind certain cities, parks, riverways, and highways. We recall pleasant stretches of New England farmland, Western ranch country, a dreamy Virginia plantation. A Columbia River salmon-fishing village has its own distinctive man-made landscape character, as does a residential park, a military installation, or a well-conceived subdivision.

In or near such areas, we experience a sense of well-being and pleasure. We say that a certain city, highway, or park is pleasant, quaint, delightful, picturesque. What we probably mean is that we subconsciously sense in the landscape certain qualities of fitness, order, or harmony that appeal to us. These we like. Other places or areas of disorder, confusion, friction, "bad taste," and "poor planning," are "ugly" and bother us. If we were travelling, we would bypass these areas. We would prefer not to live in them.

The negative qualities of such areas are those we would attempt to eliminate by planning. The positive qualities of such developed areas are those that we would strive to retain and emphasize. It would seem to follow that a fundamental principle for designers or planners developing any area, ranging from completely natural to completely man-made, would be this: To preserve or create a pleasing site or landscape character for an area, a harmony of all the various elements or parts must be retained or developed.

We make much of this word "harmony." Do we imply that everything should blend with or "get lost" in the landscape as through

To me the quest of harmony seems the noblest of human passions. Boundless, as is the goal, for it is vast enough to embrace everything, it yet remains a very definite one.

LE CORBUSIER

22

protective coloration or camouflage? No. But the planner, in developing any area of the landscape, from a small plot to vast acreage, must analyze the suitability of the land for any proposed use and then utilize its positive qualities to the maximum. If the completed project seems to blend or harmonize with the landscape, it is the happy result of an inspired design rather than the primary aim of an uninspired designer.

Contrast   Early in our study of design we learn that the best features of an object can often be emphasized through contrast. This principle applies as well to planning in the landscape, and is exemplified in the bridges designed by the brilliant Swiss engineer, Maillart.

The Garden of Rikugi-En, Tokyo, Japan

All who have seen them marvel at the delicacy and grace of the white reinforced concrete arches that span the wild mountain gorges in Switzerland and Bavaria. Surely the lines and materials of these structures are foreign to the natural character of the craggy mountain background. Are they *right* for such a location? Or would the bridges have been more suitable in native timber and stone?

In our national parks bridges are usually constructed, whenever possible, of indigenous materials. Although some may quarrel with this concept (and many do — with some reason), it has produced many bridges of high design quality and spared the park-using public from

23

The Salginatobel Bridge, Switzerland, leaps the wild chasm as lightly and as surely as a native stag.

more of the typical fluted and fruited cast-metal or balustraded cast-stone monstrosities that clutter up so many of our American river crossings.

With his bridges Maillart has simply and forthrightly imposed a necessary function — a highway crossing — on the natural landscape. He has expressed with logical materials and refreshing clarity the force-diagram of his structures. Moreover, by sharply contrasting his elegantly dynamic bridges and the rugged mountain forest, he has dramatized the strongest qualities of each. The gorges seem more wild, the bridges more precise, more eloquent.

To understand this application of the principle of contrast, we may recall that color theory states that to produce an area of greenest green, we should add a fleck of scarlet. And to make a spot of scarlet sing with fire, an artist contrasts it with the greenest possible background.

It follows that before introducing contrasting elements into a landscape we should fully understand the nature of those qualities that we wish to accentuate. The contrasting elements would then be contrived to heighten these landscape qualities. Conversely, if we want to emphasize certain qualities of the structure or element introduced, we should search the landscape for those qualities that will effect the desired contrast.

A second principle in the use of contrast, as illustrated by the work of Maillart, is that one of two contrasting elements must clearly dominate the other. One is the feature, the other the supporting backdrop. Otherwise, with two contrasting elements of equal power, visual tensions are created that weaken or destroy, rather than heighten, the pleasurable impact of the visual experience. A contrasting element, then, is properly planned as either feature or foil.

We have said that to preserve or create a pleasing site or landscape character for an area, we should so develop it that all elements work in harmony to effect the greatest unity of site expression. We find some striking and fine examples that would seem to violate this principle: Maillart's bridges, for instance, and Frank Lloyd Wright's "Falling Waters" at Bear Run. These structures at first appraisal would

The precision and whiteness of the concrete forms contrast boldly with the natural forms, colors, and textures of the site. Yet the structure seems at home here. Why? Perhaps because the massive cantilevered decks recall the massive cantilevered ledge rock. Perhaps because the masonry walls that spring from the rock are the same rock tooled to a higher degree of refinement. Perhaps because the dynamic spirit of the building is in keeping with the spirit of the wild and rugged woodland. And perhaps because each contrasting element was conciously planned to evoke, through its precise kind and degree of contrast, the highest qualities of the natural landscape.

Cone nebula, 2,000 light years away

seem to be completely alien to their specific landscape areas. Yet with study one senses in each example an insistent and compelling quality of fitness. With thoughtful analysis, the root of this fitness may be discovered — a fitness of spirit, purpose, material, or form that has brought into harmonious unity the structure and the site.

NATURAL FORCES, FORMS, AND FEATURES

We have come to learn through the centuries that the spinning orb on which we live is a minor planet suspended in limitless space — an infinitesimal speck of matter in the universal scheme of things. Yet it is our world — vast, terrible, and wonderful to us, a world of marvelous order and boundless energy. It is illumined and warmed in rhythmic cycles by the heat of our sun, bathed in a swirling atmosphere of air and moisture; its white-hot core is a seething mass of molten rock, its thin, cool crust pocked and creased with hollows and ridged with hills, mountain ranges, and peaks. The greater part of its area is covered with a saltwater sea, which ebbs and flows with heaving tides and is swept to its depths in vast and intricate patterns of current.

The earthscape   From the ice-sheathed poles to the blazing equator, the earthscape varies endlessly. Wandering over it for something close to a million years, man, the earth-dweller, has learned first to survive and later to thrive through a process of adaptation. This process, if wisely continued, should gain for him an ever-improving way of life. The study of the man-nature relationship is as old as man himself. In long-range perspective it is probably still a very young science, but, all things considered, it is perhaps the most basic science of all.

In our lifetime, man has for the first time scaled earth's highest peak, sounded its deepest ocean trench, and penetrated outer space.

Underwater atomic explosion at Bikini. Man has learned to unleash the power contained within the atom. Now he must learn constructive ways in which he may apply this boundless energy.

We are tempted to believe that we have *conquered* nature. There are those who hold that in the era ahead, man will finally subject nature to his control. Let us not delude ourselves. Nature is not soon to be conquered by puny man.

Conquer nature! How can we conquer nature? We are — blood, bone, fiber, and soul — a very part of nature. We are spawned of nature, rooted in nature, nourished by nature. Our every heartbeat, every neural impulse and every thoughtwave, our every act and effort is governed by nature's all-pervading, all-embracing law. Conquer nature! We are but fleeting traces of life in nature's eternal process of evolving life and growth. Conquer nature! Far better that we turn again to nature's way, to search out and develop an order consonant with nature's vast and intricate systems of order. That our living may tap the vital nature forces. That our cultural development may have orientation. That our form-building, form-organizing, and form-ordering may have meaning. That we may know again the rich pulsing harmonies of a life attuned to nature's way.

The history of man's progress on this earth is the history of his increasing understanding of nature's vast vitalities and powers. The wisdom of our wisest men is no more than their comprehension of nature's simplest laws. The knowledge of our most perceptive scientists is gained through their faint insight into the wonder of nature's plan. Our labored development is the development of those sciences that reveal to us a way of life more closely attuned to nature's immutable way.

Men living in the forests and jungles and on the sea are extremely sensitive to the ways of nature and instinctively shape their pattern of life in harmony with nature's rhythms, cycles, and orders. They have learned that to violate nature is to court inevitable disaster.

Years ago the urge to wander to strange new lands led the author to live for some months on the lonely, wonderful island of British North Borneo. There he came to be profoundly impressed by the tremendous joy of these people in simply being alive — exultantly healthy and happy sons and daughters of nature. On the islands all men live not only close to nature, but *by* nature. Their whole life is guided day by day and hour by hour, by the sun, the storms, the surf, the stars, the tides, the seasons. A full moon and ebbing tide give promise of successful milkfish spearing on the shoal. The wheeling and screeching of the birds gives warning of an approaching storm. In the quiet freshness of early morning a hunter may draw his little daughter to his side and, crouching, point a long brown finger to the peak of Mt. Kinabalu looming high above the palm fringe. "Tiba, little Tiba," he may caution. "Look now at the clouds on the mountain top. Soon will be blowing and raining there and the streams will be rushing full. So stay away from the banks today and play at home with your mama."

On the islands, clearly, the closer a man's life is attuned to nature the happier that man's life will be. But not only on the islands. This observation is fully as true of our life on our farms and in our suburbs and cities. Sometimes we tend to forget this salient fact as we go about our living and planning for living. And often this forgetting is the root of much distress:

The city of Toronto, for example, is surging northward for no apparent reason, into an area seven miles from its harbor on Lake Ontario. Aside from the convenience and more favorable topography of the lakeshore, which has ample room for expansion, the summer temperature at the lake is often 26° cooler and the winter temperature 30° warmer than at the areas of new building concentration.

A popular ski resort in Pennsylvania was laid out with the major runs facing south and southwest, directly exposed to the melting winter sun. On the same property, undeveloped northerly slopes have excellent snow two days for every day the planned slopes are usable.

In the city of Wheeling on the Ohio River, 25 per cent of the developed area of the city is inundated at least once every thirty-five years, and extensive areas of the built-up city are flooded out every three and one-half years on the average.

An experienced architect has noted that not 1 per cent of all the buildings in his modern city give evidence of having been planned with any regard for prevailing winds, solar radiation, or natural thermodynamics. The meanest thatched hut in Borneo is planned in well-considered relation to all three. It is a jolting experience for most of us to reflect on the natural landscape potential of the site on which our city was built and to realize the pathetic results of our efforts at city building.

Tao, the Way — the basic Chinese belief in an order and harmony in nature. This grand concept originated in remote times, from observation of the heavens and of nature — the rising and setting of the sun, moon, and stars, the cycle of day and night, and the rotation of the seasons — suggesting the existence of laws of nature, a sort of divine legislation that regulated the pattern in the heavens and on earth. It is worth noting that the original purpose of ritual was to order the life of the community in harmony with the forces of nature (tao), on which subsistence and well-being depended.

MAI-MAI SZE

27

The Great Wall of China, raised in the third century B.C. against the invasion of the Tartars, extended for 1,400 miles along the northern border. This fortress-wall, built through supreme effort, was a deliberate attempt to extend and reinforce the protective conformations of the natural mountain ridges.

Gravity is one of man's greatest enemies. It has shaped man himself, conditioned his body as well as his thoughts, and put its unmistakable stamp upon his cities. Thus in the narrow winding valleys of the world, life is a continual battle with gravity. One must live on the valley's bottom, or "fight the slope" until his dying days.

GRADY CLAY

If our planning is basically a studied attempt to improve our environment, it would seem only logical to plan in full awareness of nature's forces, forms, and features — the sweep of the sun, the air currents, the peaks and hollows of the earth, rock and soil strata, vegetation, lakes and streams, watersheds, and natural drainage ways. And this awareness should obviously entail planning in harmony with these elements of nature. If we disregard them, we will engender countless unnecessary frictions, and preclude those experiences of fitness and compatibility that can bring so much pleasure and satisfaction to our lives.

Major landscape elements   There are major natural landscape forms, features, and forces that we can alter little, if at all. We must accept them and adapt ourselves and our planning to them. These unalterable elements consist of such major forms as mountain ranges, river valleys, coastal plains, lakes, oceans, and other dominant topographical components; such major features as precipitation, frost, fog, the water table, and seasonal temperatures; and such major forces as winds, tides, sea and air currents, erosion, the process of growth, solar radiation, lightning, and gravity.

We can only analyze these overwhelming landscape elements to determine their potential effect on our planning, and then, if we are wise, shape our plans in fullest possible harmony with them. Such considerations are fundamental to the placing of cities, the zoning of a community, the projected alignment of highways, canals, or railroads, the siting of industries, the orientation of a simple structure, and to all planning projects.

The majority of the notable planning projects of any age demonstrate with striking clarity the adaptation of a structure or function to a major natural landscape element in such a way that the best qualities of natural element and function complement and dramatize each other. In such works not only the functional elements but the natural elements as well appear to have been designed by the planner, as in one sense they were, for both are well considered and integral parts of the total plan concept.

Minor landscape elements   There are also *minor* natural landscape elements that we as planners *can* modify — hills, woods, streams, and swamps for example. In the developing of any natural landscape area or feature there are four general courses of action. Let us illustrate these varying approaches with the hill as an example:

Preservation of the natural form   The landscape character of a hill may be such that its best use is realized if it is carefully preserved from change. Thus the hill may best function as a park feature, a game preserve, or the focal point of a residential community. In its undisturbed state it might better produce its crop of timber, maple sap, nuts, or fruit. Throughout our country we find huge tracts of land that have been set aside in their natural state as game preserves, parks, and forests. Many a village or town in Japan is nestled among hills or islands that have for centuries been left undisturbed by decree, in the best interest of the community.

A harbor, a town, and every structure within it fitted to the natural topographical forms. Here man and nature are seen working together in harmony.

Preservation

Accentuation

Alteration

Destruction

The four alternatives in the development of a hill

Destruction of natural form A hill or knoll may be destroyed or removed by grading; it may be split with a deep highway cut; it may be covered with water; or it may be buried in construction. If any such treatment is proposed, its original landscape character need not be considered as a design factor.

Alteration of natural form The basic landscape character of a hill may be altered or changed completely by modifying its shape through grading, by removing its natural cover of trees, or by planting, terracing, or otherwise developing it. Such changes may be detrimental — as with a denuded, eroded, or mined-out hill — or may effect an improvement, as in the terraced hills of Bali, with their contoured rice paddies, quiet pools, and clear trickling water.

Accentuation of natural form The essential landscape character of a hill may be accentuated. Its apparent height and ruggedness may be increased to such a degree, for instance, that a small hill may appear to be mountainous.

Let us assume for example that we are the owners of a small resort hotel in New Hampshire to which summer guests come each season for fresh air, rest, and quiet. We have noticed that many of the guests, when they tire of the rocking chairs set on the wide front porch, walk the easy path to the top of a nearby hill, from which they can view the countryside. It occurs to us that the hill has become an important part of resort life, and we decide during the off season to "improve" the hill by giving it more interest and affording more of a climb to its top.

First, by transplanting a patch of hemlocks, we block off the easy

The Red Rocks Theatre, Denver, Colorado. This theatre of dramatic power and beauty has been conceived in studied harmony with the existing rock formations of the native terrain.

Mont St. Michel, France, surrounded by its rushing tides and reached only by a single causeway. Here seawalls, fortifications and structures extend the island forms — producing a man-made character more insular than the natural island.

path that led toward the hill and break a new path to a spring that bubbles from the rocks at its base. From this spring a view is opened up across the steepest face of the hill to a weathered old pine, which hides the hilltop beyond. A rough trail leads up through a pile of lichen-splotched rocks to a fallen tree trunk, on which the hiker can sit and rest. Already the hemlocks and spring and rocks have given a new perspective to the hill. Next the path leads easily *down* through a native birch clump to the far side of the hill, to a place where the only way ahead leads steeply up the roughest, wildest part of the hillside. Up, down, and around the trail leads, from ferny ledge, to fallen tree, to view, and finally to a point where it breaks out on top. There we place a rough slab for a seat, in the shelter of wind-blown juniper.

Next summer when our guests leave the porch and set out to "walk" to the hilltop, they find themselves hiking and climbing over a beautiful natural terrain they have never seen before. Through tangled wild grape cover, around narrow granite outcrops, pulling themselves from rock to rock, they carefully pick their way until they finally break out at the very top. They have made it! Nothing, they may think, as they rest enjoying the view, is more exhilarating than mountain climbing. While 500 ft. away and 200 ft. below them, the oldsters sit rocking on the wide front porch and looking placidly out at "the hill." For our purpose we have eliminated the negative aspects of our hill and accentuated its positive qualities.*

Any natural landscape area can be developed in this way — a mountain-side, a valley floor, an island, a river, a bay.

Years ago the author was engaged by the Michigan State Department of Parks to plan some recreation areas. His first assignment was to develop a site in northernmost Michigan as a State Park for tourists, who would come to camp and experience the joys of "wilderness living."

31

* Adapted from Hubbard and Kimball's *Landscape Design*

Upon arrival at the park site, he found a large white "Public Park" sign at the entrance of a farm road that led in through a flat field of wild carrots to a trailer parking lot beside a muddy pond. Not much of a "wilderness campsite."

The planner's first step was to spend several weeks exploring the tract to become aware of all its natural features, good and bad. His aim was to exploit these features to the fullest. He planned, in short, to accentuate the native landscape character of the site.

As a first step in the development of the park area, the entrance road was moved from the open field to the thickest stand of balsam. Here a rough trail was carved through the rock and snaked up a winding ridge between the tree trunks, so that a camper's car or trailer could just squeeze through. The yellow clapboard caretaker's cottage with its red window boxes was demolished and replaced with a log cabin at the base of a tremendous old white pine, the most magnificent tree in the whole park. This step was taken because the campers' first impression of the park would be of this tree and the cabin in its shadow, and first impressions are usually the most lasting.

The main attraction of the park, a spring-fed pond, was drained, scooped out, and developed as a swimming pond with a clean sand and gravel bottom. Above it, a large area of water was impounded to form a settling basin, and here the marsh birds, muskrats, and other wildlife could be seen from a timber bridge that was arched across the dam. At the lower end of the swimming pool a second bridge was built across

The jagged ruins of Dunluce Castle in Ireland extend the natural rock conformation into the very sky — an ancient structure conceived in full harmony with nature's forces and forms.

The precise lines of this structure and the rough character of this rocky slope are both drama-tized by their well-planned juxtaposition.

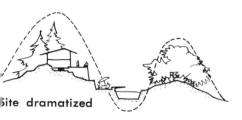

The natural site profile

Site negated

Site dramatized

The essence of land planning for any project:

1. Seek the most suitable site
2. Let the site suggest plan forms
3. Extract the full site potential.

the waterfall and spillway where large speckled trout could be seen as they rolled and swam in the sparkling water below.

Trails were slashed through the densest cover and between the most jagged ledges. Every point of interest in the area was strung on the new trail system like a bead.

In one of the most remote areas, a colony of beavers inhabited a stream where they had built a dam. Much thought was given to the best way of displaying these shy creatures, a prize in any park. It was decided that to view them, the hikers must find their way along an un-marked game trail as it threaded tenuously through a deep cedar swamp, until, from the sloping trunk of a great fallen tree that overhung the dam, the hikers could look down to "discover" the beaver workings below them.

In the development of such a landscape area or feature, the skillful planner should focus on the essential effect he desires to convey (one inherent in the raw materials with which he is working). By emphasis, by articulation, by creating a suitable sequence of revealment, he will lead the observer to discover for himself the natural elements of the landscape and thus exact its maximum pleasurable impact.

Man-nature plan   The world is richer for those memorable places where man has planned his life and his structures in full accord with nature's forms and forces. There come to mind as examples:

The Rhine River valley with its vineyards, farms, villages, small factories, beer gardens, boating clubs — all oriented to and planned in spirit with the flowing river.

The lovely Italian villas terraced down the steep, wooded slopes above the dazzling white sands and azure waters of Lake Como.

33

The Swiss alpine villages fitted to their mountainside, their lush meadows, their torrents, and their precipitous roads.

A cluster of Tahitian rhumas braced among the coco palms at the edge of a quiet lagoon.

A study of such examples should convince us that in the developing of any natural landscape area or feature the planner must by analysis determine its greatest potential effect on, or contribution to, his proposed project. He must then conceive and develop his plans to achieve between natural elements and imposed function the best possible relationship.

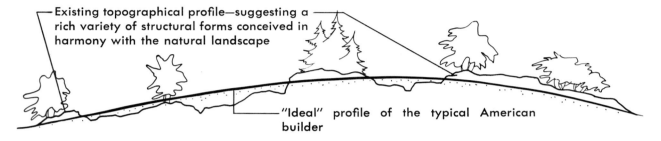

Existing topographical profile—suggesting a rich variety of structural forms conceived in harmony with the natural landscape

"Ideal" profile of the typical American builder

The Code of the American Subdivider and Homebuilder
(as it would seem to the casual observer)

Axiom 1. Clear the land; Axiom 2. Strip the topsoil (or bury it and haul in new if this saves one operation); Axiom 3. Provide a "workable" land profile (that is, as flat as possible); Axiom 4. Conduct all water to storm sewers (or else to the edge of the lot); Axiom 5. Build a good wide road — inexpensive but wide; Axiom 6. Set the house well back for a big front yard; Axiom 7. Keep the fronts even (this looks neat); Axiom 8. Hold to a minimum sideyard; Axiom 9. Throw on some lawn seed.

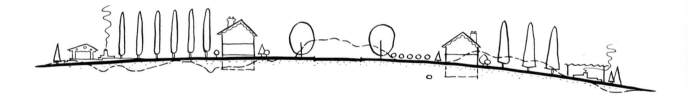

The American Suburbanite Dream
(as seemingly interpreted by the suburban builder and by our present building restrictions)

A revised topography by courtesy of the bulldozer and carryall. The boulders are buried, the natural cover stripped, the brook "contained" in storm sewer or culvert. The topsoil is redistributed as a four-inch skin over sand, clay, or rock. There sprouts a new artificial fauna of exotic nursery stock.

This is our man-made paradise.

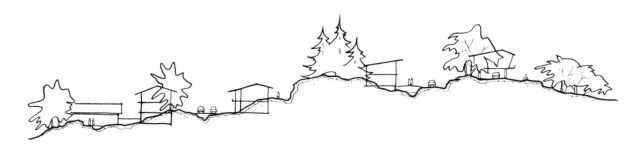

A better way is building *with* nature and in compression, which provides the human scale and charm we find so appealing in the older cultures where economy of materials and space dictated a close relationship of structure and landscape form.

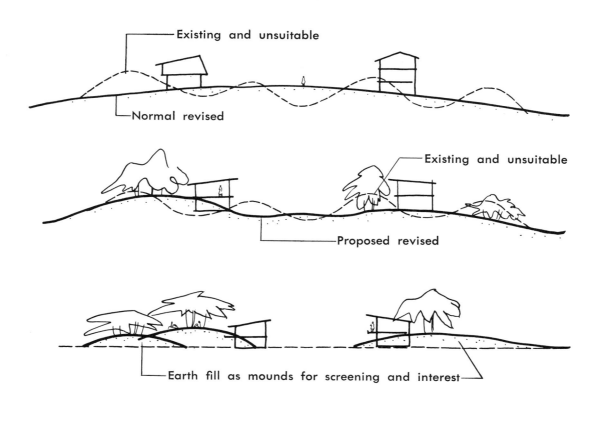

Existing and unsuitable

Normal revised

Existing and unsuitable

Proposed revised

Earth fill as mounds for screening and interest

Regrading to provide backdrop and baffle

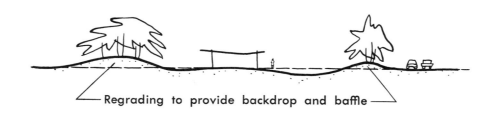

If we must use our earthmovers to create a new landscape (and sometimes we must) let us use them to create a landscape of topographical interest and pleasant and useful forms.

MAN-MADE FORMS, FEATURES, AND LINES OF FORCE

We have considered *natural* landscape elements and their importance to the planning process. Man-made forms, features, and lines of force are major planning factors too — often far outweighing the natural elements of a project site.

As we look at any roadmap, we find it criss-crossed with lines of various kinds and colors that we recognize as highways, minor roads, streets, railroad or streetcar tracks, ferry boat routes, and even subways. These lines seem innocuous enough on paper. But those of us who have pounded along with the streaming traffic of a turnpike, or stood

35

by the tracks as the "Limited" roared by, or tried to maneuver a catboat through the churning wake of a ferry, will agree that the map lines that show their path indicate powerful man-made lines of force. Such lines are useful, yes, but also lethal. Every fifteen minutes someone in the United States is killed by an automobile, and the incidence of serious injury is much higher. It must occur to us, if we ponder these facts, that we planners have as yet failed to treat traffic with the proper respect, or else we have not yet learned to design our traffic ways with imagination and foresight.

There are countless other man-made features in the landscape that, if perhaps less dramatic, still have great effect on our planning. A trunk-line sewer buried in the earth may pose an insurmountable problem in one case and in another may be a major asset, and the same may be said of a gas main or a high-voltage power transmission line. To understand the importance of such factors better, we might list those man-made forms, features, or lines of force that would deserve thorough consideration in the siting of a typical project, say a downtown hotel. Such factors would include:

Street width and alignment
Established street grades
Projected street improvements
Gas pressure and capacity
Sanitary sewer location
Sanitary sewer capacity
Sanitary sewer invert elevations
Storm sewer location and size
Streetcar access
Bus routing
Proximity to bus terminal
Proximity to railroad station
Proximity to airport
Railroad noise
Traffic noise and fumes

Projected use of property by authorities
Zoning use restrictions
Zoning height restrictions
Zoning setback restrictions
Deed restrictions
Existing structures to be demolished
Underground mines or construction
Adjacent structures — height, type, use, materials, and character
Neighborhood character
Man-made view or vistas

This list may seem long, yet we have not mentioned general site aspect, nor mineral rights, nor the difficulties posed by high-pressure utility mains, conduits, and underground cables that are expensive to relocate or remove. Nor have we considered a satisfactory pattern of automobile and pedestrian access from the standpoint of volume and type. We might well be concerned with the relation of the proposed hotel to such facilities as theatres, shopping centers, office buildings, restaurants, parks, and other hotels. Any single one of these man-made elements of the community might spell the success or failure of our project.

The list of factors considered would, of course, vary with different projects — motel, dairy, golf course, or civic auditorium, for example.

36

A prescribed planning procedure   We planners, then, must also contend with major, man-made landscape elements. How do we proceed? Assuming the element to be, for instance, a mainline railway, we might:

Consider the positive factors we may utilize — private freight sidings, favorable raw material and finished product shipping rates, proximity to passenger station, availability of the utilities that service the railroad, and so on. We would then so devise our plans as to take full advantage of the positive aspects of the railroad.

Consider the negative factors. If the railroad (in relation to the proposed project) is a total liability, take the bold steps necessary to move the railroad. Such a procedure, involved as it may be, is often the prescribed clinical procedure in community planning or replanning operations. If moving such a dominant feature is not feasible and the feature has a telling and unfavorable impact on a proposed project, it will often prove wise to move the project to a more favorable site. If unable to remove either the disturbing element or the project, the planner must conceive his project in such a way as to best nullify the offending features of the railroad and to best realize its advantages. An ingenious solution has often converted a liability into an asset.

Villa Gamberaia   To the east of Florence is the war-ravaged shell of a beautiful country villa, Gamberaia, built in 1610 by Gamberelli for the Duke of Zenobi Lapi, and, until recently, considered one of the most perfect in all Italy. Yet when it was planned many said that the site was in all ways impossible and that the villa should never be built. In many ways these critics were right, for most of the natural and man-made elements of the landscape seemed detrimental. The property was unusually small. It was split by a busy trade road with its attending confusion and dust. The property to the north of the road was steep and rocky. The buildable area had only a passable view to the south, and the major view, to Florence and the cathedral, lay to the west — into the hot, cruel, slanting rays of the evening sun.

But for reasons that would seem all too familiar to the planner of today, the Duke was determined to build there. As he forcibly declared:

He already owned the property.

It had belonged to his family and had sentimental value.

There were few better sites available, and they were frightfully expensive.

On the other hand, if he didn't use this property, who knows when he could sell it.

Besides, he wanted his villa right here.

Time was of the essence. He must waste no more time in hunting a better site. He must get this program rolling.

He had engaged a good architect to build it here, and if this architect couldn't do it, the Duke would find another one who could.

One can imagine Gamberelli roaming the site, noting each facet of the landscape, carefully observing each tree, each rocky outcrop, each varying sector of the view. At last he felt confident that the unfortunate features of the site could be minimized by skillful handling and that the commendable features of the site could be accentuated to create a delightful villa. After all, the passing road did provide good access to Florence; there was a view of the city; the land did slope generally to the south for warmth in the early spring and late fall. The northern cliff, although craggy, was covered with gnarled and picturesque trees. Best

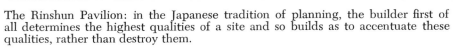

The Rinshun Pavilion: in the Japanese tradition of planning, the builder first of all determines the highest qualities of a site and so builds as to accentuate these qualities, rather than destroy them.

Interlocking wood post with stone base

of all, a mountain stream could be tapped to provide a flow of that most essential element, clear, cool water. Gamberelli set to work.

To connect the divided property and to provide a point of high interest at the road, he constructed across it a great walled ramp supported by a wide, deep arch through which traffic could pass. Near its base he fashioned a fountain basin where travellers could pause and be refreshed. In the shaded court thus formed by the walls and steep road shoulders he set the entrance gate that would lead to the house and gardens. The residence he fitted to the solid rocky contours of the slope, raising it above the entrance gate for privacy and a command of the best exposures.

Southward from the structure he leveled a garden panel, which terminated at an arched wall of clipped trees. The wall of trees effectively screened all but a selected arc of the southerly view, and this sector of view was brought into sharp focus and modulated into a rich montage by the dark green arches of architecturally treated foliage.

To the east, and parallel with this panel, Gamberelli developed a long axis through the tangled trees and across the road by a ramp, to sculpture and a quiet pool set amidst tall cypress trees at the extreme limit of the Duke's land. This long axial vista not only completed the unification of the split property but gave a pleasant impression of great distance and expansive freedom within the limited property confines. Moreover, the rigidly towering cypress and the narrow vista thus created accentuated, by telling contrast, not only the wild but also the precipitous natural character of the site.

The ultimate principle of landscape architecture is merely the application and adjustment of one system to another, where contrasting subjects are brought into harmonious relationship resulting in a superior unity called "order."

STANLEY WHITE

While the western view was unpleasant in late afternoon, Gamberelli must have reasoned, it was most pleasant for the rest of the day. This view was screened from the other garden areas, but from the west terrace it was displayed in full sweep. In the evening, after the sun had dropped behind the horizon, the western sky, ablaze with high color or muted in pastel twilight, served as a backdrop to Florence and her bridges, domes, and spires; then, from the terraced gardens of Gamberaia, with their splashing fountains and scent of boxwood and lemon trees, the view was of such haunting beauty that it could not soon fade from the memory of those who saw it.

The changing landscape   The most constant quality of the man-made landscape is the quality of change. Man is forever tugging and hauling at the land. Sometimes senselessly — destroying the good features of the land as he found it. Sometimes intelligently — developing a union of function and site with such sensitivity as to create a landscape improvement, as at Villa Gamberaia. Each time man-made elements, tangible or intangible, are imposed, wisely or unwisely, on a land area, it must be reconsidered by the planner in the light of its revised landscape character.

The physical planning of any land area is a continuing process. It is forever seeking the best expression of that function or complex of functions (present or anticipated) best adapted to the natural and man-made elements of the environs.

39

THE SITE

2

FOR EVERY SITE there is an ideal use. For every use there is an ideal site.

SITE SELECTION

If we as planners are concerned with wedding a proposed function to a site, let us first be sure that the parties are compatible. We have all seen structures or groups of structures that seem foreign to their site. No matter how excellent these structures or how well contrived their plan, the total result is disturbing and unpleasant.

It would seem obviously foolish to site, for instance:

A shopping center without adequate parking space
A farm without a source of water
A tavern near a city church
A new fabricating plant with no room for storage or expansion
A school fronting on a major traffic artery
A roadside restaurant with zero approach-sight distance
A new home at the end of a jet landing strip
A meatpacking plant upwind of a suburb
An apartment building thirty feet above a mined-out seam of coal.

Each would seem, on the face of it, doomed to failure. Yet each, to the author's knowledge, has been attempted. It is reassuring to those of logical mind to note that in the due course of events each has been subjected to disrupting strains, scathing antipathies, or bankruptcy — all rooted in the choice of an inappropriate site for the given use.

In far too many cases, a project has started with the planner's acceptance of an unsuitable location. This is a cardinal planning error. An important, if not the most important, function of a planner is the sometimes delicate, sometimes brutal task of guiding the entrepreneur to the selection of the best possible site for his project.

A symphony of flowing horizontal planes

Alternative sites   Of all men concerned, we, as experienced planners, should be the most capable of determining the detailed site requirements for a given venture; we should be the most keenly aware of all site features and their relative importance; and we should be the best

41

qualified to weigh the relative merits of alternative locations. <u>First,</u> <u>clearly, we must know what we are looking for. We must thoughtfully,</u> <u>perhaps even tediously, list those site features that we consider necessary</u> <u>or useful for our proposed project</u> — be it a power dam, a new town, or a frozen custard stand. <u>Next we should reconnoitre. We should scout out</u> <u>the whole territory for likely locations.</u> For this job we have a number of helpful tools, such as aerial photographs; U.S. Geological Survey maps; roadmaps; transportation maps; planning commission data; redevelopment authority data; zoning maps; chamber of commerce publications; plat books; and city, county, township and borough maps.

Of these, the U.S. Geological Survey maps warrant special mention. They may often be purchased locally at map or stationery stores, or they may be ordered directly from the U.S. Geological Survey Office, Washington 25, D.C. An index may be obtained that shows which map should be ordered for a given location. Several series are available, at different scales, but the one most often useful to the planner is the 7.5-

U.S. Geological Survey

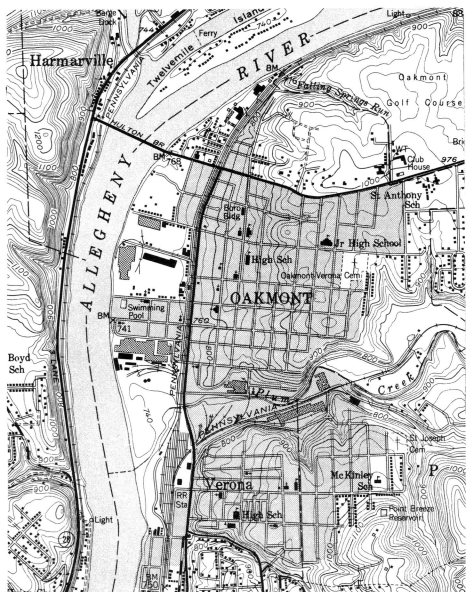

minute series, in which each map (or quadrangle, as they are called) covers an area of about 55 sq. mi. at a scale of 1 to 24,000, or 1 in. to 2,000 ft. These survey maps show most of the pertinent topography of the area, including relief, wooded areas, all bodies of water, roads, tracks, and buildings.

With such a map or other materials as a guide, we should visit the most likely places and explore them. Such scouting parties may be launched by automobile or plane or, even better, by helicopter. The latter method not only makes one immune to barbed-wire fences, cockle burrs, and no-trespassing signs, it gives also an ideal over-all perspective of likely properties. Much can be noted from an automobile, especially the relation of proposed project sites to traffic. But sooner or later, to be effective, we must get up off the seat cushions and cruise about on foot.

Having narrowed our choice to several alternative tracts of land, we analyze them — their natural and man-made forms, features, and forces — in detail. The favorable and unfavorable aspects of each are carefully noted and assayed. Sometimes we discuss the comparative analysis of the various properties informally with the client. On the other hand, we may prepare a well-documented report for presentation, to a board of directors, an authority, or a city council, for example. Such a report, oral or printed, may list the sites in order of suitability. Often, for reasons of politics, public relations, or tact, it is better to present only the relative merits of the alternative sites, in clear, concise terms, and leave to the "august body" the business of discussing the pros and cons of each and making the final decision.

The ideal site   We have all seen buildings that appeared to be happily wedded to their site. One example is the magnificent temple group at Nikko,* Japan. Its planners wanted to build a temple compound of great religious force and spiritual beauty, and spent long hours in quiet contemplation of those high qualities it should express. Being a Buddhist temple, it had to be rooted in nature, spring from nature, grow with nature, and become a very part of nature's essence. With these qualities clearly in mind, they began the long search for an ideal site. They did not consider any of a number of sites that they owned and might well have used. Nor did they consider land along a main road or street from which the proposed temple could be easily seen and admired. They believed that the native character of the site had to be as much a part of the architecture of their temple as the curve of its roof, the proportion of beam and rafter. After months of searching and reflection, the site was finally chosen — an isolated forest plateau, lying dark and cool in a grove of venerable pines above a cascading mountain torrent. Here, with infinite care, the builders marked off the temple buildings and spaces. From timbers felled on the mountainside, they fashioned their columns. With huge blocks of stone quarried from a hidden mountain face, they laid up their walls and bridge abutments. They shaped and finished each paving stone, each gate hinge, each

---

* Architecturally, the temples of Nikko are so ornate and lavishly overdecorated that to the critical eye they seem almost bizarre. (This must have seemed particularly so to the Zen Buddhist architects who, in the same era, produced the superbly refined and simple Katsura Palace in Kyoto.) But for mastery of siting and for space-structure-landscape development, there are few temple groups to compare with that at Nikko.

lantern post, to bring out the best of the native qualities of the materials with which they worked.

Today, as we approach the temples of Nikko as pilgrims, we leave the travelled road and turn into a great shadowy allee of pungent cryptomeria trees, a double row that winds for miles through the quiet rural countryside. Emerging from the half light of the lacy tunnel, we find ourselves crossing a red-lacquered bridge arched high above the stream. Here we sense that the white rushing waters cut us off from and cleanse us of the worldly things behind. Ahead, the massive foundation walls of the temples seem to merge with the mountain rock. The compound sheltered by great pine boughs seems a part of the forest. As we enter by stone and timber gates to move through the serenely beautiful courtyards toward the sacred inner shrine, everything is pervaded by a sense of timeless beauty and peace — the distant sound of the splashing water far below; the soughing of light wind above us in the pinetops; the sharp, spicy fragrance of incense; the lushness of fern and forest; the glow of light on mellow, carved wood and rich lacquer; the low, throaty sound of the deeply patinaed temple gongs; the cadenced chant of tonsured priests. Here, in the temple grounds of Nikko, man and nature, structures and site, are merged as one, and a function is truly wedded to its ideal site — not by expediency, nor by happenstance, but by thoughtful, meticulous planning.

We remember with pleasure other man-planned developments that seemed to be a natural outgrowth of their sites. A subdivision, for instance, artfully fitted to the contours, trees, and other topographical features of a pleasant valley. A school with its playgrounds in a parklike setting placed at the community center and approached along safe and inviting walkways. A factory with ordered production units, tanks, storage yards, and shaded parking space all planned in admirable relationship to approach roads, railroad spurs, and piers.

We must establish the landscape features, natural and man-made, best suited to our project and then search for a site that provides them. The ideal site is the one that, with least modification, best meets the project requirements.

SITE ANALYSIS

Now that we have selected the site, what is our next concern? At this stage we have, in fact, two concerns, which may be dealt with simultaneously — the design of a detailed program and an analysis of the site.

Design of a program   Many completed projects function poorly, or actually preclude the very uses for which they were planned. An unsuccessful project often has no reason for being. Perhaps it is doomed by being forced on an unsuitable site, or because it is not well-designed, not a beautiful expression of its function. Sometimes it may be destroyed by the frictions it generates. Most often, however, the root of failure lies in the fact that a program for it was never fully considered; the complete project with all its essential relationships and impacts was never actually envisioned or totally conceived.

It is our tacit responsibility as planners to carry each work to the most

A "leisure house" perched amidst the tree tops on a steeply sloping site seems as much at home here as trunk, limb, foliage, sun, or air.

successful conclusion possible. To accomplish this aim, to plan a project intelligently, we must first understand its nature. We must develop a *project program*. By research and investigation we must organize a logical and accurate program of requirements on which we may base our design. This program will be as detailed and as complete as possible. To this end we might well consult with all interested persons and draw freely upon their knowledge and views — with the owners, with those who will use the project, with maintenance men, with planners of similar undertakings, with our collaborators, with anyone who can contribute constructive thought. We will look to history for the lessons of time, for as Santayana has concluded, "Those who refuse to learn the lessons of history are condemned to repeat it." We will look ahead to envision possible improvements based on newly developed techniques, new materials, and new concepts of planning. We will try to combine the best of the old with the best of the new. Since the completed work will be the physical manifestation of this theoretical program, the program itself must be *designed* — thoroughly, imaginatively, completely.

Analysis of the site   At the same time the program requirements are being studied, we must thoroughly investigate and analyze the project site. Not only the specific site contained within the property boundaries, but the total site, which includes the site environs to the horizon and beyond.

It is usually necessary to conduct a survey for the specific site. Just what do we mean by a "survey" and how is one procured?

The licensed surveyor is professionally trained to produce survey information of a wide range of types and of varying degrees of accuracy. If we ask for a "property survey" we may very well get no more than a plan showing the property lines with their bearings and distances. If we ask for a "topographic survey" we may expect, in addition to the property lines, contour lines indicating the relative height above a point of known or assumed elevation. It would seem that to be sure of getting any particular information, we must ask for it. The best way of indicating to the surveyor the precise information required is to give him a survey specification, which is generally prepared for each project.

The extensional aspects of a site

Such a specification asks for all information needed, but no more. The following hypothetical survey specification may be too general for some projects and too detailed for others. It is intended only as a guide.

SPECIFICATION FOR TOPOGRAPHIC SURVEY

Property: Lawson farm and portion of Beeler Mill property.
(See sketch attached).
Location: Perry Highway, Kilbuck Township, approximately
one mile north of P. & L.E. tracks.

General

Surveyor shall do all field work necessary to determine accurately the physical conditions existing on the site.

Surveyor shall prepare a map of the given area in ink on tracing cloth at scale of 1 in. to 50 ft. Four blackline prints of the survey map shall be furnished the owner.

Datum

Elevations shall be referenced to any convenient and permanent bench mark with assumed elevation of 100 ft. The bench mark shall be clearly indicated on the map.

Information required

1. Title of survey, property location, scale, north point, certification, and date.
2. Tract boundary lines, courses, and distances.
3. Building lines, easements, and rights-of-way.
4. Names of abutting parcel owners.
5. Names and locations of existing road rights-of-way on or abutting the tract.
6. Position of buildings and other structures, including foundations, piers, bridges, culverts, wells, cisterns, and the like.
7. Location of all walls, fences, roads, drives, curbs, gutters, steps, walks, paved areas, and the like, indicating types of materials or surfacing.
8. Locations, types, sizes, and direction of flow of all existing storm and sanitary sewers on or contiguous to the tract, giving top and

invert elevations of all manholes and inlet and invert elevations of all other drainage structures. Location, type, and size of all water and gas mains, manholes, valve boxes, meter boxes, hydrants, and other appurtenances. Locations of all utility poles, and telephone lines. For utilities (gas, storm and sanitary sewer, water, telephone, and electricity) not traversing site indicate, by key plan if necessary, nearest offsite utility leads, giving all pertinent information on ownership, types, sizes, and inverts.

9. Location of swamps or boggy areas, springs, streams, and bodies of water; include spillways, drainage ditches, and the like.

10. Outline of wooded areas. Within area so noted on sketch show all trees that have a trunk diameter of 4 in. or more at waist height, giving approximate trunk diameter and type of tree.

11. Road elevations. Elevations shall be taken at 50-ft intervals along center lines of roads and flow line of gutter on property side.

12. Elevations shall be taken and shown on a 50-ft grid system as well as at the top and bottom of all considerable breaks in grade, whether vertical as in walls, or sloping as in banks. Spot elevations shall also be indicated at finished grade of building corners. In addition to elevations required, the map shall show contours at 2-ft. intervals. All ground elevations shown shall be to nearest tenth of a foot. Permissible tolerance shall be 0.1 ft. for spot elevations and one-half the contour interval for contours.

As an aid in comprehending the total site and its pertinent planning factors, we may again consult city and county maps, road maps, zoning ordinances, transportation routes and schedules, mining surveys, deed-books, geological surveys, rainfall charts, weather maps, and plans of existing and proposed utility systems. Of particular help on large scale preliminary investigations, as has been noted before, are the U.S. Geological Survey maps.

The feel of the land   Graphic survey information is essential, but it must be supplemented with at least one and preferably repeated visits to the site. Only by actual site observation can we get the "feel" of the property, sense its relationship to the surrounding areas, and become fully aware of the lay of the land. Only in the field can we sense the dynamic lines that are its bounding roads, the insistent lines of pedestrian approach, the arc of the sun, the prevailing breeze, the good views, the ugly views, the sculptural land forms, the springs, the trees, the rock outcrops, the usable areas, the features to be preserved if possible, and the features to be eliminated — in short, the character of the site. We must climb from hollow to hill, kick at the sod, dig into the soil. We must look and listen and fully sense those qualities that are peculiar to this specific landscape area.

Whatever we can see along the lines of approach to the site is an extensional aspect of the site. Whatever we can see (or will see in the probable future) from the site is part of the site. Anything that can be heard, smelled, or felt from the property is part of the property. Any topographical feature, natural or man-made, that has any effect on the property or its use is, from the planning point of view, a property feature and must be considered as a planning factor.

In our present power-happy and schedule-conscious era, this vitally important aspect of developing *sympatico* for the land and of learning to know and understand the land — learning to analyze the total project site — is too often overlooked. And too often our completed work gives tragic evidence of our haste and neglect.

In Japan (as, historically, in the highest planning cultures of all countries) this keen awareness of the site is of great significance in the planning process. All structures seem a natural outgrowth of the site — preserving, accentuating, and extending its best features. Studying in Japan, the author was struck by this consistent quality and once asked an architect how he achieved it in his work.

"Quite simply," said the architect. "If designing say, a residence, I go each day to the piece of land on which it is to be constructed. Sometimes for long hours with a mat and tea. Sometimes in the quiet of evening when the shadows are long. Sometimes in the busy part of the day when the streets are abustle and the sun is clear and bright. Sometimes in the snow and even in the rain, for much can be learned of a piece of ground by watching the rain play across it and the run-off take its course in rivulets along the natural drainage ways.

"I go to the land, and stay, until I have come to know it. I learn to know its bad features — the jangling friction of the passing street, the awkward angles of a wind-blown oak, an unpleasant sector of the mountain view, the lack of moisture in the soil, the nearness of the neighbor's house to an angle of the property.

"I learn to know its good features — a glorious clump of maple trees, a broad ledge perching high in space above a gushing waterfall, which spills into the deep ravine below. I come to know the cool and pleasant summer airs that rise from the falls and move across an open draw of the land. I sense, perhaps, the deliciously pungent fragrance of the deeply layered cedar fronds as the warm sun plays across them in the morning. This patch I know must be left undisturbed.

"I know where the sun will appear in the early morning when its warmth will be most welcome. I have learned which areas will be struck by its harshly blinding light as it burns hot and penetrating in the late afternoon, and from which spots the sunset seems to glow the richest in the dusky peace of late evening. I have marvelled at the changing, dappled light and soft fresh colors of the bamboo thicket, and watched for hours the scarlet-crested warblers who nest and feed there.

"I come to sense with great pleasure the subtle relationship of a jutting granite boulder to the jutting granite profile of the mountainside across the way. Little things, one may think, but they tell one, 'Here is the essence of this fragment of land; here is its very spirit. Preserve this spirit and it will pervade your gardens, your homes, and your very life.'

"And so I come to understand this bit of land, its moods, its limitations, its possibilities. Only now can I take my ink and brush in hand and start to draw my plans. But, strangely, in my mind the structure by now is fully planned, planned unconsciously, but complete in every detail. It has taken its form and character from the site and the passing street and the fragment of rock and the wafting breeze and the arching sun and the sound of the falls and the distant view.

A study in harmonious relationships

"Knowing the owner and his family and the things they like and the life they would like best to lead, I have found for them here on this land the pattern of living that brings them into the most ideal relationship with their land and the space around them, with their living environment. This structure, this house that I have planned, is no more than an arrangement of spaces, open and closed, accommodating and expressing in stone, timber, and rice paper a delightful pattern for their life on this land. How else can one plan the best home for this site?"

There can be no other way! This, in Japan as elsewhere, is in simplest terms the planning process — for the home, the church, the city, the national park, and the superhighway.

Therefore, let us build houses that restore to man the life-giving, life-enhancing elements of nature. This means an architecture that begins with the nature of the site. Which means taking the first great step toward assuring a worthy architecture, for in the rightness of a house on the land we sense a fitness we call beauty.

FRANK LLOYD WRIGHT

In America, rightly or wrongly, we planners approach our problems in a less contemplative frame of mind. We are "less sensitive" (of which fact we are proud) and "more practical" (a pathetic misnomer). We are rushed by pressure of time, economics, and the present public temperament. The planning process is accelerated, sometimes to the point of frenzy. But the principle remains the same — to realize a project on a site effectively, we must fully understand the program, and we must be fully aware of the physical properties of the site and of the total site environs. Our planning then becomes the science and art of arranging the best possible relationships.

The site analysis diagram   One effective means of understanding the site is to prepare a site analysis diagram. A print of the topographic survey furnished by the surveyor is taken into the field and, from actual

49

There is an area of the conceptual and forming process that is common to the four major physical planning disciplines and often others as well. This is the formulation of the basic *plan concept* by which in sketch or diagram the use-areas and plan forms are conceived in harmony with the natural and man-made forms, forces, and features of the total project site. Usually the plan concept is best arrived at through collaborative effort in which all participants contribute freely of their experience and ideas.

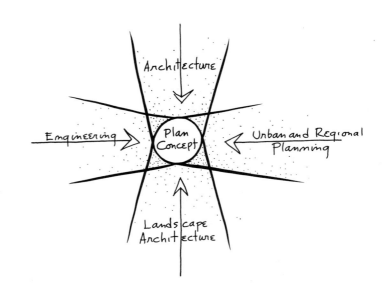

Survey

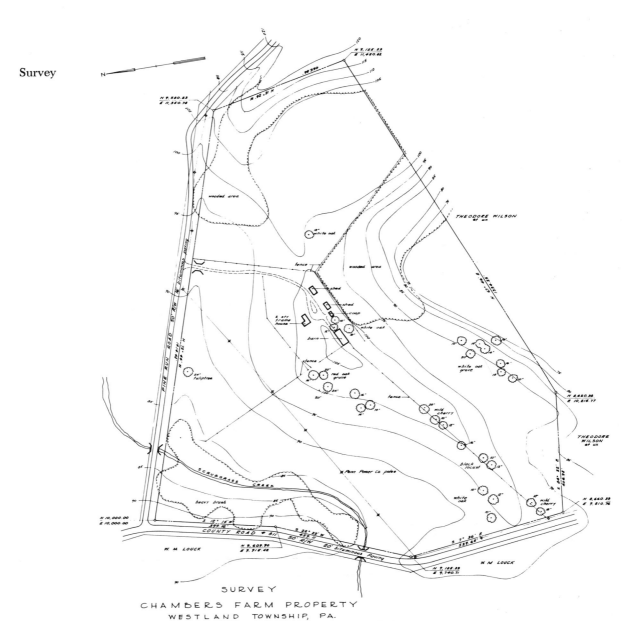

SURVEY
CHAMBERS FARM PROPERTY
WESTLAND TOWNSHIP, PA.

site observation, all site features or factors that supplement or interpret the survey are plotted on it in the planner's own symbols. Such additional information might include:

1. Best views, poor views, objectionable views
2. Which trees of those plotted should be preserved, if possible, and which removed
3. Flood level from site evidence; undrained or swampy land
4. Off-site nuisances with their bearing and approximate distances
5. Logical building areas of the site, logical points of ingress or egress
6. Sectors where high or low points on the horizon give protection from or add force to sun and wind
7. Sun diagram

Site analysis diagram

8. Prevailing wind and breezes
9. Frost study; low-lying pockets of trapped air
10. Micro-climatic analysis of the area
11. Other natural features such as springs, an unusual shrub, well-knitted ground cover, depth or lack of topsoil, eroded ground, sunken areas — as over mined out coal — and the like
12. Any other factors of especial importance to the particular project proposed.

In addition to such information observed in the field, supplementary data gleaned from careful research may be plotted directly on the survey or included in the survey file. Such information might include:

1. Gas and water pressures, normal and guaranteed
2. Names of utility companies whose lines are shown, company addresses, phone numbers, engineers

Site-structure diagram

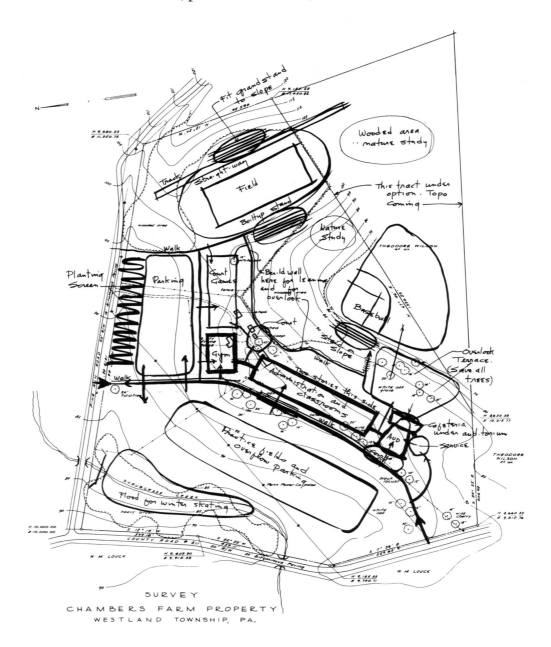

SURVEY
CHAMBERS FARM PROPERTY
WESTLAND TOWNSHIP, PA.

3. Routes and data on projected utility lines
4. Power capacities
5. Projected approach roads
6. Approach patterns of existing roads, drives, and walks
7. Traffic counts
8. Easements, rights of way
9. Zoning restrictions, building lines
10. Mineral rights, depth of coal, mined out areas
11. Water analysis, if drilled wells are proposed
12. Core boring data and logs.

In developing a sound planning approach, the planner should analyze, through survey information, research, and actual site observation, all site factors and reduce these factors, by symbols, to a site analysis diagram. To this analysis can then be logically related all plan areas and elements.

Site-structure study number two

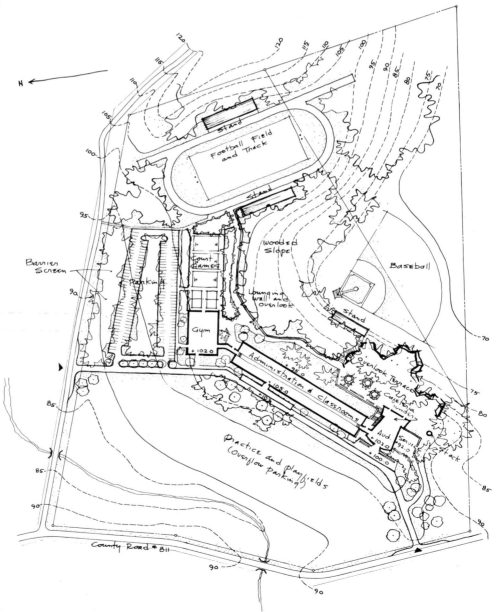

ADAPTATION OF PROJECT TO SITE

A seed of use — a cell of function — wisely applied to a receptive site, should be allowed to develop naturally, organically, in harmonious adaptation to juxtaposed functions and to its total environment.

We have by now developed a comprehensive program clarifying the proposed nature and function of our project. We have, through survey information, site observation, and the preparation of a site analysis diagram, become fully aware of all features of the total extensional site. We are now ready, for the first time, to start designing. Up to this point, the planning effort has been one of research and analysis. It has been painstaking and perhaps tedious, but it is of vital importance because it is the only means by which we can achieve full command of the data on which our design is to be based. From this point on, the planning process becomes one of integration of function, structure, and site.

Plan concept   If structure and landscape development are contemplated, it is impossible to conceive one without the other, for it is the relationship of structure to site and site to structure that gives meaning to each and to both.

This point perhaps raises the question of who, in a team of collaborating planners — architect, landscape architect, city planner, engineer, and others — is to do the "conceiving." Strangely, this problem, which might seemingly lead to warm debate, rarely arises, for an effective collaboration brings together experts in various fields of knowledge who, in a free interchange of ideas, develop a climate of perceptive awareness and know-how. In such a climate, plan concepts usually evolve spontaneously. Since the collaboration is arranged and administered by one of the principals (who presumably holds the commission), it is usually he who coordinates the planning in all its aspects and gives it expressive unity. It is the work of his collaborators to advance, under his direction, their assigned planning tasks and to aid the development toward perfection of the main design idea in all ways possible.

The site-structure diagram   When planning a project or structure in relation to a land area, we should first analyze and determine all the site functions. For a high school, for instance, we would determine the approximate architectural plan areas and their shapes — the general plan areas required for service, parking, out-of-doors classrooms, gardens, game courts, football fields, track, bleachers, and logical school expansion. On the topographic survey (or site analysis diagram) we would then indicate, in soft line, use-areas of logical size and shape in studied relation to each other and to the natural and man-made features of the total project site. Having thus roughed in the site use-areas, we may at last block in the architectural elements of the project. The result is the site-structure diagram.

The balance of the planning process is no more than a procedure of reanalysis, logical development, and refinement of detail — a process of creative synthesis.

A good plan, reduced to its essentials, is no more than a record of logical thought. A dull plan is a record of ineffectual thinking or of very

Thus we seek two values in every landscape: one, the expression of the native quality of the landscape, the other, the development of maximum human livability.

. . .

Site planning must be thought of as the organization of the total land area and air space of the site for best use by the people who will occupy it. This means an integrated concept in which buildings, engineering construction, open space and natural materials are planned together at one time by one thoroughly coordinated team of technicians, to form a complete, balanced, wholesome and pleasant development or community.

GARRETT ECKBO

Perhaps the planning process can best be explained as a series of subconscious conversations which the planner has with himself — the question posed, the factors weighed, and then the recorded conclusion. The more lucid the thinking, the more coherent the powers of idea communication . . . the better is the plan.

B. KENNETH JOHNSTONE

Planning is a process of creative synthesis.

little thinking at all. A brilliant plan gives evidence of sound analysis of all site and plan factors, clear perception of working relationships, and a sensitive expression of function and total site integrated in such a way that each complements the other and both work together in harmony.

The creative aspect of planning   A planner may create in the materials, forms, and symbols of his trade a three-dimensional thing or group of things that he believes will create for the user a certain predictable experience. If the plan is a good one, the user will *recreate* the thing or group of things through his perception of them, and will thus be led to the desired experience. For, when we experience any object, we actually *recreate* it through our senses. An understanding of this idea leads us to a clearer concept of the creative function of design.

The planning attitude   In his distinguished treatise, *On the Laws of*

55

Japanese Painting, Henry P. Bowie has written, "One of the most important principles in the art of Japanese painting — indeed, a fundamental and entirely distinctive characteristic — is that of living movement, *sei do* . . . it being, so to say, the transfusion into the work of the felt nature of the thing to be painted by the artist. Whatever the subject to be translated — whether river or tree, rock or mountain, bird or flower, fish or animal — the artist at the moment of painting it must feel its very nature, which, by the magic of his art, he transfers into his work to remain forever, affecting all who see it with the same sensations he experienced when executing it." And again, "Indeed, nothing is more constantly urged upon his attention than this great underlying principle, that it is impossible to express in art what one does not feel."

And so it is with planning. We can only create that for which we have first developed empathetic feeling and understanding. A shopping center? As designers, we must *feel* the quickening tempo, the pull and attraction, the bustle, the wonder, the excitement of the place. We must sense the chic shop windows, the mouthwatering sights and smells of the bakery shop; we must see in our mind the jam-packed displays of the hardware store, and the drugstore windows with the pyramids of mineral oil, cough syrup, shoe polish, hot-water bottles, and jelly beans. We must see in the market the heaps of grapefruit, oranges, rhubarb, Brussels sprouts, bananas; whiff the overpowering fragrance of the floral stalls; picture the shelf on shelf of bargain books, the bolts of cotton prints, the sloping trays of chocolate creams and peppermints. We must feel the brightness of the sunshine on the sidewalks, and the coolness and protection of the doorways and arcades. We must feel crowds and traffic and benches and trees, and perhaps a fountain or two. And then we can start planning.

A children's zoo? If we would plan one, we must first know and understand the flocking children, the gawking, clapping, squealing children; we must appreciate the delight, the laughter, the chatter, the confusion, and the rollicking thrill of the place. We must feel the diminutive, squeaky "cuteness" of the mousetown, the bulk and immensity and cavelike hollowness of the spouting whale with its dimly illumined interior displays. We must know the preening strut of the elegantly wandering peacocks, the quack, quack, quacking of the waddling ducks, the soft furry whiteness of the lop-eared rabbits, and the clop, clop, clopping and creaking harness and the awed delight of the youngsters at the pony ride. We must, in our minds, *be* at the children's zoo, and we must see it, hear it, feel it, and love it as a child would love it — before we can plan such a thing.

Are we to design a bridge approach, a parkway, a hotel plaza, a freight terminal, a seaside bathing beach? If we would create such projects, or any other project, we must first feel them completely. This self-induced sensitivity toward the nature of the project we might call the "planning attitude," and before we mature as planners, we will find it to be essential.

SITE-STRUCTURE EXPRESSION

If to design a project or structure in harmony with its total site is a

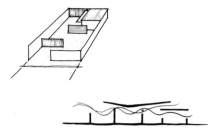

Interplay of horizontal and vertical spaces

Rigid property lines may be softened to relieve the sense of tight enclosure.

Consider carefully the scale of objects introduced.

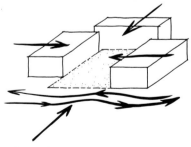

The feel of the city lot

generally valid aim, it then follows that the "design expression" of a given project will vary from site to site in accordance with the variation in site character or site expression.

To illustrate, let us consider a summer weekend vacation lodge. If this lodge were to be built on a sheltered rock-rimmed inland lake in northern Maine, its abstract design form would vary greatly from the form it would have if located anywhere along the wind-whipped coast of Monterey, California, or in the smoky Ozark Mountains, or on Florida's shell-strewn Captiva Island, or along the lazily-winding Mississinewa River in central Indiana. Forgetting for the moment the design implications of a specific site, we can see that there are strong general design features suggested by each of the varying types of landscape character.

It might therefore be helpful design procedure to classify a site according to its general landscape expression and to determine what design characteristics of a proposed structure or project are suggested by the site characteristics revealed. For example, let us consider, for four typical sites, what abstract design characteristics of a residential development may be deduced from the perceived site characteristics (given in italics).

City lot site

Area is at a premium. The plan will be compact, of necessity. To utilize the area fully, a maximum of the lot area may be included, by plan ingenuity, in the visual scheme.

Space is limited. Plan forms will probably be contrived to expand the apparent space by multiple use of areas and interplaying spatial relationships.

The city environs impose a sense of confinement and oppression. Perhaps here the embattled city dweller will wish to entrench, dig his cave, or build his fort, and feel secure. But more likely he will seek relief and release from pressure. If so, in his dwelling, the hard, the rigid, the confining forms will give way to the light, the nebulous, the transparent, and the free.

Areas and spaces are limited in scale. Scale, both induced and inductive, is an important design consideration. The object that seemed attractive in the open field may, if introduced into the cityscape, seem overwhelming. A giant tree, for example, might dwarf an urban complex, while a dwarf tree might give it increased and more desirable visual dimension.

City streets and pedestrian walks are major lines of approach, observation, and access. They are the elements most strongly relating the home to the community. The driveway throat and front entrance will normally be designed to express a receptive "harbor" quality. The relationship of the structure to the insistent lines of the city street becomes a major consideration.

The city street is a source of fumes, noise, danger, and other frictions. Plan elements adjacent to the street may well be contrived to provide "depth." Perforated screens or studded barriers have useful application here.

The city is, microclimatologically speaking, a desert of pavement and masonry. A city is often twenty degrees hotter than the surrounding

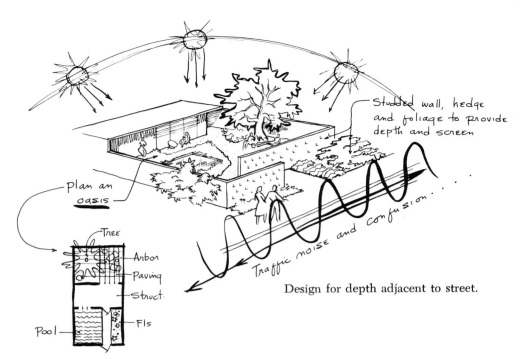

In the city desert, plan an oasis.

Design for depth adjacent to street.

countryside in the summertime. Design an oasis, make maximum use of breeze, shade, shadow patterns, sunscreens, treillage, and the refreshing qualities of water in fountain, pool, or jet spray. The climate may be further modified artificially — by refrigerated paving or panels, by air movement fanned through pierced or baffled screens, by mist sprays, moist fabric, gravel, or other evaporative surfaces. In cool weather, heat may be introduced in radiant elements or in warm water circulated in fountains or pools.

Natural features — trees, interesting ground forms, rocks, water — are scarce and therefore have increased value and meaning. They are no longer part of the natural scene but are now isolated objects to be treated in a more stylized way. Exploit natural features to the full, design them into the scheme, orient to them. "Import" additional landscape materials for optimum interest and climate conditioning. Earth, plants, and water in the city may well be treated as sculptural elements or as architectural elements. Since in the city all materials appear to be introduced, exotic plants and materials are particularly appropriate.

City materials and forms are, at their best, sophisticated. Where sizes and quantities are limited, richness of material and refinement of detail gain in importance. Sills of polished marble, handles of brass, cases of hand-rubbed teak are fitting here.

Surrounded by neighbors, we become an integral part of the community, a unit in a group of related units, an important part of the whole. Neighborhood character cannot be blithely violated without social repercussions. We are tacitly obliged to conform. To achieve a measure of conformity while designing a residential complex of individuality and distinction is a difficult art, mastered long ago by the Japanese. Their modular homes of stone, wood, tile, and grass mats are arranged tightly along their city streets with an artistry that produces a pattern of infinite variety, yet great harmony. Even the smallest structures, through ingenious plan arrangement and flexibility, are made to feel spacious.

From the street to the farthest limits of the city lot, there is little room for the necessary transitions from the compelling lines of traffic to

The orientation of the city house may well be inward to garden or patio.

In the city, a rock, a tree, or a single potted plant may represent all of nature.

areas for quiet family living. Designed transitions are a mark of the successful city house. The Japanese speak of a quality called *wabi* that has application here. This quality may be exemplified by a black walnut with its outer covering a rough, splotched, grey-green husk. With husk removed, the exposed walnut shell is seen to be a handsome case of horny ridges arranged in a structural pattern. Cracked open, the shell reveals the walnut kernels encased in a membrane of delicate veining and fitted to smooth chambers of perfect shape and richness of finish. And finally, the ivory-white kernel itself is a marvel of beautiful sculptural form. A progression inward from the unostentatious to the highly refined.

A city property has a "fishbowl" quality resulting from the proximity of the neighbors. Privacy, a prime design requirement in a city house, may be achieved only through able planning. A logical orientation of such structures is inward, to private gardens, patios, or courts.

Living space in the city may extend from property line to property line.

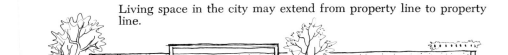

59

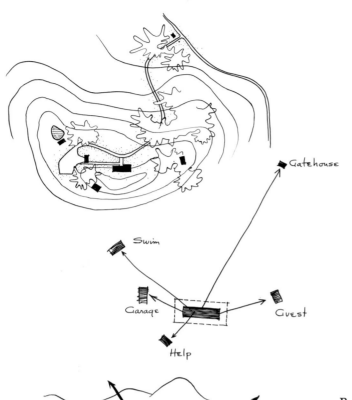

Ample area permits an exploded plan — each element being related to the most compatible topographic features.

Rural property has an expansive feel. Streams, groves, distant hills, all features of the landscape that can be seen or sensed, are a part of the extensional site.

Major landscape features are established; build to, around, and among them.

Structural forms conceived in sympathy with ground forms borrow power from, and return power to, the landscape.

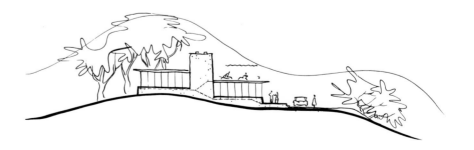

Rural site

Land area is plentiful. The plan is more open, free, and "exploded." *Although the specific site may be limited by property boundaries, the visual site may include vast areas.* Our plan scope is increased, since fence lines, orchards, paddocks, even a mountaintop miles away may become design factors and elements. Our scheme must be planned to the horizon.

Freedom, with open view of fields, woods, and sky, is the essential landscape quality. We may logically orient our plan outward to embrace the total site's best features and to command the best views.

The choice of a rural site would indicate a desire to be "at one" with nature. Make nature appreciation a design aim and theme. Insofar as possible, we will disturb the natural environment only to improve it.

The major landscape features are established. Build to the landscape, feature the best landscape elements, screen out and deemphasize the less desirable elements, and contrive structural forms in best relation to landscape forms. Site use-areas, sympathetically fitted to topographical features, may well dictate the architectural arrangement. The structure is ideally conceived as a series of architectural elements best relating man and man's functions to the landscape.

The landscape is dominant (in character and mood). Presumably the site was chosen because of this landscape character. If existing landscape character is highly desirable, the site-structure diagram should be contrived to best preserve, capture, and accentuate it. If an altered landscape character is desired, we may modify or completely change the landscape character only in such a way as to take fullest possible advantage of the existing landscape features.

Earth and ground forms are strong visual elements. A structure conceived in studied relation to ground forms gains in architectural strength and in harmony with the site.

The pleasant landscape is one of pleasant transitions. In the planning of transitions between structure and site, intermediate areas relating structure to the land are of key importance.

Structures become elements imposed on the landscape. Either structure or site must dominate. Either the site is considered as basically a setting for a dominant structure, or the structure is conceived as subordinate to the landscape and designed to complement it and blend with the natural contours and forms.

The rural landscape is a landscape of subtleties — of foliage shadings, sky tints, and cloud shadows. Man's planning must recognize these qualities and treat them sympathetically, or he will destroy them.

In a rural site, one is more exposed to the elements and the weather — rain, storms, sun, wind, snow, frost, winter cold, and summer heat. The site-structure diagram and structural forms should reflect a thorough study of, and adaptation to, the climate and microclimate.

A rural site implies increased land area and greater maneuverability. The automobile and pedestrian approaches, important elements in our design, may often be controlled within the property boundaries.

The indigenous materials of a rural site — ledgerock, fieldstone, slate, maple, birch, cedar — contribute much to its landscape character. The intelligent use of such natural materials in buildings, fences,

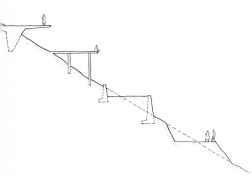

On a sloping site the level plane is achieved by terracing, retaining walls, the supported platform, or the cantilever.

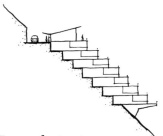

Imposed structures may hug the slope,

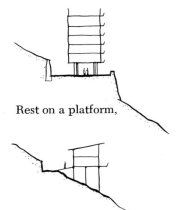

Rest on a platform,

Or stand completely free.

bridges, and walls helps relate the structure to the site.

The essential quality of the landscape is the natural and the unrefined. Our structural materials may well reflect this naturalness and forego high refinement.

Steeply sloping site (unobstructed inclined plane)

Contours are major plan factors. Contour planning (the placing of plan elements parallel with the contours) is generally indicated.

The areas of relatively equal elevation are narrow bands lying perpendicular to the axis of the slope. Narrow plan forms as bars or ribbons are suggested.

Sizable level areas are nonexistent. Essential level areas must be carved out of, or projected from, the slope. If shaped of earth, the earth must be retained by a wall or by a slope of increased inclination.

The top of the slope is most exposed to the elements. The planner may exploit or evolve a land profile similar to the "military crest" of the artillery manual — an adaptation or modification of the slope to preserve or enhance the view while affording increased protection.

The essence of slope is rise and fall. A terraced scheme is suggested. Levels may separate functions, as in split-level or multideck structures.

The slope is a ramp. Ramps and steps are indicated.

The normal slope grade is perhaps too steep for wheeled traffic. Access is easiest along contours. This fact dictates a normal approach to the project from the sides.

The pull of gravity is down the slope. Our design forms must not only have stability, they must *express* stability to be pleasing. An exception, of course, would be those structures in which a feeling of daring or exhilaration is desired.

The sloping site has a dynamic landscape quality. The site lends itself to dynamic plan forms.

The dramatic quality of a slope is its apparent change in grade. Natural grade changes may be accentuated and dramatized through the use of flying terraces, overlook platforms, and terraced balconies.

A slope inherently emphasizes the meeting of earth and air. A level element imposed on a sloping plane often makes contact with the earth or rock at the inner side and is held free to the air at its outer extremity. Where the element makes contact with the earthbound

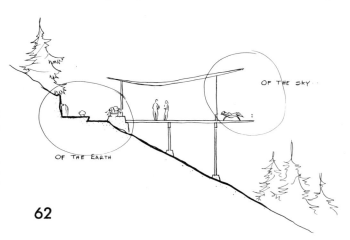

62

A structure imposed on a sloping site belongs to the sky as well as the earth.

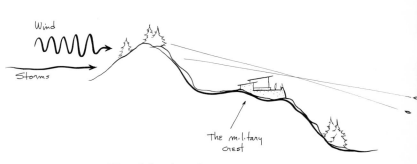

Use of the slope for protection

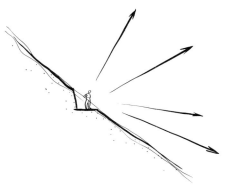

On the sloping plane, orientation is outward.

materials, we must clearly express this contact. Where the leading edge flies free, this union of element and air might well be expressed design-wise.

A sloping site affords great interest in view. Artificial site development to create landscape interest may be minimized, for where a sloping site commands a fine view, little other site interest may be required.

The slope is oriented outwards. Plan orientation is normally outward and down. Since the view side is exposed, the plan relation to sun, wind, and storms is of vital design importance.

A sloping site has drainage problems. Ground water and surface runoff from above must be intercepted and diverted, or allowed to pass freely under or through the structure.

A slope brings out many of the most desirable qualities of water. The play of water in falls, cascades, spouts, trickling rivulets, and films is an obvious plan opportunity.

Level site   (theoretically unobstructed plane extending to horizon)

A level site offers a minimum of plan restrictions. Of all site types, the level site best lends itself to the cell-bud, crystalline, or geometric plan pattern.

A level site has relatively minor landscape interest. Plan interest depends on relation of object to object, space to space, and object to space.

A flat site is essentially a broad-base plane. All elements set on this plane are of strong visual importance, as is their relation one to the other, since each assumes a sculptural quality. Each vertical plane es-

The strong horizontal characteristics of the site evoked these sympathetic forms.

Four studies of an exhibition group by architectural students of Professor John Pekruhn of Carnegie Tech illustrating the free plan arrangements made possible by a level site.

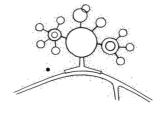

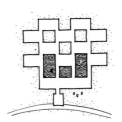

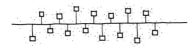

The level site adapts itself to the cell-bud, crystalline, or geometric plan.

Where flatness equals monotony, maximize every topographical opportunity.

tablished must be considered not only in terms of its own form but also as a background against which other objects may be seen or across which shadows may be thrown.

A flat site has no focal point. The most visually insistent element placed on this site will dominate the landscape.

Lines of approach are not dictated by the topography. The possibility of approach from any side makes all elevations important. Lines of exterior and interior circulation are critical design elements since they control the visual unfolding of the plan.

The dome of the sky is a dominant landscape element of infinite change and beauty. We may well feature the sky through the use of reflecting basins, pools, open courts, and patios.

The sun is a powerful design factor. We may use it as a sweeping beam or flood, and design in terms of light and shade. We may explore the myriad qualities of light and utilize the most effective in relation to our forms, colors, textures, and materials. We may dramatize cast shadow — solid as from a wall, moving as from water, sculptural as from objects, dappled as from foliage, or as a dark background and foil for luminous objects displayed against it.

A level site has a rather neutral landscape quality. Site character is created by the elements introduced. Bold form, strong color, and exotic materials may be used here without apparent violation of the site.

The site provides a minimum check to, or protection from, the elements. Weather barriers, screens, converters, and modifiers are important. Areas or spaces of controlled climate are desirable.

The site offers little privacy. The creation of privacy is a function of the plan orientation, for privacy may be inward to private spaces, or outward to infinity from subtended areas on the project periphery.

Third dimension is lacking. Third dimension in the ground plane may be achieved through the creation of earth or architectural platforms or pits. Slight rises, drops, and steps assume exaggerated significance on the level site.

The flat site offers no obstruction to lateral planning. An expanded scheme with connective passageways or elements is a logical plan expression.

A flat site is monotonous. Since interest is in structure rather than in natural landscape, the structure should be enhanced and dramatized in all ways possible.

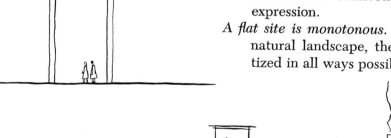

On the level site the pit, the mound, and the vertical assume telling significance.

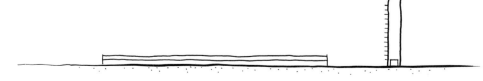

On the scaleless level plain, scale is what one makes it.

The horizontal in harmony, the vertical in dramatic contrast.

The monotony of the flat site is here relieved by the boldness of the structures and by the exhilarating thrust of the jets in the great water panel.

The horizon is an insistent line. Striking effects may be achieved through the use of low, sweeping horizontal forms (complementary) or incisive verticals (contrasting).

Flat landscape under the open sky is often oppressive and lacking in in human scale. Scale is therefore easily controlled, from the intimate to the monumental. Human scale, if it is to exist must be consciously created.

Other sites   This same procedure of determining (by perception and deduction) the abstract design characteristics suggested by a given landscape type may, of course, be applied to sites of an infinite variety, for example:

The snow-covered site
The swampy site
The pastoral site
The forest site
The boulder-strewn site
The hot, flat site
The cold, flat site
The flat and wooded site
The resort site
The business-district site

The heavy-industrial-area site
The site approached from above by air
The site oriented to major vistas
The site dominated by a highway
The site approached and viewed from below
The site oriented to a stream
The windswept site

In planning any project or designing any structure in relation to a given site, it is important first to deduce the general plan or design characteristics that are dictated or suggested by an analysis of the character or landscape expression of the total site.

SITE-STRUCTURE PLAN DEVELOPMENT

It can be seen from the foregoing study and from the development of the site-structure diagram that the forms, forces, and features of the total site exert a powerful influence on the arrangement and shape of the functional elements of the project or structure. In the refinement of the project or structural approach each element must be further developed in studied relationship to the total site and to the site areas immediately adjacent.

Outward and inward plan progression   We must consider each function from the innermost point of generation to the off-site target or terminus. In the design of a home, for example, we would consider the route of the small fry not only from bed to bathroom to breakfast table but also from breakfast table to the nearest door to play areas to walk to school — all in a natural and pleasant progression. Or, in more prosaic terms, we would plan the route of refuse from kitchen to service area to refuse truck to street — all with inconspicuous convenience. The relationship of dining table to window to view involves enframement and development of the view to the property limits, and an appreciation of the view to the far horizon.

Conversely, each functional element or area must be designed as the logical conclusion of a function originating at the extremities of the total site. The groceryman approaching your property is subtly directed to the service drive, the parking space for his truck, the service walk, the service entrance, and storage. By design, guests arriving for the evening are alerted and invited in, welcomed to the property, directed to the parking area, and guided to the entrance door, where they enter to the vestibule, coat storage, and the hospitality of the inner home. This same inward and outward planned progression is fully as important to any planned project, be it a sawmill, a recreation park, or a world's fair exposition.

Expansion-contraction of plan concept   Most site planning problems can be fully solved only by expanding the areas of consideration to the farthest extensional aspects of the site and by contracting each problem to the minutiae of human experience and irreducible detail. For although it is true that an object or element must be judged in relation to all other elements with which it is allied, it is also true that objects can only be truly judged when they are experienced one at a time, in depth, and at the living moment.

Satellite plan   As the total structure is conceived in harmony with the total site, so must each element or area of the structure be conceived in harmony with related site areas. In an elementary school for instance, we would plan the kindergarten, its out-of-door playlot, garden, and entrance gate all as one. The gymnasium we would coordinate with the

67

game courts, equipment areas, and playfields. We would consider the boiler plant together with its service and storage areas. The auditorium with its approach court and parking, the classrooms with their related out-of-door courts, terraces, or spaces — each element with its extensional site areas would be treated as an integrated plan complex. The total scheme in the relationship of its elements would resemble a solar system with sun, planets, and satellites.

Integral planning   When a structure is imposed on a site, certain changes in site character are effected. It is important that these changes be controlled by the planner. Our elementary school is not just "plunked down" in a city block or in the midst of a suburban community. Rather, ideally, it is fitted to the city property and conceived in harmony with the community with such skill that functionally and visually the new landscape created is an improvement over the original.

For a lesson in relating structure to site we may well look to the planners of the Renaissance. In the building of the magnificent Piazza San Marco in Venice, the architect commissioned to design the cathedral, or the campanile, or the Doge's palace, or the memorial columns at the watergate never conceived of his building or columns as a design entity. Instead he instinctively considered his work as an integral part of the piazza and its street and canal approaches. He reevaluated the piazza in terms of his proposed structure. He conceived his structure, from broad plan to most minute detail, in terms of its impact on the piazza and vice versa. Each planner designed not only a structure, but redesigned the entire piazza and, in doing so, his city of Venice. Thus, and only thus, was he fulfilling his obligation to his client and his city. The secret of much of the charm and great beauty of European towns and cities lies in the conscious application of this planning axiom. Much of the hodge podge and helter-skelter appearance of the American scene results from planning with seeming ignorance of integral planning.

Proving the plan   How do we know if our structure is well related to its site? There is one sure test we can apply. We can experience it through the senses of those who will see and use it. At any stage of the planning, from rough sketch to final drawings or model, we can by our imagination lift ourselves up and look down at the project with a fresh perspective. We can bring it alive in our mind's eye. We can say, in effect, as we look down at the plans for a church:

"I am the minister. As I drive by my church or approach it, does it express those vital inspirational qualities to which I have dedicated my life? As I enter my study, do I sense that this space is remote enough to give me privacy for study and meditation, yet accessible enough to attract to its doors those who need counsel or help, or those who come on church business? As an office is it so located that I can direct and oversee the church activities? Does this church that I am to administer have an efficiently organized plan?"

"I am the janitor. As I come to work in the morning where do I park my car? How do the barrels of cleaning compound get moved from the service dock to the space where they are stored? How do I get the refuse from kitchen to service area? Where do I store my ladders and snow removal equipment? Did someone in their planning think about me and my job?"

"I am a boy scout 'homing in' to troop meeting. Are the walks planned to take me where I am going or do I cut across the grass? Some friends of mine are waiting outside. Do we have a place where we can rip around and blow off steam and maybe shoot a few baskets? Where do we park our bikes? Where do we set up a practice tent? Where do we . . ."

"I am a member of this church and I am coming to a service. Does my church invite me to its doors? Am I able to drive close to the church and Sunday school doors on a cold or rainy day? Where do I park? Is there ample room? After service is there a pleasant space adjacent to the door where we may linger and greet our friends and welcome strangers? All these things are a part of church life and must be arranged for in its planning."

The function of any project, and the relationship of a structure to a site, may thus be tested by an imaginary introduction to and through the structure (from the outer reaches of the total site) of people typical of those who would see, service, or use it.

The process of site-structure plan development is a search for logical progressions and best relationships.

Residence of Marcel Breuer, New Canaan, Connecticut.

SITE-STRUCTURE UNITY

We have discussed the importance of developing the plan of a structure or project in relation to its site. Let us now consider other means by which we may achieve site-structure unity.

We may develop the structural elements of a project so as to utilize and accentuate land forms. A lighthouse, for example, is an extension of a jutting promontory. The ancient fort or castle extended, architecturally, the craggy top of a hill or mountain. Our modern municipal water tanks and transmission or relay towers rise from and extend the height of a topographical eminence. These applications are obvious. Not so obvious is the location of a community swimming pool to utilize and accentuate the natural bowl configuration of a landscape basin or valley. More subtle yet may be the conscious planning of a yacht club to emphasize the structural, protective shoulders of a point, or the soft receptive forms of a quiet bay.

A terraced restaurant stepping down the naturally terraced banks of a river, floating structures on water, light airy structures fixed against the sky, massive structures rooted in rock — each draws from its site a native power and returns to the site this power magnified. Whole cities have been imbued with this dynamic quality — Saigon overhanging its dark river and slow-flowing tributaries, Lhasa braced proudly against its mountain wall, Darjeeling extending its timbered mountain peaks and towers into the very clouds.

A structure and its site may be strongly related by the architectural treatment of site areas or elements. Clipped allees and hedges, water panels, precise embankments and terraces — all extend the apparent limits of man's control. Many of the French and Italian villas of the Renaissance were so architectural in their treatment that the entire property from wall to wall became one grand composition of palatial indoor and outdoor rooms. These grandiose garden halls were de-

Site-structure unity: yacht club, terrace, and restaurant have been planned to the natural ground forms, which overhang and command the bay. Boat slips are fitted to the protective ridge. The beach area extends the soft receptive wash of the harbor. Cabanas follow the natural bowl. The breakwater and light extend the existing rocky shoulders of the point. The parking areas are "hidden" in the shade of the existing grove. Such *sympatico* for the existing topography insures a plan development of "fitness" and pleasant harmonies of esthetics and function.

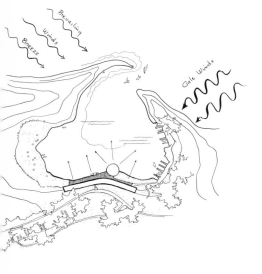

The Alhambra Palace of Granada, Spain, with the snow-covered Sierra Nevada in the distance. This assemblage of fortress-like structures fitted to the crest of the natural rock escarpment borrow both position and spirit from the native site.

70

Taliesin West emerges like boulder and cactus from the desert floor on which it lies. Low, horizontal, it spreads out into the landscape. Yet even in its blending it defines itself with forms as dynamic and sweeping as the desert wind and sun.

Complete integration of structure and site

Satellite

Buckshot

Finger

Villa d'Este at Tivoli, Italy

Checkerboard

Ribbon

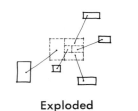

Exploded

Dispersion of plan elements

marked by great planes or arches of sheared beech, of masonry and mosaic, rows of plinths, and elaborate balustraded walls. They embraced monumental sculptured fountains and parterre gardens of rich pattern, or mazes of sharply trimmed box hedges. The integration of architecture and site thus became complete.

Unfortunately, the results were often vacuous — a meaningless exercise in applied geometry — the control of nature for no more reason than for the sake of exerting control. Many such villas, on the other hand, were, and still remain, notable for their great symphonic beauty. In these, without exception, the highest inherent qualities of the natural elements of the site — plants, topography, water — were fully appreciated by the planner and given design expression. Seldom, for instance, has water as a landscape element been treated with more imaginative control than at Villa d'Este at Tivoli, where a mountain torrent was diverted to spill down the steep villa slopes through the gardens — rushing, pouring, gushing, foaming, spurting, spewing, surging, gurgling, dripping, trickling, riffling, and finally shining deep and still in the stone reflecting basins. Here at Villa d'Este water, slopes, and plant material were handled architecturally to enhance both the structure and the site and superbly unite the two.

Alternatively, the landscape features of the site may be embraced by the dispersion of structural or other planned elements into the landscape. The *satellite* plan, the *finger* plan, the *checkerboard* plan, the *ribbon* plan, the *buckshot* plan, and the *exploded* plan are typical examples.

Just as the early French and English explorers in our country controlled vast tracts of land by the strategic placement of a few forts, so can the well-placed elements of a scheme control a given landscape. Such is true of our national parks with their trails, lodges, and campsites so sited as to unfold to the user the most interesting features of the park. Such is true, in a *linear* plan expression, of any well-planned scenic drive or highway extended into the landscape. Our military installations are often, in plan, scattered over extensive land areas, each function — be it rifle range, officers' quarters, tank proving ground, tent sites, or artillery range — relating to those topographical features that seem most suitable. For this same purpose, many of our newer schools are exploded in plan. Unlike the old three-story monumental school set *on* the land, the newer schools of which we speak are planned to the landscape, embracing and revealing its more pleasant qualities with such success that school and landscape are one.

The site and structure may be further related by the interlocking of common areas — patios, terraces, and courts, for example. A landscape feature displayed from or in such a court takes on a new aspect. It seems singled out. It becomes a specimen held up to close and frequent observation under varying conditions of position, weather, and light. A simple fragment of rock so featured acquires a modelling and beauty of form and detail that would not be realized if it were seen in

The bastion at the gate of Mont St. Michel guards its land-sea approaches. Any structural element by its placement dominates or "controls" the use of areas of its site.

This vertical panel by Burle-Marx serves not only as screen and backdrop but as pure sculpture as well.

its natural state. As we watch it from day to day — streaming with rain, sparkling with hoar frost or soft snow, glistening in the sharp sun and incised with shadow, or glowing in subdued evening light — we come to a fuller understanding of this landscape object, and thus of the nature of the landscape from which it came.

The landscape may be even more strongly related to structure by the orientation of a room or area to some feature of the landscape, as by a vista or view. A view, or a garden, may be treated as a mural, a mural of constant change and variety of interest, extending the room or area visually to the limits of the garden (or to infinity for a distant

This structure is fitted into the natural forest, around the existing boulder, and to the view of the sea.

view). It can be seen that, to be pleasant, the scale, mood, and character of the landscape feature viewed must be suited to the function of the area from which it is observed.

To the foreign visitor in a Japanese home, one of the most appealing features of many is the use of smoothly sliding screens of wood and paper by which the entire side of a room may be opened at will to "bring into the room" a cloudlike flowering plum tree, a vigorous composition of sand and stone and sunlit pine, a view through tiered rock-maple branches to the tiered roof of a distant pagoda, or a quiet pool edged with moss and rippled by a lazily fanning goldfish. Each feature viewed is contrived or controlled with impeccable artistry as part of the room, to extend the room and wed it to garden or landscape. The Japanese would tell us that they have a deeper purpose, that what they are really trying to do is to relate man and nature completely and make *nature appreciation* a part of their daily lives.

To this end they introduce into their homes the best of those objects of nature that they can find or afford. The posts and lintels of their rooms, for instance, are not squared and finished lumber, but rather a trunk or limb of a favorite wood — shaped, tooled, and finished to bring out its inherent form and pattern of grain and knotting. Each foundation stone, each section of bamboo, each woven grass mat (*tatami*) is so fashioned by the artisan as to discover, and reveal in the finished object, the highest natural quality of the material that is being used. In the Japanese home one finds plants and arrangements of twigs, leaves, and grasses that are startling in their beauty. Even in their art forms the Japanese, consciously, almost reverently, bring nature into their homes.

In such ways we, too, may relate our projects and structures to their natural environment. We may use large areas of glazing. We may so devise our approaches and circulation as to achieve desirable relationships. We may recall and adapt from the landscape colors, shapes, and materials. We may make further ties by projecting into the landscape certain areas of interior paving, and by extending structural walls or overhead planes. We may break down or vignette our structures from high refinement to a more rustic quality as we move from the interior out. This is a reverse application of the quality *wabi* mentioned before. This controlled transition from the refined to the natural is a matter of great importance. It is also a matter of such high art that only rarely can outstanding examples be found. One such example is the temple of Tofukuji in Kyoto.

If a building or plan area of any predetermined character is to be imposed on a landscape area of any other character, transitions from one to the other will play an important role. If, for example, a civic plaza and art museum are to be built at the edge of a city park, all plan elements will become more "civic" and sophisticated as one leaves the park to approach the plaza. Lines will become more precise. Forms will become more refined and "formal." Materials, colors, textures, and details will become richer. The natural park character will give way gradually, subtly, to an intensified urbane character consonant with the planned expression of the museum and its supporting plaza. Conversely, if a rolling, wooded recreational area is to be built in a highly developed urban area, plan forms and spaces will relax and be freer

Rikiu was watching his son Shoan as he swept and watered the garden path. "Not clean enough," said Rikiu, when Shoan had finished his task, and bade him try again. After a weary hour the son turned to Rikiu: "Father, there is nothing more to be done. The steps have been washed for the third time; the stone lanterns and trees are well sprinkled with water; moss and lichens are shining with a fresh verdure; not a twig, not a leaf have I left on the ground." "Young fool," chided the teamaster, "that is not the way a garden path should be swept." Saying this, Rikiu stepped into the garden, shook a tree and scattered over the garden gold and crimson leaves, scraps of the brocade of autumn.

OKAKURA KAKUZO

75

Studied transition, structure to site

Where site and structure meet we may well "structure" the site and at the same time "wash" the landscape over and into the structure.

HIDEO SASAKI

and "more natural" as one approaches the park. Such controlled intensification, relaxation, or conversion of plan expression in the relation of object to object or area to area in the landscape is the mark of skilled physical planning.

Yang and yin   The well-conceived project or structure entails more than the *application* of a function or a complex of functions to a plot of land. Planning that disregards the compelling forms, forces, and features of the total site fails to utilize the full site potential for the project. Worse, it produces needless frictions. Often, one or many of these frictions may become so insistent as to preclude the very functions for which the project was developed. Such a project fails.

The well-conceived project or structure seldom results from the all-out *adaptation* of the project to the site. By such abject submission of program to site factors, the project and site may be blended to the point of camouflage. This result may, rarely, be desirable. Usually, however, the program requirements suffer through the effort to conform.

The well-conceived project is rather more than a studied *integration* of program functions and site functions. Such integration is desirable, even essential. It may well achieve harmonies of function and harmonies of esthetics. Yet without further purpose, the mere wedding of project and site may dilute the best qualities of both and result in a new hybridized site-structure expression that is inferior to the highest expression of parent program or the existing character of the site.

The ideally conceived project is one in which the ideal program functions are conceived in awareness of the highest potential of the site and in which both are realized and dramatized together. This ideal site-project expression may be achieved through either harmony or contrast of the project with the forms, planes, or character of the site, or through a combination of both. The project plan and forms must always be determined in full awareness of the total site and its optimum relationship and contribution to the project. Unsuitable site factors are modified, ameliorated, or eliminated. Positive site factors are developed, extended, and accentuated. Project or structure and *modified* site are conceived together as *one*. Always there must result a complete unity — a fully satisfying resolution of site and project functions. Such unity is typified by the Chinese symbol *yang* and *yin* evolved in the misty beginnings of time and representing the complete and balanced unity of two opposing yet complementary elements — man and woman, earth and sea, and, in planning terms, the functions of the program and the functions of the site.

ORGANIZATION OF SPACES

3

IN THE DEVELOPMENT of the site-structure or site-project diagram we were concerned with "use-areas" and their relationship to one another and to the total site. Now we are concerned chiefly with the translation of these areas into "use-volumes" or spaces — each volume or complex of volumes having a shape, size, material, color, texture, and other qualities that best express and accommodate the function for which the space is intended.

SITE VOLUMES

Much of the art and science of land planning is revealed to the planner when he first realizes that he is dealing not with *areas*, but with *volumes* or *spaces*. A playground, for example, is not a collection or grouping of play equipment arrayed on a given base plane, but more properly, a series of volumes incorporating these things. A well-designed playground is a series of well-organized volumes, each volume skillfully devised to provide the most useful and pleasant space for its specific function.

A highway is not just a strip of pavement on an elongated land plane. A properly designed highway must be conceived also in terms of volumes; open where safe vision and pleasant views so dictate; closed for screening; varied in form, texture, and color for interest and relief from fatigue; modulated to reveal the natural landscape and complement the structural highway elements in the best possible way. The ideal highway will be a scientifically contrived, expanding and contracting, variformed volume, through which the motorist may move speedily, safely, and freely, enjoying a highwayscape designed to keep him relaxed and happy and, at the same time, alert.

A city is not just a heterogeneous conglomeration of buildings arranged about the land in a rigid pattern; the mature planner approaches it in terms of its pattern of open spaces. More than the buildings, it is the arrangement and character of the open spaces they define that give a city its essential quality. Perhaps the most disturbing fact about our disturbing American cities is that they are generally oriented to the clamor and friction of constricted city streets, rather than to

People live on the earth, on the land, but in the three-dimensional air-space, the atmospheric volume, immediately above this land surface. Plans and land-use maps may be measured diagrammatically and abstractly in square footage and acreage, but space for living is measured in cubage, in volumes of air-space enclosed or organized with tangible physical elements.

. . . .

It can be stated categorically, on the basis of our experience of great architecture and great natural scenery, that the experience of being within fine three-dimensional spatial volumes is one of the great experiences of life.

GARRETT ECKBO

Architect's model of Chase Manhattan Bank and plaza. An architectonic well of space.

Site volumes — degrees of vertical enclosure

traffic-free courts, squares, plazas, parks and open spaces. The creation of pleasantly organized spaces for any use and of any scope is our major work as physical planners.

Spatial impact   It is possible to design a volume that will torture its inhabitant. During the Spanish Civil War, it is said, an architect was ordered to design a highly refined torture chamber. He developed a translucent, multicolored polyhedron of sharply intersecting planes — an insidious enclosure in which a locked-in victim found himself unable to lie, sit, stoop, or kneel without tilting or tumbling the chamber. The surfaces were slippery, burning hot in the sun, and frigid in the cold. In any light, the colors were distressing if seen alone, and seen together, in their discordant clashing, soon became maddening.

If it is possible to devise unpleasant volumes, then we should be able to create volumes that will give an experience of pleasure. We may recall a favorite fairway of our golf course as such a space. Expansive, free, undulating, it is open to the sky, lightly or tightly enclosed with foliage and carpeted with turf. An outdoor space of far different character is the cascade approach and plaza of New York's Radio City. Walled by a canyon of metal, masonry, and glass, its base is cut flagstone and terrazzo, and its overhead plane a tower-framed segment of sky, relieved by the tracery of foliage and the moving color of waving flags. Here is a space artfully planned to attract, refresh, and excite us and condition us for entry into the sophisticated restaurants, shops, and offices that line its sides. Not far away, we can find another outdoor space of high design refinement. The garden of the Museum of Modern Art is an urbane space eminently suited as a backdrop and visual extension of the adjacent galleries — or as a place in which to wander through pleasant sunlit and shaded spaces, viewing the pools and sculp-

A site volume that clearly, and beautifully, expresses its use

80

Three moods of the Lower Plaza of Rockefeller Center: in the summertime with its gay tables set out beside the splashing coolness of the handsome Prometheus fountain, during the Christmas Holidays, and in winter converted to a skating rink — an urbane space laced with music, motion, and kaleidoscopic color.

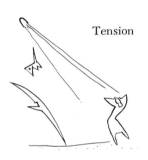

Tension

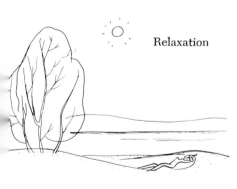

Relaxation

Gaiety

ture. There will come to mind, upon reflection, many other similarly pleasant site volumes — a sheltered picnic spot on some lake shore, a college stadium, a city square, a private swimming pool. By analysis, we find that all these spaces are pleasant because, and only because, in size, shape, and character they are manifestly suited to the purposes for which they are used.

As an instructive exercise, we might list the abstract design qualities or spatial characteristics of a series of varying volumes, each specifically designed to induce a predetermined emotional or psychological response (given in italics).

Tension   Unstable forms. Split composition. Illogical complexities. Wide range of values. Clash of colors. Intense colors without relief. Visual imbalance about a line or point. No point at which the eye can rest. Hard, rough or jagged surfaces. Unfamiliar elements. Harsh, blinding or quavering light. Uncomfortable temperatures in any range. Piercing, jangling, jittery sound.

Relaxation   Simplicity. Volume may vary in size from the intimate to the infinite. Fitness. Familiar objects and materials. Flowing lines. Curvilinear forms and spaces. Evident structural stability. Horizontality. Agreeable textures. Pleasant and comfortable shapes. Soft light. Soothing sound. Volume infused with quiet colors — whites, greys, blues, greens. *"Think round thoughts."*

Fright   Sensed confinement. A quality of compression and bearing. An apparent trap. No points of orientation. No means by which to judge position or scale. Hidden areas and spaces. Possibilities for surprise. Sloping, twisted or broken planes. Illogical, unstable forms. Slippery hazardous base plane. Danger. Unprotected voids. Sharp, intruding elements. Contorted spaces. The unfamiliar. The shocking. The startling. The wierd. The uncanny. Symbols connoting horror, pain, torture, or applied force. The dim, the dark, the eerie. Pale and quavering or, conversely, blinding garish light. Cold blues, cold greens. Abnormal monochromatic color.

Gaiety   Free spaces. Smooth, flowing forms and patterns. Loop-

81

The court of the Swedish Pavilion at the 1939 World's Fair in New York. Few out-of-doors spaces in our time have surpassed this court for sensitivity of organization, for interest, or for that quality one may call "charm."

In Japanese art space assumed a dominant role and their attitude toward it was strengthened by two important Zen concepts. Zen affirmed the reality of immediate experience and yet declared its indivisibility from a present defined as "The moving infinity" — its oneness with life in eternal flux. Space was felt to be the only true essential, for only in space was movement possible. Space was the universal medium through which life moved in constant transformation, in which place and time were only relative states.

NORMAN F. CARVER, JR.

ing, tumbling, swirling motion accommodated. Movement and rhythm expressed in structure. Lack of restrictions. Forms, colors and symbols that appeal to the emotions rather than the intellect. Temporal. Casual. Lack of restraint. Pretense is acceptable. The fanciful is applauded. Often the light, bright, and spontaneous in contrast to the ponderous, dark, and timeless. Warm bright colors. Wafting, sparkling, shimmering, shooting, or glowing light. Exuberant or lilting sound.

Contemplation   Scale is not important since the subject will withdraw into his own sensed well of consciousness. The total space may be mild and unpretentious or immense and richly ornate — so long as the structural forms are not insistent. No insinuating elements. No distractions of sharp contrast. Symbols, if used, must re-

Fright

Fright

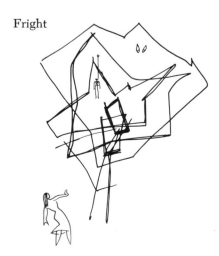

Contemplation

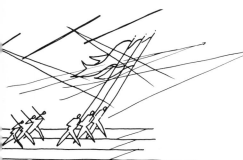

Dynamic action

Sensuous love

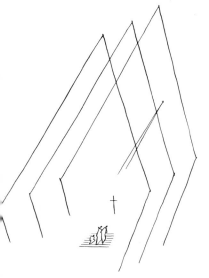

Sublime, spiritual awe

relate to subject of contemplation. Space must provide a sense of isolation, privacy, detachment, security, and peace. Soft diffused light. Tranquil and recessive colors. If sound, a low muted stream of sound to be perceived subconsciously.

Dynamic action   Bold forms. Heavy structural cadence. Angular planes. Diagonals. Solid materials as stone, concrete, wood or steel. Rough natural textures. The pitched vertical. Directional compositional focus. Concentration of interest on focal point of action — as to rostrum, rallying point, or exit gate through which the entire volume impels one. Motion induced by sweeping lines, shooting lights, and by climactic sequences of form, pattern, and sound. Strong primitive colors — crimson, scarlet, and yellow–orange. Waving flags. Burnished standards. Martial music. Rush of sound. Ringing crescendos. Crash of brass. Roll and boom of drums.

Sensuous love   Complete privacy. Inward orientation of room. Subject the focal point. Intimate scale. Low ceiling. Horizontal planes. Fluid lines. Soft rounded forms. Juxtaposition of angles and curves. Delicate fabrics. Voluptuous and yielding surfaces. Exotic elements and scent. Soft rosy pink to golden light. Pulsating, titillating music.

Sublime spiritual awe   Overwhelming scale that transcends normal human experience and submerges one in a vast well of space. Soaring forms in contrast with low horizontal forms. A volume so contrived as to hold man transfixed on a broad base plane and lift his eye and mind high along the vertical. Orientation upward to or beyond some symbol of the infinite. Complete compositional order — often symmetry. Highly developed sequences. Use of costly and permanent materials. Connotation of the eternal. Use of chaste white. If color is used, the cool detached colors, such as blue-greens, greens, and violet. Diffused glow with shafts of light. Deep, full, swelling music with lofting passages.

Displeasure*   Frustrating sequences of possible movement or revelation. Areas and spaces unsuitable to anticipated use. Obstacles. Excesses. Undue friction. Discomfort. Annoying textures. Improper use of materials. The illogical. The false. The insecure. The tedious. The blatant. The dull. The disorderly. Clashing colors. Discordant sounds. Disagreeable temperature or humidity. Unpleasant light quality. That which is ugly.

Pleasure*   Spaces, forms, textures, colors, symbols, sounds, light quality, and odors all manifestly suitable to the use of the space — whatever it may be. Satisfaction of anticipations, requirements, or desires. Sequences developed and fulfilled. Harmonious relationships. Unity with variety. A resultant quality of beauty.

If we were to list the requisites of the ideal space for each of a series of varying *uses,* we might be amazed at the variety of suggested spatial characteristics. *A child's play lot,* for example, would be designed

* It is to be noted that "displeasure" and "pleasure" are general categories whereas "tension," "relaxation," "fright," and the others mentioned are more specific. With these more specific responses we can list in more specific detail the characteristics of the volumes designed to induce them. The degree of "pleasure" or its opposite, "displeasure" would seem to depend on the degree of sensed fitness of the volume for its use, and a unified and harmonious development of the plan elements to serve this function. It can be seen that one could therefore experience pleasure and fright simultaneously (as in a fun house) or pleasure and sublime spiritual awe simultaneously (as in a cathedral), and so forth.

An exterior space endowed with many of those design characteristics that we associate with pleasure.

From its hollowness arises the reality of the vessel; from its empty space arises the reality of the building.

LAO-TSE

A creation in space is an interweaving of parts of space. . . .

MOHOLY-NAGY

Architecture . . . is the beautiful and serious game of space.

WILLEM DUDOK

84

as a space of amusing confusing complexity — a dynamic volume shaped to induce and withstand motion and action. Bright splashes of color and arresting forms and textures would be an asset, because the tactile sense of children and their response to brilliant hues and interesting shapes is highly developed. Their play space may well be variformed with curves, zigzags, and angles, evolving from tight to free, a series of tunnels, obstacles, baffles, and places to climb under, over, into, and through — a place of strong contrasts; sun-to-shadow, smooth-to-rough, bright-to-dull, open-to-closed, high-to-low. A proper playlot for a child is a plaything in itself; a place of curiosity, wonder, and fun.

A *space for private outdoor dining* would have a different set of values. As a volume it should be simple in shape, intimate in size, and refined in texture and detail. It should be shaped to induce repose. It should create a serene and pleasant atmosphere conducive to dining and conversation. For the point of highest interest, it might well focus on the surface of the table and the faces of the diners poised above it. It should no doubt be a casual, light, and airy space of studied subtleties. As can be imagined, if the child's play activities were transposed to a space such as we have described for dining, the child would soon become restive. If, on the other hand, the dining table and diners were moved to the space designed as a playlot, we could in time expect no less than nervous collapse or chronic indigestion.

Spatial qualities   The essence of a volume is its quality of imposed or implied containment.

A confined space may be static. It may hold interest, induce repose. It may direct and concentrate interest and vision inward. The whole spatial shell may be made to seemingly contract and bear, to engender a feeling of intensity or dynamic compression.

Alternatively, a space may open out. It may direct attention to its frame and beyond. It may fall away, or seem to expand. It may burst outward. It may impel outward motion.

A space may be a flowing undulating space, suggesting directional movement.

A space may be developed to have its own sufficient, satisfying qualities, and seem complete within itself; or it may be incomplete — a setting in which to introduce objects.

A space may be in effect a vacuum.

A space may have expulsive pressure.

A space may be developed as an optimum environment for an object or a use.

A space may be so designed as to stimulate a prescribed emotional response; or it may be so developed as to produce a predetermined sequence of such responses.

To grasp space, to know how to see it, is the key to the understanding of building.

BRUNO ZEVI

Architecture represents an organic unity of all space in planning considerations. The elements consisting of structurally enclosed, semi-enclosed and open spaces, in reality are parts of a wholeness or total space environment. It is apparent, then, that in this wholeness, the buildings themselves constitute merely particularized spaces in which it is desired to provide controlled environmental conditions. . . .

ERNEST J. KUMP

Space is not plastic, static, positive, projecting. It is hollow, negative, retiring. It is never complete and finite. It is in motion, connected to the next space and to the next — and to the infinite space. . . . We (who have learned to move faster — faster than anyone ever moved before) have a new experience of space: space in motion, space in flow. And because we have this new experience we are no longer concerned so much with the tiny detail, but rather with the greater unity of this new and wonderful medium: the flowing space we try to mold.

MARCEL BREUER

A space may be dominated by an object. This classic site-volume was an early work of Mies van der Rohe.

A space may dominate an object, imbuing the object with its particular spatial qualities. Or it may be dominated by an object, drawing from the object something of its nature.

A space may have orientation — inward, outward, upward, downward, radial, or tangential.

A space may relate to a force, an object, or another space, and may gain its very meaning from the relationship.

A component space in a composite space is colored by the greater space.

A total or composite space assumes to a degree the qualities of its component spaces or cell volumes, and must relate them into an effective entity.

Spaces, by nature, may vary from the vast to the minute, from the light and airy to the heavy and ponderous, from the dynamic to the serene, from the crude to the refined, from the simple to the complex, and from the somber to the dazzling. Spaces, in their size, shape, and quality, may vary endlessly. In designing a space for any given function, we would do well to first determine the essential qualities desired, and then do our best to create them.

Spatial size   Planned spaces are usually considered only in relation to man or the functions of man. Paddocks, corrals, dog-runs, canary cages, and elephant traps are exceptions, but even these spaces are best conceived with more than fleeting attention to the habits, responses, and requirements of the proposed occupants. Take the elephant trap, for instance. Few architects approach their planning with a keener awareness of their client's traits and habits than the native builder who directs the construction of the stout timber and rattan enclosure for the trapping and training of wild elephants. The canary cage too, with its light enframement, seed cups, swinging perches, and cuttlebone, is a volume contrived with much thought for the well-being of the canary. In planning spaces for man, it seems plausible that his accommodation and happiness should be of equal concern to the planner as are those of the bird and the pachyderm.

It is well known that the size of an interior space in relation to man has a strong psychological effect on his feelings and behavior. This fact may be illustrated graphically as follows:

Traditionally, the West has been concerned with the enclosers of space — in structure and in form. The East, to the contrary, has been more concerned with the quality of the spaces enclosed and with the intellectual and emotional impact of these spaces upon those who experience them.

LESTER COLLINS

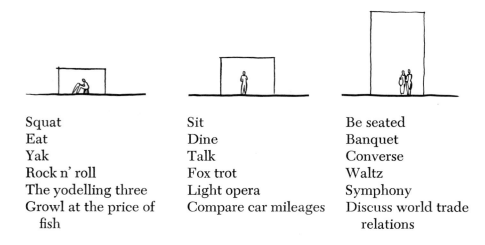

Squat	Sit	Be seated
Eat	Dine	Banquet
Yak	Talk	Converse
Rock n' roll	Fox trot	Waltz
The yodelling three	Light opera	Symphony
Growl at the price of fish	Compare car mileages	Discuss world trade relations

Man on the horizontal orients to the vertical.

Exterior spaces have similar psychological attributes. On an open plain a timid man feels overwhelmed, lonesome and unprotected; left to his own devices, he soon takes off in the direction of shelter or kindred souls. Yet, on this same plain, the bolder spirit feels challenged and impelled to action; he has freedom, room for movement, for dashing, leaping, ya-hooing. The level plane not only accommodates, but also induces mass action, as on the polo field, the football field, the soccer field, and the racetrack.

If, upon this unobstructed base, we set an upright plane, it becomes an element of high interest and a point of orientation for the visible field. We are drawn to it, cluster about it, and come to rest at its base. No small factor in this natural phenomenon is man's atavistic tendency to keep his flanks protected. The vertical plane or wall gives this protection and suggests shelter. Increased protection is afforded by two intersecting upright planes. They provide a corner into which our atavistic man may back, and from which he may survey the field for either attacker or quarry. Additional vertical planes define spaces that are further controlled by the introduction of overhead planes. Such

recurrence

87

Stonehenge

spaces assume not only their size and shape and degree of enclosure from the defining planes, but also a resultant character induced by the separate planes acting together and counteracting. This space may be one of tension or repose; it may be stimulating or it may be relaxing. It may be immense, suggesting certain uses, or it may be confining, suggesting others. In any event, we are attracted to those spaces that we feel are suited to our use, be it hiking, target shooting, eating grapes, or making love. We are repelled by, or at least have little interest in, those spaces that appear to be unsuited to the purpose we have in mind.

The Japanese, in their planning, have learned to develop spatial volumes of such intrinsic human scale and personalized character that the spaces can only be satisfied by the presence of the person or persons for whom they were conceived. The Abbot's garden of Nikko for instance, is only complete when the Abbot and his followers are seated sedately on the low broad terraces, or are wandering contemplatively among the gnarled pine trees or beside the quiet ponds. The Imperial Shinjuku gardens, sublimely beautiful and faultlessly groomed, seem always somehow incomplete except in the Emperor's presence. In all Japan, each family home and garden, planned together and as one unit, is a balanced composition of interior and exterior spaces so designed as to call for, and need for fulfillment, the master, his family, and his friends for whom they were created.

Some spaces are man-dominated, and are controlled in size by the reach of his arm or the turning radius of his car. Other spaces are intentionally planned to dominate man. The visitor to the Grand Canyon is brought into relation to the dizzying heights and yawning depths so that he thrills to their maximum impact. On the Blue Ridge Parkway, in Virginia, man is intentionally brought to the edge of a sheer precipice, and then, on some narrow rocky ridge, is thrust like an ant against

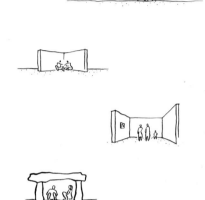

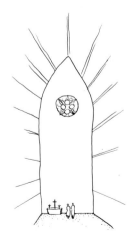

the vast, empty dome of the sky. Ancient, mysterious Stonehenge in England, a great circle of space carved out of the moors with massive stone posts and lintels, is a dramatic reminder that even the primitive Druid priests in their dim forgotten centuries already knew the power of the space to inspire and humble man. It would seem that even then they must have sensed that man's soul is stretched by the feeling of awe, and his heart revitalized by the experience of abject humility.

Between the micro and macro spaces we may plan spaces of an infinite range in size. The volumetric dimensions should never be incidental. We must calculate and contrive those dimensions that will provide the optimum space or spaces for each prescribed human experience.

Spatial form   It has been said that, ideally, in designing or planning, *form must follow function.* This statement is much more profound than it seems. It is open to some argument unless, as we have previously assumed, esthetic considerations are considered a part of function. What all this means is that any object or thing should be designed as the most effective tool (in form, materials, and finish) to do the job for which it is made; and moreover, it should look it. If the designer can achieve an actual and *apparent* harmony of form, material, finish, and use, the object should not only work well, but should also be pleasant to see. Let us take a simple example. An axe handle has for its specific purpose the transmitting to the cutting edge of an axe-head the full power of the axeman's stroke. A superior handle is made of selected, straight-grained, seasoned ash with just the right degree of toughness and flexibility. It is shaped to the grip and butted to prevent slipping. From the grip it swells in a strong force-delivering, shatter-resistant curve of studied thickness and length. When the tapered helve is fitted and wedged at precisely the right angle to the head, the axe is in perfect balance, lies well in the hands, and is good to use. It is also good to look at. To the woodsman it is beautiful.

If the woodsman were shown a new axe with a handle made of plastic he would probably shake his head incredulously — a handle that had no grain and looked like glass surely couldn't be trusted. To him the handle would appear comical, incongruous, and ugly. If, however, by experience he came to learn that the new handle was in all ways superior, in time he would come to admire it — and for him no axe with a wooden handle could ever be as beautiful again.

89

A sloop is designed to utilize the driving force of the wind in propel-
ling a floating object through the water. In the superior sloop the hull
is fastidiously shaped to best cleave the waves, slide buoyantly through
the water, and leave a smoothly swelling wake; the deep lead keel extends the conformation of the hull as a streamlined stabilizer; the spars
of clear pine are so fashioned and bent as to carry the optimum areas
of canvas; the humming stays are of finest stainless steel cable; the
halyards and sheet are of braided nylon; the chaulks and cleats are
so formed as to fairly reach for the lines; tiller and rudder are precisely
fitted and balanced to sweep and bear. Such a sloop, heeled and
scudding, is a miracle of shapes, materials, and forces working in harmony. Here again form is designed for function — and the form is a
beautiful thing. For, as the poet Keats has told us, "Beauty is truth,
truth beauty."

Not only things, but spaces as well, should be given their form with
high regard for function. We have seen that this is true of the child's
playlot, of the planned highway, and of the hypothetically ideal city.
Without doubt the greatest common denominator of all pleasant site
volumes is this very quality.

Having allocated and organized the required use-areas for a project
site, the planner proceeds to develop these areas into use-volumes,
each volume being designed in size, shape, material, and finish to best
express and accommodate the use for which it is planned, and to best
relate it to all other project functions and volumes.

Spatial color   In passing, we might mention an early Chinese theory
of volumetric color design. Man, according to this theory, has become
so accustomed to the color arrangements of nature that he has an
aversion to any violation of the accepted pattern. It follows that, in
selecting colors for any man-made space, interior or exterior, the base

An early study for the new city of Nemours in Algiers by Le Corbusier and
P. Jeanneret. Note the complete and sensitive adaptation of all use-areas and
structures to the natural topographic forms. Note also the adept way in which
use-areas have been translated into use-volumes.

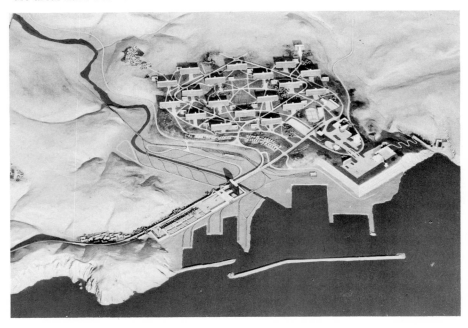

plane is treated in earthy colors — the hues and values of clays, loams, stones, gravels, sands, forest duff, and moss. The blues and blue-greens of water, recalling its unstable surface, are used but rarely on base planes or floors, and then only in those areas where walking is to be discouraged. The structural elements of wall and overhead are given the colors of the tree trunk and limb — blacks, browns, deep greys, reds, and ochres. The receding wall surfaces adapt their hue from the wall of the bamboo thicket, the hanging wisteria vines, the streaming sunlight and foliage of the glade, the pine bough, and the interlacing branches of the maple. The ceiling colors must recall the airiness of the sky, and range from deep cerulean blue or aqueous greens to misty cloud whites or soft greys. This writer has found that this tested theory of nature adaptation applies as well to the use of materials, textures, and forms.

There are, of course, many other theories and systems of color application.

One theory would keep the volume enclosure neutral, in shades of grey, white, or black, and let the objects or persons within the room thus "glow" with their own subtle or vivid color. Another theory calls for infusing a space or coloring a form with those hues and values that, alone or in combination, produce a prescribed intellectual–emotional response. Given a basic color theme or melody, it modulates harmonious overtones to soothe, contrasting ones to interest, and discordant ones to incite. Another system manipulates spaces, and objects within those spaces, by the studied application of recessive and dominant values and hues.

Another would determine for any given structure one expressive color which, running through the whole, could be used as a dominant unifying trunk. All other colors would be, to this trunk, its branches, twigs, leaves, flowers, and fruit. In such a scheme can be sensed a cohesive organic *system* of color like that of the willow, the sassafras, the mountainside, the river valley, or any other element or feature of nature. Still another theory proposes that hues and values have no meaning except in combination, and gain their impact through carefully devised relationships. All systems of color theory attest to the truth that spaces, or things within the spaces, have no meaning except as they are experienced, and that, in creating spatial experiences, the knowledgeable handling of color is essential.

Abstract spatial expression   We have learned that, just as abstract design characteristics may be suggested by a given landscape type, abstract spatial characteristics may be suggested by a given function. The spatial characteristics of a cemetery, for instance, would hardly resemble those of a Coney Island-type park. We come to the amusement park for a laugh, for a shock, for a change, for relief and escape from ordered routine. We want to be fooled, and delight in confusion and distorted, contorted, ridiculous shapes. We seek the spectacular, the spinning, tumbling, looping, erratic motion. We love the roller coaster's flash and roaring crescendo, the brassy clash of cymbals, the jarring sock-ring-a-ling-ting of the tambourines, the rap of the barker's hammer, and the raucous honkytonk. We thrill to color as gaudy as grease paint, as garish as scarlet and orange tinsel, as raffish as dyed feathers, gold sequins and rainbow–hued glitter. We expect the scare, the boff, the flirt, the shriek, the come-on, the tease, and the taunt. All is gay tumult; all is for the moment; all is happy illusion. We accept materials as cheap and as temporary as bunting and whitewashed two–by–fours. Everything is surprising, attracting, diverting, winding, expanding, contracting, arresting, amusing, and dynamic — carnival atmosphere. If we want a successful amusement park, this atmosphere must be planned. We must create it with all the planned whoop-de-doo and spatial zis-boom-bah that we can conjure into being. This is not just desirable; in such planning it is vital. Here, order and regimentation are wrong, and the stately avenue or the handsome mall would be in fatal error.

How different are the spatial requirements of a cemetery. The cemetery volumes we would expect to be serenely monumental, spacious, and beautiful. We would expect some imposing enclosure, to provide protection and imply detached seclusion. The entrance gates, like the prelude to an anthem, would give theme to the spaces within, for these are the earthly gates to paradise. Man enters here in his moments of most poignant sorrow, seeking to bury his dead in solemn ceremony, as has man from time's beginning.

He comes in grief, seeking that which will give solace and comfort. The general spatial character of a cemetery might well suggest peaceful quietude in terms of soothing muted colors, subtle harmonies of texture, soft rounded forms, horizontal planes, still water, the ethereal, and the evanescent.

Troubled and questioning, man seeks here reassurance and order. Order as a spatial quality is affected by evidence of logical progressions, visual balance, and ordered cadence of plan or spatial revelation.

Humbled and distraught by the presence of death he would orient himself to some superior power. The presence of such divine power may be suggested in plan form and by symbol. A sensitive variation of the classic axial treatment that so compellingly relates man to a concept perhaps has no better application than here. There may well be closed spaces for contemplation and introspection. There may also be breathtaking vistas and sweeping views, so long as vista and view are in keeping with the sacred and the sublime. At those thoughtfully selected plan areas where an inspirational quality is to be concentrated or brought to culmination we might use the soaring verticals that effect an uplift of the spirit. Again, an appropriate sculptural group placed at the edge of a dark reflective surface, or a simple cross of white marble lifted against the sky may evoke in the viewer an emotional response of great satisfaction and meaning.

Man seeks here a fitting and final resting place for those whom he has loved. In planning, this concept is translated into terms of the eternal and the ideal. The eternal may be suggested by planned harmony with the timeless features of the landscape — the moss, the fern, the lichened rock, the sun, the grove of gnarled and venerable oaks, the gently sloping summit of a hill. Materials must be enduring, such as marble, granite, and bronze. Idealism may be expressed through the enlightened creation of those spaces and those high art forms that will instill in man the firm conviction that here in this sacred place the living and dead are truly in the presence of their God.

Many will note that these spatial requirements are similar to those of

The design characteristics of the successful trade fair are reminiscent of the carnival.

a church chapel or sanctuary; and, just to the extent that they are similar, will the church form and spaces resemble architecturally their cemetery counterpart. These qualities refer to no one particular cemetery more than any other. They are, rather, the abstract spatial qualities suggested by the function of all cemeteries.

In like manner, any such function we may name — the shopping center, the summer camp, the outdoor civic light opera — will immediately bring to our mind desirable spatial characteristics. These, it should be apparent, are pertinent to the planner.

The elements of containment   In a large measure all spaces acquire their being and their character from the elements that contain them. Because each element so used will imbue the space in some degree with its own qualities, it must be well related not only to all other such elements, but also to the essential resultant character desired for the space.

Lines, forms, colors, textures, sounds, and odors all have certain predictable impacts on the human intellectual–emotional responses. If for example, a certain form or color *says* or *does* things to the observer, this is reason enough to employ such a form or color in the shaping of those structures, objects, or spaces that should ideally hold this same message for the observer. Surely, if the *abstract* expression of a given line violates the *planned* expression of structure, object, or space, it should be used only with studied intent and care.

Where the containing elements of a space have linear characteristics,

93

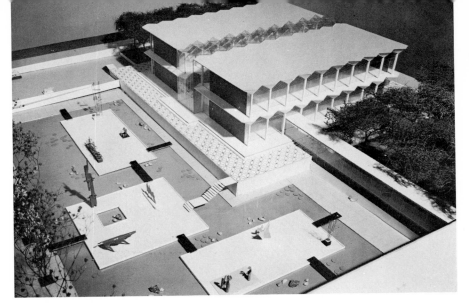

Abstract line expression is structural, solid, and strong.

the abstract line qualities are of great design importance. Every line evident in the form or surface of any element, or described by the meeting of any forms or planes, has its own abstract design expression. This expression must be in harmony with the intended nature of the space. A graphic demonstration of variations in abstract line expression follows.

Variations in Abstract Line Expression

Lines, forms, colors, textures, sounds, smells — all have in the abstract certain predictable impacts on the human intellectual-emotional responses. If, for example, a certain form *says* things, or *does* things to the observer, this might be reason enough to employ such forms in the shaping of those structures or objects or spaces that should ideally have for the observer this same message. Surely, if the *abstract* expression of a given line violates the *planned* expression of structure, object, or space, it should be used only with studied interest and care.

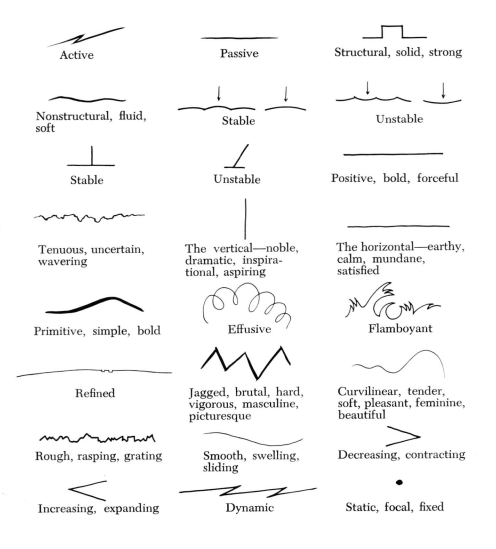

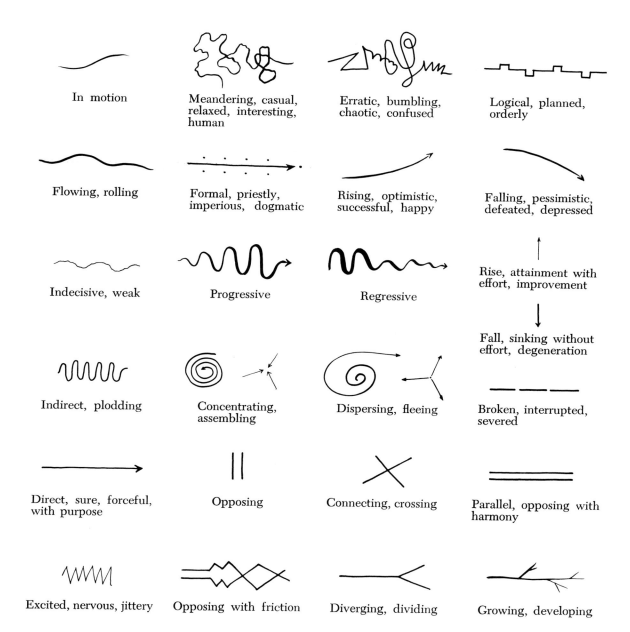

In motion

Meandering, casual, relaxed, interesting, human

Erratic, bumbling, chaotic, confused

Logical, planned, orderly

Flowing, rolling

Formal, priestly, imperious, dogmatic

Rising, optimistic, successful, happy

Falling, pessimistic, defeated, depressed

Indecisive, weak

Progressive

Regressive

Rise, attainment with effort, improvement

Fall, sinking without effort, degeneration

Indirect, plodding

Concentrating, assembling

Dispersing, fleeing

Broken, interrupted, severed

Direct, sure, forceful, with purpose

Opposing

Connecting, crossing

Parallel, opposing with harmony

Excited, nervous, jittery

Opposing with friction

Diverging, dividing

Growing, developing

Detail of pool edging. Abstract line expression is fluid.

Functions of vertical enclosure. Induced human responses vary with the type and degree of enclosure.

Complex for excitement, diversion, curiosity, surprise, induced movement

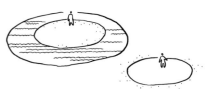

Enclosure may be effectively *implied* by strong demarcation of the base plane

Simple enclosure for concentration on idea, form, and detail

Confined for relaxation and induced repose

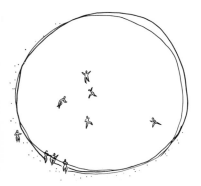

Open and free for induced action and exuberance

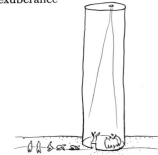

Volumes may be contrived to impart specific predetermined emotional and intellectual impacts

Space unlimited

Definition of volumes   The orientals have long understood that to have significant spaces you must have enclosure, and that the size, shape, and character of the enclosure determine the quality of the space. Openness, void, or mere expanse are not enough; they may be only emptiness.

Outdoor volumes may be of infinite scope, limited only by the distant horizon and the farthermost reach of sky. Or they may be as finite as the space between two cedar fronds or the crevices in a weathered face of limestone. In shaping outdoor volumes the planner is not limited, as in architectural or engineering construction, by material forms, sizes, or cost factors. He may employ not only the full range of structural and fabricated materials, but also all the materials of nature, from the crude to the highly refined. A seaside volume may be formed naturally of pounding surf, luminous sky, craggy rock, and a wind-battered strand of wild sea-grape. A sophisticated city park volume may be shaped largely by the masses and voids of the surrounding skyscrapers. It may be defined further by a pavement of sawed stone slabs in pattern, clipped beech, tubbed oleanders, treillage, spun brass fountain bowls, glazed tiles, and illuminated water.

An exterior space may be as loosely defined as a volume of sand for a floor, blue sky and quaking aspen foliage overhead, and the walls demarked only by low junipers scattered sparsely across the dunes. Or an out of door space may be tightly controlled by terrazzo mosaic pavement, polished marble walls, sculptured panels, fluted glass in burnished frames, ceramic murals in rich pattern, and brightly colored canopies of fabric. All exterior volumes, controlled or free, are formed of three volumetric elements, the *base plane*, the *overhead plane* and the *vertical space dividers*.

An out-of-door volume on a grand
scale — delimited only by rolling
wooded pastureland as a base, by
craggy mountain slopes on the vertical plane, and by lowering clouds
overhead.

A highly sophisticated volume focused upon a three dimensional mural constructed upon the base plane.

On the base plane we are most concerned with *use*.

THE BASE PLANE

The base plane is closely related to the site-structure or site-project diagram, with its studied arrangement of *use-areas;* for this is the plane on which we are most concerned with *use*. What we see when we look at a project plan is what is laid out on the base plane. The shapes, materials, and textures imposed here are those that best accommodate the proposed uses, and coordinate them into a cohesive plan. If the base plane is improperly developed, nothing that follows has meaning. For here we establish the kind of use, the area allocated for each use, the surface best suited for the use, and the plan relation of each use to all others. If we fail here, our plan is a failure; and, no matter how well contrived the rest of the spatial enclosure, our plan is still a failure.

The base plane surface is often the natural surface of the earth. With its topsoil strata, ranging from thin to deep, its soil moisture and fertility, and its cover of plants, this plane is veritably the base of all life. This fecundity of the land, together with its natural contour and cover, if once destroyed, is lost forever. It is interesting to note that a one-inch topsoil section is roughly a thousand years in the making, and the rash waste of this precious substance is, in America, a common and devastating sin. The wise planner will never disturb or modify this natural ground plane without reason. Any modifications he makes will be those that best implement the proposed use.

More than two thirds of the earth's surface is, as we know, submerged in water. The balance of surface area is generally underlaid with a fresh water table that fluctuates slowly in elevation, and through which imperceptible currents flow. This water rises continually by capillary action, keeping the soil layers moist and the adjacent air layers cool. From this bountiful subsurface reservoir, fresh water may be tapped and used, so long as the free water in the local water-bearing soil is not depleted. Such depletion is caused not only by overuse, but also, and more often, by the destruction of the natural ground cover, topsoil, duff, low plants, and trees, which absorb rain and snow water and store it in the earth. Without this cover, precipitation drains off the exposed land surface unchecked, causing erosion, floods, and lack of essential ground water reserves. This is another reason why we, as knowledgeable planners, must set ourselves to preserve within reason the unspoiled natural surface areas of the earth.

The general composition of the earth plane is mineral — its components ranging in hardness from diamond through solid granites, limestones, and shales to clays, sands, and loams. The supporting strength and stability of the soil and mineral strata depends not only on the nature of each stratum, but also on its angle of inclination, the presence of water, and its relation to the other strata and to the surface. Appearances are deceptive; deceptions are often disastrous. If the degree of support and stability are of consequence, then we must investigate the subsoil by drilling, testpits, or core borings, to be sure of soil types and load bearing capacities for all structural elements.

Masterfully related to its base plane, this superb structure reveals a studied transition from the mineral and moisture of the earth to the lightness and airiness of the sky. Note the posts on stone, the platform, the lightly framed balcony, the upcurved straw roof, and the poised phoenix on the roof cap.

An American home that recognizes and springs from the stone, the water, and the fecund soil of the earth's broad base plane.

Our traffic ways on the base plane are established rigid or fluid.

Because it is mineral in fact and in connotation, the earth plane suggests the use of those materials that are mineral or of mineral extraction. The soil and the moisture and frost it retains are powerful eroders and corroders. From the structural point of view, extreme care must be taken in the selection of materials that are placed on, or make contact with, the earth. In considering outdoor spaces, we associate with the earth plane such natural materials as rock, gravel, water, sand, and plant materials; and such refined materials as brick, concrete, asphalt, ceramics, and tile. Such materials seem compatible. Other materials, such as fabric, leather, finished woods, and polished metals seem unsuited; even when special processing has made them suitable, they are nevertheless visually disturbing.

It is on the base plane that we establish our traffic ways. Either rigid or fluid, within the limits of the plan flexibility, they are aligned best when they are in sympathy with the earth's natural conformation. To "buck the land" is to invite expensive cuts and fills and require costly drainage structures. Moreover, on the disturbed surface areas a tight-knit cover must be reestablished for the sake of appearance and to preclude erosion. The most stable and most beautiful drives and highways of the world are those that generally follow the ridges and the valley floors, and rise or fall across the side slopes, where the cross gradient is most naturally suitable. Perhaps such drives are pleasant because they are basically lines of dynamic force flowing in harmony with the natural forms of the earth. Our friend Plato, if we could question him on this point, would nod in sage agreement.

A highway planned to flow in harmony with the natural conformation of this beautiful valley floor.

Skilled handling of the base plane. Brick, redwood, gravel, and foliage suggest patterns of movement and repose.

Every object found on the base plane has plan significance. If the object is to be moved, the ease and means of moving warrant consideration. If the object is to be modified, the degree and type of modification must be analyzed. If the object is to be preserved, its relation to other elements of the plan must be thoughtfully considered. We must remember that the essential quality of a piece of land is the quality of the land surface and that which springs from or underlies it. If we preserve and adapt this essence, we have best used the land.

The base plane, in a world of gravity, gets the most use and wear. It requires the most care and maintenance. The planner must recognize, as does the caretaker, that all materials and textures applied to this plane should be selected with concern for their permanence and appearance during all phases of their projected use.

The earth plane — level, warped, sloped, or terraced — is the base for all construction. This is the plane *on* which, *in* which, and *around* which all things are placed. This plane sets the theme and the primary cell forms of the project. All use-cells introduced on this plane are best allowed to grow and develop in harmony with the total area and surrounding space.

The treatment of the base plane is important to the accomplishment of proper transitions. The shapes and patterns of the base, if well handled, may subtly or powerfully relate a structural element to the site. Through the treatment of the ground surfaces we may relate one structural element to others; and through the treatment of their designs we may (by contrast or harmony) accentuate, articulate, and coordinate all elements placed on the base surfaces.

THE OVERHEAD PLANE

In outdoor spaces we come to think of the overhead plane as being free — extending to the tree canopy or the sky. Seldom, if ever, has man been able to devise anything as beautiful. Even the open sky, however, has its limitations. We sometimes require shelter; and further, we know that our site spaces and volumes, to be effective, must have height control. To realize this we need only hold one hand palm upward and the other palm downward over it, and slowly bring the two together. We can at once, by this exercise, sense the spatial importance of the overhead. We will remember, as children, our pleasure in crawling under a porch floor, or, as adults, sitting under a low porch roof or under an arbor. Even in a large open area, a suspended or supported overhead surface may provide this psychological, and perhaps physiological, function.

When open blue infinity is suitable as a ceiling, we accept it and perhaps rack our powers of ingenuity to best feature the sky with its kaleidoscopic cloud forms and opalescent colors by day, and its glorious show of constellations in the night. It has been said that, if man were permitted to view the sky but one day and night of his life, he would count it his most memorable earthly experience.

When the sky is not suitable as a ceiling we contrive overhead controls. The form, character, height, and extent of overhead enclosure

A circular sunshade of plastic provides the overhead plane of this intriguing space. On the right is a space frame.

We must create pools of still-ness, areas of entrancement; and the purpose of these is not to escape from life — even the vibrant life created by the new sources of energy that charac-terize our modern civilization — but to enjoy life in its pro-foundest essence.

SIR HERBERT READ

104

will have a telling effect on the spatial character of the volumes they help to define.

The new overhead plane may be as light and airy as treillage or canvas; it may be as solid as reinforced concrete, or beams and planks; it may be perforated, pierced, or louvered; or it may be a pattern of solids and voids. If solid, it controls not only the sun and rain, but, by its degree of translucence or limit of overhang, the amount and quality of light. To appreciate the effect of light on a given space we need consider but a few of its unlimited qualities. In color, light may be pearly, milky, amber, cobalt, lemony, aqueous, inky, sulphurous, or silvery. In intensity, it may range from pale, soft, or limpid to bril-liant, blazing, dazzling, or blinding. Light has motion, as shooting, piercing, quivering, dancing, scintillating, creeping, flooding, or stream-ing light. It has distinctive character, as dappled, splotched, or mot-tled light; as subdued, harsh, or glaring light; as searching, glinting, shadowy, gleaming, or glowing light. Light has mood, as gloomy, haunt-ing, or mysterious; as cozy, inviting, or exciting; as relaxing, refresh-ing, or cheering light. These are but a few of its qualities and effects that have design application.

The solid overhead plane may serve as a shield or modifier of natural light, or it may act as a source of direct or reflected illumina-tion.

If pierced or partially open, the overhead plane is not in itself as important visually as are the shade and shadows it casts. We may consider such a plane as a disc, or film, or patterned screen held up between the sweeping orbit of the sun and the textured surfaces upon which its shadows fall and over which they move. Generally the man-made spatial ceiling is kept simple, because it is to be sensed more often than seen.

Light fabric on the overhead plane.

THE VERTICALS

The vertical elements are the space dividers, screens, baffles, and backdrops. Of the three volumetric planes, the verticals are the most easy to control. Conversely, they have the most important function in the creation of outdoor spaces. They contain and articulate the use areas; and may tightly control and enclose such areas, as with masonry walls, or more loosely, as with a tracery of foliage.

By plan manipulation, the vertical elements may extend and expand the use-areas to apparent infinity, by screening out the near or obtrusive features of the landscape and revealing such receding or expansive features as the distant view, the horizon, or the limitless spaciousness of the open sky.

Enclosure for privacy   It can be seen that neither enclosure nor openness is of value in itself. The degree and quality of enclosure must be considered in relation to the function of a given area. Enclosure is desirable where privacy is desired. The orientals have a faculty for creating their own privacy by mentally blocking out those things or spaces they find to be distracting or disturbing. They seem able to bring into sensed focus a space or volume suited to their pleasure or their needs. This ability enables them to enjoy a degree of privacy even in a crowded market place. For the occidental mind this is more difficult, and such privacy as we may require must usually be sought out or achieved by planning.

It has been said that, in our modern civilization, privacy is at once **105** one of the most valuable and one of the rarest of commodities. We may readily observe this lack of privacy by walking down almost any city street. Inexplicably, our contemporary homes have been

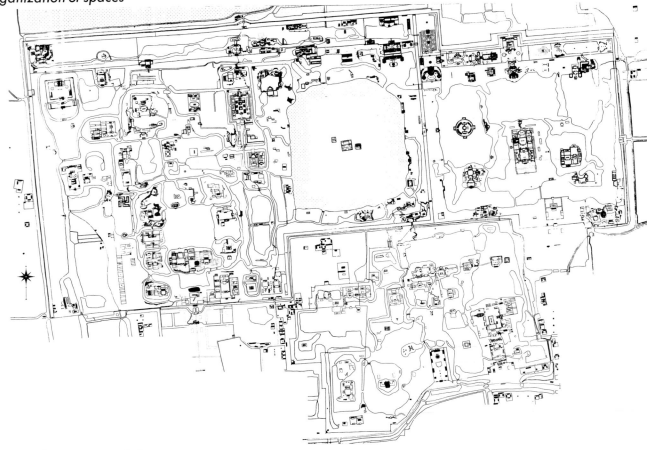

The Garden of Perfect Brightness

The articulating power of the vertical. Without these upright posts, the low rock masses, or the enclosing wall of foliage, much of the charm and interest of this garden space would be lost.

106

oriented to the street and avenue — designed as showpieces and displayed for public approbation. Our gardens, our terraces, even our interior living areas, through the use of large glass window walls, have been opened to the public. This bizarre compulsion to be seen at all times, and in most all situations, is unique to our times. If it be mistaken for an evidence of democratic freedom, we have perhaps overlooked the most significant freedom of all — the freedom of privacy. We may hope that this tendency toward public display is just a passing phase, for privacy has long been recognized as essential to human well-being and to the cultivation and appreciation of those things that are of highest human value.

We are only now beginning to realize again the advantages of private living and working areas that are screened from the street and oriented to the enclosed court or garden. In Egypt, Pompeii, Spain, Japan, and in all mature cultures, such walled residences, palace courts, and temple grounds were, and still are, the most functional and pleasurable of all planned spaces. Perhaps we, in our new and experimental culture are rediscovering the logic and charm of the walled or screened enclosure.

Enclosure for privacy need not be complete or rigid. It may be achieved by no more than a strategically placed screen. It may be attained by a loose arrangement of elements providing a screen in depth. Such a screen is the wall of woodland–trunk, twig, and foliage. Such a screen might also be effected by the dispersed arrangement of any standing elements.

Privacy

Scale induction

Sun
Wind
Sound
pollution

Filter and diffuser

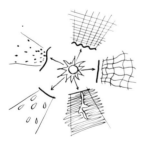

Mystery

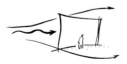

Transmitter (cast shadow pattern)

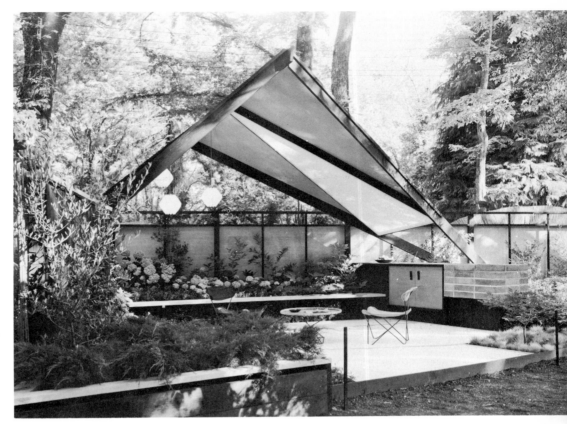

Wind control

A pleasant out-of-door volume that provides both shelter and privacy.

Qualities of enclosure   Vertical enclosure may be as rugged as the rocky face of a cliff or a wall of piled-up fieldstone. It may be as sophisticated as a panel of carved or molded glass or rich ceramic mosaic. <u>The range of form and materials is limitless</u>. But whether massive or delicate, crude or refined, simple or ornate, the essential business is to suit the enclosure to the use of the space or the use of the space to the predetermined enclosure. The nature of the vertical elements providing enclosure must be in keeping with the nature and use of the space enclosed. Usually, in fact, the verticals, more than any other design elements, develop and produce the character of a given volume. If the space is to be gay, bright, or exciting, the "walls" of the space must be bright and light, and induce gaiety and excitement. If the space is to connote serenity, dignity, and order, so must the enframing vertical elements express and induce a sense of serenity, dignity, and order in their form, materials, color, and arrangement.

Visual control   All things seen from a space are a visual function of that space. Not only the extent and nature of the enclosure, but also the extent and nature of the revealment must be in keeping with the use of the space that is framed. For anything that can be seen from a space is visually *in* the space and must be taken into account. Often an object far removed may be introduced to the space by opening to, enframing, and focusing on the object. A far off mountain peak or a nearby tree may thus be "brought into" a garden. The bustle and clamor of a sprawling city and its harbor may, for its therapeutic value, be "brought into" the convalescent spaces of a

107

Functions of the screen

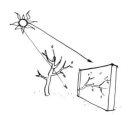

Receiver (shadow plane)

Decorative surface

Proper background

Background should not compete in interest

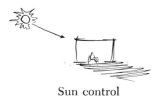

Sun control

Visual control

military hospital grounds. A distant cathedral campanile may thus be "transported" to a church yard, or a quiet pond to the dormitory terrace of a girls' academy.

The verticals may direct attention inward or outward. Enclosure is desirable for those areas where interest is to be centered upon an object or where detail is important. It is evident in such cases that distractions should be eliminated and that we must devise an enclosure to best display or complement the object or reveal the detail. It would be difficult, for instance, in viewing a piece of sculpture to appreciate those subtle nuances of light and shade that reveal the modelling of a torso, if the sculpture were seen against a moving stream of city traffic or a line of flapping laundry. Even against a vista of great serenity much of the startling beauty of an individual rose, for instance, would be lost to the observer. For the backdrop of anything to be featured should rarely compete in interest. Spatial enclosure, when doubling as a backdrop, should be so devised as to bring out the highest qualities of the object to be seen against it.

In general it may be stated that, where interest is to be directed to an object within a given area, we must contain the area in such a way as to focus attention inward. Where the interest is to be directed outward to object or view we will pierce or open the enclosure in such a way as to best accentuate and frame that which is to hold our attention.

Elements within a volume   Vertical elements provide not only containment, screen, and backdrop, but often become the dominant

The observer, on an elevated pathway, moves across and over the garden. Thus, through a precisely described pattern of circulation, the changing colors and patterns of the horizontal floral "mural" are revealed.

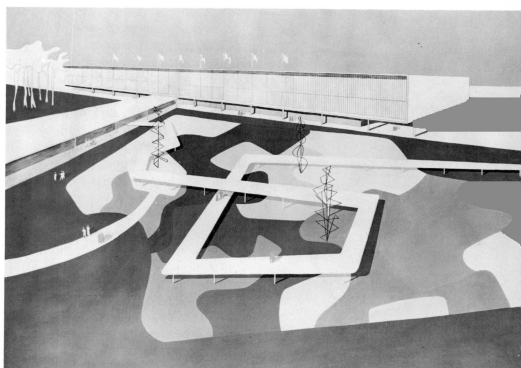

A vertical element as the focal point of a volume. The spirit of the figure and the spirit of the space are one. Note how the heavy structuring and deep shadows of the volume give emphasis to the airy, luminous quality of the moving sky.

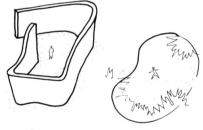

Enclosure may be light to solid

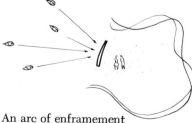

An arc of enframement may give adequate privacy

Enclosure by dispersed plan elements

spatial feature. Such verticals may include furniture or equipment set about on the base plane — a specimen magnolia of striking branching habits and flower, a cool jet of rising and falling water, or a children's slide or climbing structure of welded metal tubing. Such objects standing free assume a sculptural quality and may well be considered in sculptural terms. In scale and form they must satisfy the hollowness of the space, enrich it, pick up and accentuate its character. Its shapes may counterplay with the shapes of the space, may "read" against the enclosing planes as against a carefully selected backdrop. If the object is to dominate, the plane is subdued to serve as a foil and to make the object "sing." If the spatial plane is to dominate, as in a mural, or a building facade, the standing object is so placed or designed as to heighten the interest and spatial impact of the plane.

When an object is placed within a space, the object *and* enclosure may "read," but often more important is the expanding, contracting, evolving relationship of the spaces between the two.

The roundness or squareness or simple solidity of an object may best be dramatized by placing it off-center in a variformed volume, so as to develop dynamic spatial relationships between it and the enclosing planes.

109

Functions of enclosure

Concentration of interest

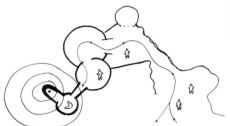

Controlled progressive development of a concept

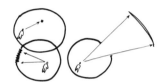

Visual control

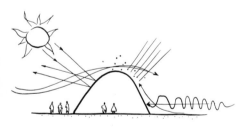

Privacy, shelter, protection

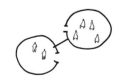

Classification of interest

The vertical elements of the house are used to define, enframe, and interplay with the richly composed interior-exterior volumes.

An object that itself has dynamic or intricate lines is usually best displayed in a volume of simple shape so that the spatial relationships enhance and "explain" the object rather than confuse or detract.

When several objects are placed in a volume, the interacting spaces between objects, as well as between objects and the enclosing planes, are of high design importance.

Structures as vertical elements   Often buildings are the dominant vertical elements within or surrounding a space. If within, they may be treated as sculpture to be experienced in the round. Within or without, the space is so developed as to focalize attention on the major facades and to impel movement toward the entrances.

The space may be designed to serve as foreground or setting, or as an anteroom, or a functional compartment of the building. The function of the building may even be concentrated in the space and the building itself be incidental. Such structures, as vertical elements, may serve in themselves, and perhaps primarily, as spatial enclosures, dividers, and backdrops. In planning any structures in relation to a space, or vice versa, we need first be clear as to the purpose or purposes of each before we can determine their proper character and form.

Public squares, circles, or plazas flanked by structures pose a complex problem in design, for structures, plazas, and the people who use them must all be "in scale." Which is to dominate — the space, the buildings, or those who use them? St. Peter's clearly dominates its piazza and the crowds assembled there. Boston Common rules as verdant queen over the edifices at her sides. The tiny town squares of Capri, Italy, and of Tasco, Mexico, on the other hand, are in effect no more than charming stage sets for the lounging, dining, parading townsfolk and tourists who gather there from early sunup to the late cool hours of the evening. People, spaces, or structures — which? There is no rule.   Accept, surely, that each, in turn and together, must be taken into full account and that all relationships are made pleasant through a sense of fitness.

The vertical as a point of reference   In planning any area for any purpose, except where mystery, bewilderment or confusion is to be an intended function of the plan, it is well to set up enough signs or symbols to give orientation to those who will use the areas. Usually such signs will give not only points of reference but also a *theme* to the spaces they dominate or explain. A revolving ferris wheel, for example, draws one to and sets the key of the amusement park. A venerable beech tree on a rise, the library companile, or the ceremonial flagstaff of the parade ground may so "explain" and guide one through a campus — just as the bright greens with their numbered flags induce one from hole to hole around the golf course.

In the treatment of large spaces, the author has discovered a curious planning phenomenon that has many useful applications. He has found that a freestanding vertical element or panel brought near to a small use-area within a large space may have such a strong visual relationship to the use and the user that it imparts its own scale to both. For example, a given plaza may be vast and overwhelming to a person who enters or wanders through it. If, say, a small bench is placed within the space, the volume by contrast may seem even more over-powering. A person seated on the bench would sense only his relation-

Precise control of form, materials, light, acoustics, temperature

Elimination of distractions

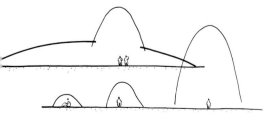

Emotional implications of varying spacial volumes

Fence, white poles, foliage, sun, and shadow

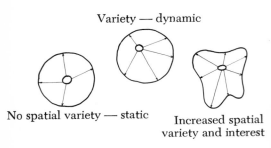

Variety — dynamic

No spatial variety — static

Increased spatial variety and interest

Piazza Umberto I, Capri

Form clarity lost by improper enframement.

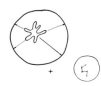

Complex form interest heightened by simple enframement.

Several objects placed in a volume relate to the enclosure not only singly but also as a group.

112

ship to the total space. If however, near the bench, we were to place a small honey locust tree, a stone fountain or a decorative screen, our intimidated friend would first sense that he was seated under the tree, beside the fountain, or near the screen and only incidentally within the greater space. He would relate himself to the scale of the object introduced.

Within a large space many such human reference points may be placed and, indeed, these must be furnished if the individual is not to feel himself overwhelmed. (We recognize, of course, that historically the primary objective of many great public spaces has been to humble and even humiliate the crowds that mill about within them.) Where awe, wonder, or humility are to be instilled by spatial concept, the human reference points are removed or distorted. Where human comfort and assurance are desirable, a human scale must be made evident. Generally, the steps, doorways, or windows of adjacent buildings suffice to give a sense of human scale; if not, such human reference points must be otherwise provided.

The vertical in relation to pix   In spatial design, the verticals generally have the greatest visual impact. Since, either moving about or seated within a volume, we are normally face to face with the verticals, we are usually more conscious of them than of either the base or overhead planes. We may assume that such standing surfaces or objects present the most design possibilities. It seems logical, then, that features of greatest interest or refinement should normally be placed or incorporated on the verticals and at eye height — *pix*. It would seem obvious that pix for a seated person is lower than pix for a person who is standing, but because this critical design factor is too often ignored, the point is emphasized.

One of the most distressing of all visual experiences is to have a vertical terminate at or near eye level, particularly if the vertical is a fence or wall. The top of such a wall or screen seems to slice or saw across the eye of those who pass by or see it.

One of the most pleasant of visual treats, on the other hand, is to have the eye come comfortably to rest upon an object or plane placed so that it falls into pleasing perspective and focus. If, moreover, in the thing observed, the viewer discovers subtle and delightful relationships to the space, the use, and the user, the pleasure is intensified.

Such relationships may be accidental, but more often they are consciously planned.

Verticals as articulators   Verticals reinforce and modify the traffic and use-patterns of the base plane. Just as the gate piers of a driveway say "enter," and just as the sweeping curbline says "follow me," and the entrance platform says "come to rest and alight here," so must the verticals of any space elucidate the plan. They must attract, induce, arrest, amplify, explain, receive, deflect, direct, detain, and accommodate the planned use, as the area demands. The plan pattern of the base plane most often sets the theme of a space, and the verticals most often modulate and reinforce the theme and produce those variations that develop the rich harmonies.

Verticals as controlling elements   The verticals, providing as they do the degree and kind of spatial enclosure, are important in the control of wind, breeze, sunlight, shadow, temperature and sound. The wind may be diverted, checked and, to a large extent, eliminated. Desirable breezes may be channeled to play across moist cooling surfaces or used to give motion and sound by activating flags, foliage, mobiles, or those most delightful of oriental divertissements, wind-flutes or wind-bells. Sunlight may be blocked, filtered, diffused, or admitted in its full glorious, healing, life-giving force.

Like the overhead plane, the verticals have an important function in casting shadows that may lightly wash across a paving, dapple a wall surface, dance, creep, flicker, tremble, stretch, blank out a space in dim coolness, or incise a bold architectural pattern onto the surfaces of the area.

Plant materials   The whole of the earth's land surface, as it were, is broken into variformed volumes by trees — free standing, in rows, clumps, or in masses. As he is to water, so is man instinctively drawn to trees and the inviting volumes they embrace and define. The attributes of trees are so manifold that, in the conceiving of any site volume, we usually first consider its construction in relation to existing trees. If we cannot use trees as a spatial frame, we usually draw upon the inexhaustible palette of plant materials that range from the wildly free to the stiffly architectonic in their native or manicured forms.

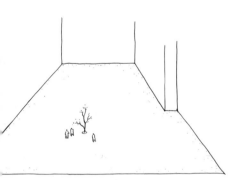

An object introduced within a large space may impart, within the area of its influence, its own lesser scale.

Effective enclosure   It must be remembered that the vertical space enframers are not usually seen from within the volume alone, but "in the round" as well. They, together with the volumes they enclose, become in total a unified landscape element to be related to all other landscape features.

An axiom   Lack of effective enclosure is the key to most unsatisfactory spaces or places. We cannot stress too strongly the need for the proper type and degree of vertical enclosure. All good site development is marked by the organization of vertical (and overhead) planes, to provide both optimum enclosure and optimum revealment. By such means, it can be seen, we must synthesize not only the micro-landscape, but the extensional landscape as well.

VISUAL ASPECTS
OF PLAN ARRANGEMENT

4

THE VIEW

A VIEW is a scene observed from a given vantage point. Often an outstanding view is reason enough for the selection of a site. But far too often, once attained, the view is poorly used or only partially exploited. Indeed, the proper treatment of a view is one of the highest and least understood of all the planning arts. A view must be studied, analyzed, and developed with keenly perceptive artistry to utilize even a fraction of the full dramatic potential. Like other landscape features, the view, by its handling, may be preserved, neutralized, modified, or accentuated. But, before we attempt to deal with the view, we must learn more of its nature.

A view is a picture to be framed, a kaleidoscopic picture of many blending facets.

A view is a theme. Its proper realization resembles the musical creation of variations on a theme.

A view is a constantly changing mood.

A view is a limit of visual space. It transcends the boundaries of the site. It may evoke a feeling of soaring freedom.

A view is a backdrop. It may be a garden wall, or a mural in a room.

A view is a setting for a structure.

Suitability as a plan factor   To be enjoyed, a view must be related to man and to those areas and spaces that he uses. But we must be sure that the use of an area and the view seen from the area are compatible. A scene of great activity, excitement, or tension, for instance, should hardly be introduced visually into an area of quiet repose. How could the schoolboy concentrate in a classroom facing a ballpark, or a river lock with its whistles, bells, and shouting gatemen and its straining tugs and tows? Or how, cajoled by such a view, could the draftsman keep his eyes on his board, or the librarian her thoughts on her card files? A scene of gentle pastoral tranquility may neutralize the effectiveness of a space designed to exhort men to action or inspire them to lofty thought. For such a purpose, the view should be lofty

A view is a mural.

115

A view is a theme that may suggest and give added meaning to well-related functions.

A view is a garden wall.

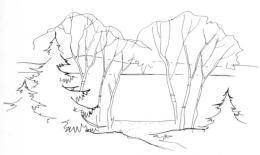

The best view is not always, or often, the full view.

A view is usually better if enframed or seen through an appropriate screen.

and awe-inspiring, vast and grand, or there should be no view at all. The invigorating qualities of a rocky chasm scene with craggy fir and the thunderous roar of rushing, tumbling water might well negate the serenity or passive atmosphere intended for an introspective space. A dynamic industrial scene of belching smoke, leaping flame, and switching freight cars, has its design applications, and its qualifications too. Even a sweeping night scene of a sprawling river city with its jewel-like constellations and patterns of light, its cubes and prisms of shadow and illuminated surface, its luminous vapors of smoke and steam, its crawling beetlelike traffic glows, its arcing river wakes and shooting beams, its trembling cloud reflections — even such a wondrous view as this may be unsuited to a number of use-areas, while for many others it would clearly be ideal.

Design treatment of a view   A view has landscape character. This will of course determine those areas or functions with which it should be combined. If the view is a dominant landscape feature, the related use-areas and spaces should be developed in harmony with the view as it exists or as it may be treated.

A view need not be seen full front, or approached from a fixed direction. It is a panorama, or segment of a panorama, to be seen from any or all angles. It may be viewed on the oblique, on the sweep, or broadside.

A view is an impeller. A powerful magnet, it will draw one far, and from one position to another, for the opportunity of better commanding its limits or seeing some part in a new and intriguing way. The planner should let a view develop as the viewer moves across it, just as a mountain climber experiences more and more of the view as he ascends, until he sees it in total.

The modulation of a view.
From a glimpse through loose
foliage, to enframing slot, to
wider sector, to reverse interest, to vista, to object seen
against the view, to reverse
interest, to objects placed
against the view seen through
a film of fabric, to concentration in cave-like recess — to
full, exuberant sweep.

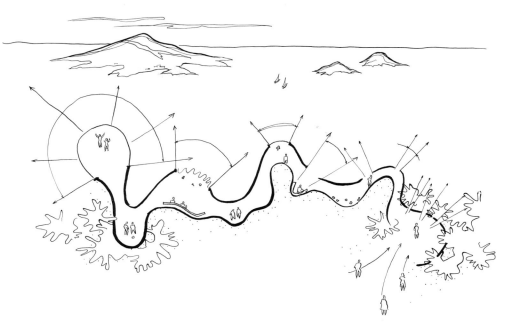

Light or incongruous detail
placed against a view may result in split interest and annoyance.

If the view is to serve as a
backdrop, the object placed
against it must be in character, and it must be dominant.

117

A view may be subdivided. It may be appreciated facet by facet, with each bit treated as a separate picture and so displayed as to best capture its special qualities. Through precise planning, a view may be deftly modulated as one moves from area to area. Each area will, by direction, foreground, framing, or by the function of the space, relate man to some new aspect of the scene until, at last, the complete panorama is revealed.

A view gains in force when certain plan areas are developed as a counterpoint or foil. If we stand for long at one vantage point comprehending a view in its entirety, it begins to lose its first fresh appeal and strikes the senses with less impact. The interest of the open view may be sustained and much accentuated when certain plan areas are developed in balanced opposition. Such an area might be enclosed, with a narrow slot or constricted aperture opening on some absorbing detail of the scenery. It might be a chaste volume kept simple and severe in form, and white, grey, or black in tone, so that the wide and colorful mural of the view might glow more vividly. It might be a recessive area, leading one away from the view into some cavelike interior space for contrast, so that, emerging to the expansiveness of the view, one senses an emotional response of great release and freedom. A plan volume may incorporate some feature subtly or powerfully related to the view — a ship relic related to a view of the ocean; black hammered iron to a spectacle of blazing furnaces; a fruit bowl to an orchard view; a trout etching to a scene of splashing brook; a fox, grouse, or wild turkey, or hunting accoutrements to a panorama of rolling gameland; or a candle to a distant cathedral campanile.

Some areas, to give respite, might best be planned with no apparent relation to view. For a heady view, like a heady drink, should be absorbed slowly and in moderation. Split interest is a hazard in the treatment of a view. Light detail placed in front of a scene is usually lost, or seems, rather than an element to be enjoyed, an element of annoyance. If the broad view is used as a backdrop the object or objects placed before it must, singly or as a compositional group, have the power to dominate the backdrop.

The power of suggestion   If a view, or an object in the landscape, is by design *suggested* only, the mind will multiply the possibilities of perception and thus expand the scope and richness of the suggested experience. The silhouette or shadow of a pine branch seen through a translucent panel or screen, or projected upon it, is often more effective than a direct view of the branch itself. The dim outline of an abstract form seen at a distance or in half light is thus often of more value than the same form seen fully and in detail.

It has long been the belief of the Zen Buddhists, writes Okakura Kakuzo in *A Book of Tea,* that "true beauty could be discovered only by one who mentally completed the incomplete. It was this love of the abstract that led the Zen to prefer black and white sketches to the elaborately colored paintings of the classic Buddhist School."

Concealment and revealment   A view should be totally revealed in its fullest impact only from that position in the plan where this is most desirable. It is not to be wasted in one first blast, but is to be conserved and displayed with perhaps more refinement, but certainly with no less feeling for suspense and timing, than shown by the striptease artist.

It has been told that near the village of Tomo in Japan, a celebrated tea master planning to build a teahouse, purchased, after much deliberation, a parcel of land with a startlingly beautiful view of the idyllic Inland Sea. His friends were most curious to learn how this great artist would exhibit his scenic prize, but during the time of construction were, of course, too polite to investigate, and waited to be invited.

On the day when the first guests finally arrived at the entrance gate, they could hardly contain their eagerness to see the fabulous ocean view as eloquently displayed by the great artist. As they moved along the narrow stone pathway toward the teahouse, they were aware that the sea was teasingly hidden from sight by the alignment of the path through the thin bamboo clumps. At the door of the teahouse, they reasoned, the view would be opened to them in some highly sensitive enframement. They were more than a little perplexed at finding the view there to be effectively *concealed* by a shoulder of lichened rock and a simple panel of woven straw fencing. As is the custom before entering a teahouse, they paused and bent over a stone basin brimming with water, to rinse their hands. As they raised their eyes from this bowed position they caught a glimpse, no more than a glimpse, between the great rock and a low dark branch of ancient pine, of the shining sea below them. And as they looked they sensed with tingling comprehension the relationship of the mother sea and the cool water at their finger tips.

Inside on the mats of the teahouse with the paper screens closed around them they performed the simple ritualistic rites of the tea ceremony, still mindful of the lesson of the sea. Relaxed and refreshed at the ceremony's conclusion, the guests were half surprised when their host rose quietly to slide back the screen walls of one side of the room, revealing in its perfect completeness the overwhelming beauty of a seascape that stretched from the edge of the grass floor mats at their feet to the farthest distant limits of the sky.

THE VISTA

A vista is a confined view, usually toward a terminal or dominant element or feature. It may be a natural vista, as an allee opened through a grove of Japanese maples to give a view of Mount Fujiyama; or it may be structural, as the majestic vista from the palace of Versailles toward the lavish Neptune fountain.

A vista, unlike a view, may be created in its entirety and is therefore subject to close control. Each vista has, in simplest terms, a viewing station, an object or objects to be seen, and an intermediate ground. The three together should make a satisfactory unit and are usually **119** conceived as an entity. If one or more of the elements already exist and are allowed to remain, then the others must, of course, be designed in conformity.

The view is a scene observed.

The vista is an enframed segment of a view.

Vista and allied use-areas must be compatible. If the vista is planned as an extension of a use-area or space, we must be careful of the relationships of character and scale. For example, the vista from the boardroom of a powerful bank, if there is one, should hardly terminate at the ferris wheel of an amusement park or the gates of the state penitentiary. Commanded by such a rarified viewing box of marble, gilt, and paneled rosewood, the vista and its terminus should be equally impressive and richly conservative and even, perhaps, equally as pompous. The vista toward a national monument should hardly commence at a service station, factory, or drug store. It might well start at another monument, civic building, or public gathering space. It is fundamental to the fine vista that the end justifies the beginning, and the beginning justifies the end. And just as the beginning and terminus of a vista are related in character, so must the middle ground and enframement of either be related to both.

The terminus The terminal feature on which the vista is focused sets the theme to be developed. All other elements must fall into cadence, support the theme in harmony and counterpoint, and carry the work to a final satisfying crescendo. There is no room for discord, the superfluous, or the inappropriate. A well-conceived vista has the balance, rhythm, and polish of a symphony or, perhaps, a string quartet.

For the vista is not always grandiose in scale, not even the memorable ones. The world is, in fact, laced and interlaced with beautiful vistas, and vistas within vistas, some no longer than the length of an arm. And these are often the delightful ones — not necessarily pretentious, not necessarily planned, but always the right thing seen from the right place with just the right enframement.

If it is planned that the terminal feature also becomes a viewing station, then the reverse vista should provide a new and rewarding visual experience. A terminal feature may serve as a focal point for several vistas. Such vistas need not, of course, be identical. Even if the viewing stations were identical, the middle ground treatment and enframement might well vary. If the same focal point is viewed from stations of varying character, each vista will, of necessity, vary also — since a vista is in essence a progressive visual transition from point to point.

A terminal feature may be seen in full or in part. It might be that a feature chosen tentatively as a focal point is too large in mass or plan area for the suitable termination of a proposed vista. Some portion of such a focal point might be selected in terms of appropriate quality or scale, and this segment used instead. It is only essential that either the entire terminal feature *or a visually satisfying element* of it be brought into proper perspective as the vista's focal point.

Enframement   A vista has three planes of enframement, all of which are usually best kept simple in form, texture, and color. The vertical planes may be natural or architectural — as loose as unclipped foliage or as severe as cutstone masonry or fabricated panels. The base plane or planes may be sloping, level, or terraced; in turf, water, paving, or other surfacing. Often the overhead plane is the sky, or the foliage arch provided by overhanging trees. It is to be noted, however, that by the manipulation of overhead planes at the viewing station, or else-

Enframement and vista must be compatible.

121

where, we may exercise great control over the quality and scale of the vista. In all cases we must prevent distraction through interest in the form or the detail of the overhead enframement.

A monumental vista, particularly, is often reflected in a water panel. If so, the water basin must reflect from the viewing station or stations a visually pleasant unit of the terminal feature. "Of course," we say, "of course, of course."

In this regard, the author recalls a shattering experience during a recent visit to our national capitol. Wishing to view the Washington Monument across the full sweep of the mall, he assumed that the most handsome vista would be enjoyed from the raised entrance platform of the Lincoln Memorial. As he mounted the grand stairway to the monument and the impressive seated figure of Lincoln, he was shocked to find the top stepline rising higher and higher in perspective on the figure of Lincoln, until it cut him off at his chin. Here was an unbelievable error in sightline design, a science long ago perfected by the Egyptians and the Greeks. Flushed with embarrassment for the planner of this stairway, the author at last gained the main platform and turned to look back across the grand mall to the towering shaft of marble at its far terminus. Surely, from here, the viewing platform, reflecting panels, and shaft must have been coordinated into such a flawless vista as would be a marvel of civic design. Panels must have been thoughtfully shaped in materials and proportion to best mirror the monumental image and hold it perfectly enframed in the long rectangle of water against the majestically moving reflections of the background sky. But the image of the imposing shaft hardly reached the basin! From the platform at the base of the stairs the effect was equally disastrous. Crossing the avenue to the viewing stage at the basin's end, the author found the reflected image of the monument to be no more than an abortive stub projecting foolishly onto the far half of the panel's water surface. Nowhere along the mall's entire length could viewer, panel, and terminus, let alone enframement, be brought into satisfying relationship. Shades of Le Notre, Amon Ra, and wise old Pericles!

Progressive realization   The terminal feature may be revealed in progressive stages. If a vista can be seen from several stations along the approaches, the section seen from each station must be considered as a separate vista and so staged. Sometimes a terminus may be viewed along an entire approach. In such a case, it should be so revealed by its evolving spatial containment as to exact the full potential of its changing perspectives. If the approach is long, the vista becomes tiring and should be divided into stages by change of level, by expanding or contracting the frame of reference, or by changing the character of the spaces through which and from which the focal point is seen. Often, as one moves toward a distant focal point, he can at first discern no more than the outline of the terminal feature. As he continues, the feature reveals itself progressively — the component masses, the texture and colors, and finally the details. Approaching a focal tower, for example, we perceive first its outline, then the general forms of base and tiers or soaring verticals. As we get nearer, we distinguish the shapes and colors of masonry, metal, and glass, and we recognize windows and doors. Finally, we are attracted to the rich handling of the entrances; and as we extend our hand at last to the polished door latch, we are invited inward by a glimpse of the pleasant lobby space beyond.

Any vista may be staged satisfactorily in an infinite variety of ways. It is only necessary that, from all viewing stations or lines of approach, the vista is a pleasing visual entity.

A vista may induce motion or repose. Some vistas are static, to be enjoyed from one fixed stage, and are seen in their completeness from this point. Others, by the promise of unfolding revealment, by interest in detail, or by the attraction of the terminus, invite movement and draw one from point to point. All vistas subject the viewer to a compelling *line* of sight. A vista is insistent, a directional magnet to the eye. As such, a vista is a visual function of a plan *axis*.

THE AXIS

The axis, essentially, is a linear plan element connecting two or more points. In use it may be a court, a mall, or a drillfield. It may be a path, a drive, a city street, or a monumental parkway. But always it must be regarded as a connecting element.

An axis, because it is an arbitrary line of plan diagram, can be precisely controlled.

In the planning process, the axis has many important applications. It also has its limitations; for, once an axis is introduced into a landscape, it generally becomes the dominant landscape feature. Established in a plan complex, it becomes so insistent that all other design elements must be related to it directly or tacitly. Any area or structure impinging upon the axis, adjacent to the axis, or leading toward the axis must draw much of its use, form, and character from this relationship. Any planned experience of view or movement from a peripheral point of origin toward the axis must be regarded as an experience of transition, culminating at the area of juncture.

At the garden of Versailles, for example, when we wander through the shady groves and diverting spaces far to the side of the axial canal, we are always aware that the canal is there, and somehow subconsciously adjust to this relationship. We sense that a certain path, for instance, leads *away* from the canal, and thus we expect it to relax its discipline of form and finish and dwindle into gradual rustication. Should the same path moving *toward* the great canal grow thin and less well defined, we would be perturbed; for we would know that just ahead we should soon be surveying the full grandeur of the great axis, and we would expect the path to be preparing us for the experience. Even if surprise were intended by the planner, the relationship of path to axis would be as significant. For, in such a case, the planner, by spatial manipulation, would soothe the viewer into a state of pleasant complacency, then suddenly, around a seemingly casual turn, confront him abruptly with the most astonishing aspect of breathtaking axial splendor.

Because it is a strong landscape element, the axis tends to subjugate or neutralize other landscape features. This can happen in more ways

The axis

An axis imposed on a free plan area demands a new and related order.

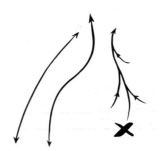

An axis may be bent or deflected but never divergent.

than one. It has been told that, in building the palace of Versailles, King Louis XIV questioned the fact that the three approach avenues were unequally spaced on the drawings. When he was advised that the offending avenue was so aligned to miss a nearby village, Louis replied that he failed to understand the point. The plans were revised. To preserve a perfect symmetry, one axial approach was of necessity driven throught the hapless village. Demolition crews set to work and the village was neutralized.

Almost as effective would be the driving of an axis through any established landscape area. Because the existing order of things would be disrupted, a new order would have to be devised — and this in relation to the intruding axial line, for there is little of polite gentility to the axis. It is forceful; it is demanding; and, as a result, things usually go its way.

> An axis is directional.
> An axis is orderly.
> An axis is dominating.
> An axis is often monotonous.

This is not to say that the axis is always best avoided. It is only to suggest that none of these attributes are conducive to relaxation, pleasant confusion, appreciation of nature, freedom of choice, or many other such experiences that we humans tend to enjoy.

A powerful axis requires a powerful terminus.

Axial characteristics   From a given use-area an axis is a strong plan line leading *out* and thus orienting the area outward. Such an area, both as a viewpoint and as a source of axial movement, might well express this outward flow. How can this be accomplished? By shaping the space to induce movement outward. By constructing in effect a viewing box with its aperture well focused. By fanning the paving lines out and away, or by sighting them accurately down the axial centerline. By concentrating interest at the forward edge of the staging area, inducing flow to and past it. By directional forms. By use of concentric arcs circling outward, as from pebbles tossed into a pond.

Often, in an axial plan, the viewing point and terminus are interchangeable. It can be seen that the forms and lines and details that dispatch us from one station would, if we approached from the opposite direction, seem to beckon and receive us. This is fortunate, because most axial treatments allow for looking both up and down the line of sight and for moving from one end to the other and back again. We find that each transmitting area thus becomes, in turn, a receiving area. We may correctly conclude that, where viewing point and terminal feature are interchangeable, each must express the characteristics of the source as well as the terminus of axial view and movement.

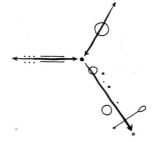

The axis is a unifying element.

An axis, being a line of *movement* and *use* as well as *vision*, must satisfy all three functions. The axis, like the vista it creates, combines primary, intermediate, and terminal spaces in the same volume. It would seem only reasonable that all three need be planned as integral parts of the whole. If the axial plan area is intended as a boulevard, it should,

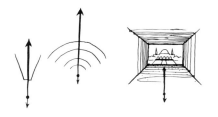

Terminus as a generator of axial movement.

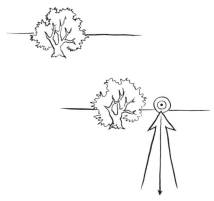

Often objects adjacent to a strong axis suffer in the relationship.

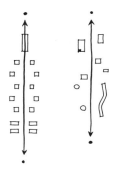

An axis may be symmetrical. But usually it is not.

from start to finish, look like a boulevard and function as a boulevard. Every building at its flanks should "belong" to the boulevard. Every space projecting or leading into its central volume should partake of the boulevard character.

Much lyrical praise has been heaped upon that prototype of all grand boulevards, the Champs Elysées of Paris. Much criticism has also been leveled at its sociological and economic impact on the city. But, for the moment, let us cast off the weighty implications of such charges and let ourselves rise up in our imagination until we can gaze down upon the whole stirring sweep of this magnificent axis.

Below us we see the grand Etoile, a wide traffic circle with forcefully radiating streets that disappear in the distance. The circle is massively defined by the stately trees and severe grey buildings at its sides. Its glistening pavement of clipped granite blocks is precise in pattern. The whole martial space has about it a stiffly proud and solemn air, as well it might, for there at its center looms the Arc de Triomphe, and at its wreath-lined base the Tomb of the Unknown Soldier, with its eternally glowing flame of tribute. The Etoile is a volume remarkably suited to its use. A focal point, the arch is seen fittingly framed for miles in all directions. A marshalling space, the circle is a converging space and a point of generation — for, as well as being the powerful terminus, the Etoile is also the head of the Champs Elysées, and its archway commandingly rallies attention to the wide start of the boulevard.

The axial boulevard marches on, out to the east, still crisply military in spirit, progressing firmly in measured cadence of structures and trees until, almost imperceptibly, we note less of a military and more of a regal character — less of the coldly regimented, more of the ornately monumental; for now we approach the palace group. Here the royal Grand and Petit palaces flank the Esplanade des Invalides as it sweeps in grandeur across the Seine to join the boulevard. The transition is now from palatial to civic as we continue along the Champs Elysées to the

The Arch of Triumph on the Etoile, at the head of the Champs Elysées

125

Place de la Concorde, with its pretentious ministries, secretariats, and Chamber of Deputies.

In our journey eastward from the Etoile we have passed resplendent apartments with silver entablatures, elite shops with high velvet curtains, proud restaurants with glittering chandeliers, and, finally, small cafes with their trim green awnings and crowded sidewalk tables, between which bustle the white-aproned *garçons* with trays poised lightly on fingertips. Here the boulevard takes on a lively air. Colors are gay, spirits are light, the smile is quick, and the heart is glad on the boulevard in Paris.

Beyond the ordered spaces of the Place de la Concorde we come to the Tuileries, the magnificent public gardens and park. At the gardens' end, and handsomely framed, we behold the palace of the Louvre, with its warm stone walls and richly ornamented gables and turrets. Fronting the majestic Louvre we see the clipped allees of sycamore, the wide gardens rolling with colorful flowers, the screeching traffic, trim nursemaids, perambulators, barking dogs and dodging children, the white bearded, pink cheeked old men in blue berets drowsing on the benches in the sun, the well-scrubbed jaunty sailors and their *belles jeunes filles*. All — all that is in this whole exuberant space belongs to it and is of its very essence.

And where along the length of this great axis do we find the discrepancies in plan, the discordant notes? Some there must be, and many perhaps, but they are lost in the captivating and ringing experience of moving down through this evolving complex of boulevard volumes, the "Elysian fields." From the hushed memorial solemnity of the arch at the Etoile, to the palatial, then stately governmental core, to the splendid apartments, the chic shops, the lively cafe district and on through the carefree expanse of the public gardens, to the grandiose museum of decorative arts. We feel ourselves to be in turn, in one brief morning's stroll, the soldier, the courtier, the statesman, the man of wealth, the gay dilettante, the poet, the lover, the relaxed, free, and happy boulevardier, the stimulated observer, and finally the distinguished connoisseur.

If planned today, this Champs Elysées would have a different mien. And so it should. For, since its conception, times have changed and conditions have changed, and plan concepts and forms have changed with them. The new "Champs" would have less of the old despotic formality, less unbending symmetry. Retaining its hallowed monuments, it would be less monumental. It would open out and free the teeming residential districts at its sides. It would be less of the classifier and more of the synthesizer. It would be more flexible and allow more flexibility. It would take its form from an empathetic understanding of the individual Parisian and his emerging culture. It would express his new freedom, new ideas, new techniques, and new aspirations. But let those who will change the present "Champs" first study it long and thoughtfully, for, in light of the times and society for which it was built, and for its masterful handling of forms and space, there is no boulevard that is its equal.

An axis has sometimes a negative, sometimes a positive effect on landscape elements within its field of influence. We have said that areas and

The good life is not a matter of good gimmicks or of physical ease; it is a matter of things that uplift the spirit. High averages will not define it. The Arch of the Etoile and the tree-lined streets that come to it and depart are more important to the good life of the poorest Parisian than a tenth of one per cent improvement in his substandard dwelling. I mean this rejection of the high average to apply to all elements of the good life — to the poetic life, to the political life, to the visual life, to the spiritual life. It is a life which occasionally though not too often must reach to ecstasy. Not too often because ecstasy can not be prolonged, as the readers of Dante's Paradisio can discover. But a life without these high points is not the good life.

JOHN ELY BURCHARD

126

An aerial view of Washington, D.C. The imposition of radial axes upon a rectangular street pattern leaves in its wake many awkward slices and undesirable properties. The freer urban street and land patterns of the future will eliminate this difficulty. Yet in our future urban planning we would do well to learn from Washington its lesson of the power of the radial axis to organize and unify a vast and sprawling city.

What is the monumental? The word, by the way, in the architectural sense, is quite new. Ruskin a hundred years ago spoke only of power. Actually it is a recent borrowing from from the French. "Monumental" they tell us is said of a building "qui a un caractère de grandeur et de majesté," *for a monument is an* "ouvrage d'architecture considérable par sa masse, son étendue, sa magnificence." *Grandeur, majesty, magnificence!*

HENRY H. REED, JR.

Today, we are more honest, more practical, and quite functional, but it has been at the expense of grace and gentility . . .

PIETRO BELLUSCHI

Yes, we have forgotten the simple courtesy of pleasing. What is true of architecture is even more so of city planning where the chief object seems to be to get the driver from A to B sitting down.

HENRY H. REED, JR.

objects adjacent to an axis are perforce related to it. Sometimes they suffer from the relationship, because the interest is less in the things themselves than in the thing-axis relationship. A fine sweetgum tree, for example, if standing alone, is observed in terms of trunk and limb structure, twigging, burgeoning foliage, sunlight and shadow patterns, interplaying forms and spaces, the beauty of its broad outline, and the detail of its leaves and twigs. If related to a strong axis, however, the same tree is noticed primarily as an object along the axis, and in relation to other axial elements. The subtle, the natural, the detailed, is lost to the axial line.

Sometimes, however, by the fact of their relationship to an axis, plan elements gain in interest and value. If as units they are dull, in pattern they may be attractive. If in form they are meaningless, in total axial composition they may gain significance. If by position they are inconspicuous, by axial frame of reference they may gain in prominence.

The axis as a unifying element A terminal or intermediate station of one axis may function also as the terminal or intermediate station of another axis. Thus two or more major plan areas may be focalized on a common point. Washington, D.C., whose plan diagram exemplifies this principle, has thereby developed one of the most cohesive metropolitan plans yet devised. Its long, radial, tree-lined avenues, converging on park, circle, structure, or monument, enframe compelling vistas of inspiring beauty and elegance and bind the city's complex and extensive component parts into coherent unity. If we distinguish in the plan arrangement the outline of monumentality, this seems preeminently fitting. Historically, in planning terms, monumentality has been man's *only* means of glorifying a concept.

Certainly Washington, by monumental plan, spaces, and architecture, as well as by mural, sculpture, and the enrichening contributions of all the visual arts, should epitomize the glorious idea of democratic freedom. This same (now inexplicably suspect) quality of monumentality is still sadly lacking in most other American cities. In truth, our towns and cities are in the main bleak and barren, made so by our overriding compulsion to be, first and last, *practical*, without regard for the visual aspects of function. By skillful use of the axis, widespread and heterogeneous plan areas may be related into a simple and comprehensible plan diagram. In such a case, the axis with its cross axes or intersecting axes becomes a skeletal plan element.

127

The lessons of Central Park in New York: its effect on real estate values, its inestimable value to the city, its ineffable meaning to all who see and sense and use it. These lessons should never be forgotten by the urban planner, yet how seldom. on even the smallest scale, do we see such urban parks envisioned, let alone brought into being?

Two examples   It is generally conceded that, in terms of its plan layout, the Chicago World's Fair of 1933 was a failure. It was simply too vast, too sprawling, and too disorganized. The fairgoer entering its gates felt overwhelmed, which was desirable in some respects; but he also felt confused, which was not. The visitor sought direction and points of orientation; he wanted to know where he was, where he was going, and how he might return. Seeking a particular exhibit, he wanted to know how best to get there. Finding himself in any one area of the fairgrounds, he wanted to know his relationship to the other fairground areas, the features, and the gates. He wanted, simply, to understand the Fair's plan and relate himself to it. Frustrated in this, he felt confused and lost, and often didn't pay a return visit.

The planners of the 1939 World's Fair in New York had the advantage of the Chicago experience. Carefully analyzing the Chicago Fair plan, they determined that it lacked most a dominant reference point or area to which all other areas were directly and clearly related. Translating this deduction to their studies of the New York Fair, they evolved as the dominating feature the trylon and perisphere that became at once the Fair's symbol, theme, and focal point. The trylon and perisphere commanded a great central axis of sculptural water panels, linden allees, exhibit groups, great fountain basin, and finally, in the distance, the impressive Court of the Nations. Leading to this axial core, and the features placed along it, were axial streets generated in the outlying reaches of the fairgrounds. These streets, of varying lengths, widths, and alignments took their character and flavor from the areas through which they passed. Visually, and actually, these axes and counter axes laced all plan areas simply into a cohesive whole that could be easily com-

The "Century of Progress," the Chicago World's Fair of 1933. Its site on the man-made lagoon was superb. But post-facto judgment has criticized the plan for lack of clarity and visual organization.

The New York World's Fair of 1939. The central theme symbols, the trylon and perisphere, became the focal point to which the vast grounds were oriented by broad axial ways. Visitors could "take a frequent bearing" and thus sense their relationship to the plan. The axes were treated mainly as decorative connective elements. With further study, and a more asymmetric treatment, they might well have become desirable and important "use-areas" of the Fair.

The 1958 World's Fair in Brussels. While the scheme was compact, the rambling plan diagram again led to visitor confusion. The theme symbol as an orienting feature would have been more effective if more centrally or dominantly placed.

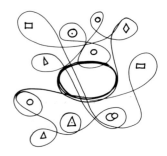

A small exhibit area may function well without a major vista or axis. Such a scheme permits a crowd to filter freely through the entire complex. In this case a powerful focal center is mandatory.

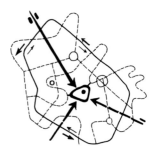

A diagrammatic and workable circulation plan for a large-scale exhibition area has the following features: main entrance, secondary entrances, major vista, minor vistas, strong focal point, major circulation loop, minor paths, and secondary focal areas and reference points for easy orientation.

Major and minor vistas need not be perpendicular.

prehended. Visitors took delight in moving through the extensive fairgrounds as exciting view and inviting vista were revealed to them, and as they easily found their way about.

Additional characteristics   A powerful axis requires a powerful terminus. Conversely, powerful design features are often, in the abstract, of such form or character as to require an axial approach. Such features are those best seen "head on,"

Or on the oblique from a fixed direction
Or those best seen in total at the hub of converging plan lines
Or those to be comprehended at a distance
Or those to be revealed phase by phase, or element by element, along a given approach line
Or those which in scale require a linear plan extension
Or those requiring controlled enframement and established viewing points
Or those that gain through a direct relationship to other plan elements.

The axis presents the most imposing foreground or approach to a structure or other plan feature. The key word in this axiom is "*imposing*," because the axis imposes a discipline upon spaces and forms as well as upon the viewer. The movement, attention, and interest of the viewer are imposed upon by axial composition and induced to alignment with the direction of its strong polarizing forces.

The axis subjects man to a fixed line of approach and thus subjects him to the thing approached. An impressive, dogmatic design form, the axis expresses the supremacy of man over nature and subjects man to a structure, feature, or idea. It denotes authority, discipline, the military, the civic, the religious, the imperial, the classic, and the monumental. To understand its full significance when properly applied, we may well look to the ancient city of Peking, the northern capital of the Khans. Kublai Khan, its founder, and the great city builders who followed him, understood the power of the axis as have few men before or since. Centuries ago, in the building of their city, they and their planners scrupulously avoided the use of the axis in those areas where its insistent lines were unsuited. The refreshing parks, market places, and winding residential streets were relaxed and free in their forms and spaces. In the whole fabulously delightful summer palace grounds, planned for sumptuous divertissement, there is scarcely a conscious axis to be found.

But where the imperial will was to be made manifest, or the people were to be subjected to a concept of supreme deity, omnipotence, or military might, the axis was employed with sensitive understanding: As witness the military roads that stretch in broad grandeur from the city gates to the entrance courts of the golden-roofed Forbidden City of the emperor; or the wide tree-lined axial boulevard that sweeps southward from the shrine atop Coal Hill at the north, through parks, past temple groups, through the teeming city centers, to and through the Forbidden City's imperial gateways, and on beyond through parade grounds, fields, and forests to the farthest hills on the distant horizon — a wide and pulsating line of force, subjecting the whole city and countryside to the will

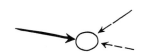

The terminus of a vista may be a space as well as an object.

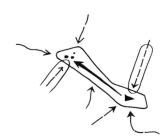

A major or a minor vista may be a function of an *area* or *volume* as well as a *line* of approach.

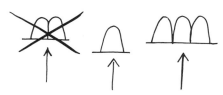

When the axis terminates in a structure that is to be entered, one or three openings are better than two since they provide a receptive element rather than an obstruction.

and authority of the all-powerful beneficent emperor, who sat astride it on his royal throne of jade.

Axial planning also highlights the Temple of Heaven that lies on the wide plain to the south of the Imperial City. Here, each year at the time of the vernal equinox, the great Khan rode in magnificent pomp and ceremony to welcome the coming of spring. The approach to this sublimely beautiful temple was by a wide causeway of white marble that commenced at a circular platform of noble proportions, rising in elegantly balustraded tiers. The spacious causeway, elevated above the level plain, extended in a long grand plane to the gilt and deep-red lacquered gates of the temple. Spaced out along the causeway sides, at regular intervals, were sockets to hold the heavy standards of hundreds of banners, and between the standards were carved fire pits, in which pitch-faggots were burned to illumine the long processions that moved past them in the night.

On the night before the great annual event, the people of Peking flocked through the streets of their city and out through the gates toward the temple, where they massed along the wooded edges of the plain to stand in watchful wide-eyed wonder and respect. Then, through the gates, the foot soldiers came marching, division after bristling division of the Khan's seasoned warriors, in dark helmets, chain breastplates, and padded felt boots, to mass in ordered formation along the causeway flanks. The courtiers and nobles followed in dazzling·procession, thousands upon thousands on horseback, each noble and mount in trappings of silk, gold, costly furs, and precious gems, and each proudly taking his appointed place along the white marble pavement. The high priests, with smoldering incense pots, then moved in solemn procession, chanting, fur-capped, and in silken robes and gowns of unbelievable splendor. Slowly, with vast dignity, they took their august posts on the tiered platform, commanding the length of the ceremonial causeway.

Finally, as the first faint traces of light tinged the eastern sky with pink, the glorious Khan and his mounted retinue pranced through the golden gates of the Forbidden City and out through the throngs to the head of the causeway. There, to the cadenced booming of drums and the crashing of brass and silver gongs the Khan rode imperiously past the blazing fire pits, down the avenue of waving flags and wafting banners, on through the massed troops and kowtowing nobles to the resplendent temple and the gleaming altar seen through its opened doors. Precisely at that hushed moment when the Khan reached the high altar and bowed his head in grave salutation, the blazing red orb of the rising sun arced above the purple hills to the east, and every face and every eye and every thought in all Peking was focused down the length of that great axis to the sacred place at the temple altar where the exalted Khan, their emperor, knelt to greet the spring.

THE SYMMETRICAL PLAN

The use of the axis does not necessarily dictate the development of a symmetrical plan.

The elements of a symmetrical plan are the same and in equilibrium

Symmetry
Plan elements in equilibrium

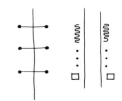

About a point or area

About an axis or plane

Bilateral — as the double wings of a maple seed

Trilateral — as the grappling hook

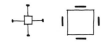

Multilateral — as the snowflake

Quadrilateral — as by geometry

about a central point or on either side of an axis. The central point may be an object or an area, as a memorial fountain or the plaza that contains it.

The axis may be a line or plane of use, as a path, a street, or a broad avenue. It may be a powerfully induced line of sight or movement, as through a series of imposing arches or gates, or between rows of rhythmically spaced trees or pylons, or toward an object or space of high interest. It may be a quiet vista across an open panel of turf on either side of which things appear to be equally and pleasantly balanced.

A symmetrical plan may be as minute in its ordered arrangement as a tiny plot of parsley, onions, and cooking herbs outside a cottage garden. Or it may be as vast in its outlines as the plan of a sprawling city; for many a town or city, from ancient times to the present day, has been laid out, rightly or wrongly, in balanced patterns of streets, squares, structures, and open spaces.

Symmetry may be absolute, as in the pillared and carved and polished perfection of Alhambra's Court of the Lions. Or it may be as loose and casually implied as in the balanced order of fence rows and haycocks along a country road.

Growing things, including humans, are often symmetrical, for the seed or the cell or the crystal may be by nature symmetrical, and thus also are the products evolved through their development or growth. But, in the natural landscape, *plan symmetry* is a rarity. Where it is observed, therefore, symmetry generally indicates a system of order imposed by man.

It is revealing to note that in the western world the word *symmetrical* is synonymous with *beautiful* and has the connotation of pleasant and handsome form. Perhaps this is because it implies an order to the scheme of things that is easily comprehended and thus enjoyed by man. Perhaps it is because the word "symmetry" has come to be associated with plan clarity, balance, rhythm, stability, and unity, which are all positive qualities. Perhaps it is because man himself is symmetrical and takes pleasure in the relationship.

Dynamic symmetry   When, by symmetry, two opposing elements or structures are seemingly held apart, an apparent attraction and tension develops between them. The two are strongly related, to the point where the opposing elements read as one, together with the intervening space and all that it contains.

The symmetrical plan has a quality of polarity. Each pole generates its own field of force, and between these two fields is a field of dynamic tension. Each element within this field is at once in tension and repose. By definition, every symmetrical composition must be in balance and, therefore, repose. But the repose of symmetry is the more compelling for the fact that it bespeaks the resolution of myriad opposing forces held in equilibrium.

Each object in a symmetrical plan creates a need for fulfillment — a fulfillment that can only be achieved by its opposite number. This becomes apparent when in a symmetrical arrangement even the smallest element is removed. The equilibrium is lost at once, and the entire composition seems to strain at the gap.

The Court of the Lions in the Alhambra Palace of Granada, Spain.

The plan layout of this pleasure garden is well deserving of study. While the general appearance is exuberant and free, it is given cohesive unity by several plan devices that are fundamental to every successful large-scale area in which large crowds are to move about. The pleasantly sprawling areas are bound together by *major and minor vistas*, which are in this case generally symmetrical. The complex has a *focal point* — the large tented dance hall. There is a well-defined *pedestrian circulation loop*, which leads one through and around the major points of interest to points of reference. Many *minor paths* have been provided to articulate the main pattern of the plan, to disperse and again collect the crowds, and to lend variety. The *total volumetric composition* is of compelling exhibition scale and the planned experiences of *volumetric sequence* are rich and satisfying. The exhibition is admirable too in that it has taken full advantage of the best features of the existing landscape.

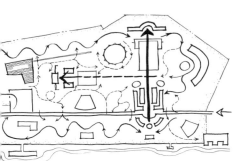

133

Symmetry in nature — growing objects in nature are often symmetrical due to the bilateral formation of their germ cell or seed; the natural landscape, a product of infinitely divergent forces, is rarely symmetrical.

We find from experience that the perception of repetition, sequence, and balance in landscape composition causes us an immediate pleasure, an amount of pleasure which seems insufficiently explained by the repetition, sequence, and balance of muscular motion or tendency to muscular motion involved in their perception. But we should remember that the emotions associated with repetition, sequence and balance are associated also with and often automatically expressed by repeated, sequential, or balanced muscular motions and positions of the whole body, and these in turn intensify the emotion that suggested them. The delicately balanced nervous and muscular machinery of the body is thus in a way a reverberator for the increasing of the effect of these experiences.

HENRY V. HUBBARD

134

An interesting experiment might be to develop an elaborate symmetry, leaving one such gap at that crucial point where all interest is to be concentrated. It would be an interest of annoyance, for the tendency would be to mend the gap and restore the balance. When, in perceiving a plan, the eye discovers a rhythm of objects and intervals, it develops an anticipation of the next object and interval, and is shocked if this anticipation is not satisfied. If the break in rhythm reveals only a void, one senses a plan imperfection, and the reaction is disappointment. If, however, the experience of shock coincides with the discovery of an interesting plan feature, the reaction is one of pleasure, and the feature is thus emphasized.

The despotism of symmetry   The symmetrical plan subjects plan elements to a rigid or formalized pattern. As with objects within the field of axial influence, objects within a symmetrical frame of reference have meaning mainly in their relation to the pattern of the whole. Each feature must always be considered, first and last, as a unit in the grand composition.

Sometimes a symmetrical plan may give added emphasis to objects. Such an object, for instance, might be featured as the terminus of a major or minor axis. Or it might be given more importance through a progressively evolving sequence of approach, or by its relationship to complimentary or complementary features. Usually, however, it may be said that the more powerful the total plan, the less potent the individual plan unit.

A symmetrical plan subjects a landscape to control. It systematizes the landscape. It organizes the landscape into rigid patterns. The natural environment at best is reduced to a setting or background for the plan composition. As a background it must be of suitable character and scale. By screening, enframing, or opening wide, the landscape environment may be neutralized, embraced, or modulated into views, vistas, or backdrops. But always the relationship of plan diagram, plan element, and natural landscape must be controlled, a study in harmonies. The landscape may be forced to compliance, its new symmetry achieved by extensive cutting, filling, and reshaping; or a complete new landscape may be deliberately devised.

A symmetrical plan subjects man to plan conformity. Not only the landscape and all plan features are subjected to an organized plan of things, but so is man, as well. He is held transfixed by a diagram of pattern. His lines of movement are limited to the lines of the plan. The plan forms control his vision. He is consciously stirred or lulled by developing cadences, balanced repetitions, the subjugation of all things to one concept. Even his subconscious mind is attuned, as if by hypnosis, to the rhythmic symmetrical order of things, and he finds himself in all ways conforming to the order of the plan. This conformity induces a sense of harmony.

It can be realized that symmetrical plan forms, if skillfully handled and directed, may be used to dramatize a concept and to evoke in man a sense of discipline, high order, magnificence, power, monumentality, stirring idealism, and even divine perfection.

The nature of symmetry   Being precise and disciplined in plan, symmetry requires precision in detail and maintenance.

Bold in concept, it demands bold forms.

The symmetrical plan becomes a structural framework, compartmenting site features or functions. To be successful, such an arrangement must be an expression of the logical relationship of the features or functions so grouped. The rhythmically recurring elements of a symmetrical scheme divide the plan field into units. All that occurs within the measured beat becomes in itself a unit and must be considered in all ways as a design entity. Each such unit, complete in itself, must still be related, as a segment, to the total plan.

Through the whole of this beautiful town on the Inland Sea asymmetry prevails, except at the central temple, where discipline, ceremony, and the implied presence of the supreme being demand symmetrical order.

When for any reason the eye is to be habitually directed to a single point — as to an altar, a throne, or a stage — there will be violence and distraction caused by the tendency to look aside in the recurring necessity of looking forward, if the object is not so arranged that the tensions of eye are balanced, and the center of gravity of vision lies in the point which one is obliged to keep in sight. In all such objects we therefore require bilateral symmetry.

GEORGE SANTAYANA

The Louvre, Paris. Site and structures are here combined in a grand plan of geometric symmetry. Imperious and inhuman planning unfortunately characterized most of the work of the Renaissance.

Usually the symmetrical plan has a strong relationship to adjacent structures. Often it is designed as an extension of such structures, or is employed to directly and positively relate two or more structures. Such a plan is the familiar "campus quad," a sweep of greensward crisscrossed with walks, flanked by dorms and classrooms, and featuring on its long axis the library or chapel at one end and, on the other, the commons or administration building. For this treatment to be effective, the buildings must not only be compatible with the physical expression of the symmetrical plan, but also with its abstract qualities.

A symmetrical plan must express a symmetrical function. A symmetrical arrangement for an army tent street might be fitting, for the essence of the military is order and organization and the subservience of all units to the whole. Or a symmetrical grouping of civic structures about a central court might give to the court a more forceful civic character than if the structures were seen individually. At the same time, such a grouping might also best define the relationship of each unit to the ordered entity.

College buildings symmetrically placed on their quadrangle may express a closely knit and well-balanced community of learning. Such a grouping is more suited to buildings of classic context, and to areas where a sense of established order, discipline, perfection, and high idealism is to be engendered. A symmetrical grouping is not valid where the context of the structures or area is the natural, organic growth, or the experimental, or where the human eye, mind, and spirit are to be set free.

Symmetry is unsuccessful if it obviously forces unsymmetrical functions to a symmetrical plan arrangement. This is one of the most frequent errors in plan organization. It is painful to discover an important function balanced against the trivial. It is pathetic to find a plan area

There is no such thing as *"beauty of symmetry,"* with the exception of those cases where, because of the nature of the problem and its logical solution, the *"balance"* line of design happens to coincide with the middle line of symmetry. Only in such cases is symmetry logical and thus beautiful.

ELIEL SAARINEN

constricted or contorted beyond workability in order to visually balance an area of dissimilar use. It seems dishonest to disguise a function or falsify a form to conform to the dictates of symmetry. If Keats was right in his observation that truth and beauty are one and the same, then such symmetry can never be beautiful. For a plan — as an object, as an experience — to be beautiful must not only be truthful, it must be eloquently truthful.

Symmetry has little merit if its pattern cannot be realized from at least one point or line of observation. If this is not possible, we fail to comprehend the unity of the composition or the repose gained through the parts in balance. It can be seen that the positive qualities to be gained from a symmetrical plan organization are lost if the plan is too large or extensive to be perceived as a unity. This explains in part why, historically, no such extensive symmetrical plan layout has ever been successful. There are symmetrical gardens, villas, and estates of great charm. There are symmetrical squares, circles, and civic parks. There are innumerable avenues, courts, and approaches of complex symmetry. Where they are successful, the symmetry of the plan, or a cohesive unit of the plan, may be taken in at a glance.

It can be seen that this same quality of symmetry that seems essential to its success may also be a negative quality; for a plan that can be grasped *in toto* is generally static and, once seen, loses interest.

Symmetry is a coordinator. Symmetry as a system has use wherever it might be helpful from an understanding of one part to better comprehend the whole or the relationship of the parts.

A symmetrical plan may be of crystalline form. This may be ideal if the function is by nature crystalline in its pattern of growth and expansion.

A symmetrical plan may be of geometric design. Such plan geometry may be excellent, but only if the function can be expressed geometrically.

There are those who believe that geometry is the root of all beauty, and that beauty of form and pattern can be consistently achieved by the application of mathematical formulas to the planning process. Such thinkers would recommend bilateral, trilateral, or multilateral symmetry as a highly desirable and universal kind of order. This thinking, they hold, gains support from the fact that people take pleasure in the comprehension of order. The author contends that the preference is generally for order over chaos, rather than for symmetry over asymmetry.

A plan that imposes geometry without reason may destroy desirable landscape character or may neutralize the inherent design qualities of the areas or objects affected.

A geometric plan, direct and obvious, is quickly comprehended. It thus has the advantage of clarity. It also has the disadvantage of monotony, if seen often or for long.

Far too often, symmetrical plans are conceived by their authors as a design expedient, a sort of geometric doodling. Such plans are only repetitious and dreary, as uninspired as their authors. If symmetrical plans are successful — and this is, in fact, but rarely — it is found that their symmetry is derived through clear logic and a conscious synthesis

137

Occult balance

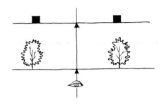

Symmetrical balance — equal and like masses balanced on either side of an optical axis or fulcrum

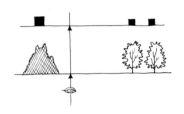

Asymmetrical occult balance — unequal and unlike masses balanced on either side of an optical axis

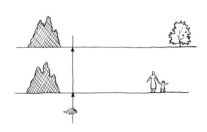

Asymmetrical occult balance — equilibrium achieved by mind-eye evaluation of form, mass, value, color, and association.

of all plan forms into symmetrical plan arrangement, as the highest and best expression of the function.

Symmetry, when appropriate, and when intelligently applied, is a plan form of unique and compelling power.

THE ASYMMETRICAL PLAN

In nature, we can seldom, if ever, find the elements of a landscape symmetrically balanced on either side of a line of sight. Visual balance is fundamental to all satisfactory composition and to all art. It is generally conceded that any design, any picture, or any view or vista that lacks such balance is disturbing and unpleasant. Because we usually think of the natural landscape as being pleasant to look at, we might conclude that visual balance must somehow be inherent in such natural landscapes. This brings to mind two intriguing questions.

First, until an observer wanders along, how can the landscape be so balanced, for without the vision or the imposed line of sight, how can there be visual balance? Second, does it not seem highly improbable that, from any given point of observation, the landscape should *happen* to balance visually on either side of a line of sight? Upon reflection, it would seem, rather, that the eye must *find* in any landscape those vistas or views or sightlines that *produce* a satisfactory visual balance. This is, in fact, precisely the case. The trained eye is repelled by the unbalanced and attracted to the balanced, and tends constantly to seek out and bring into register those sections or portions of the visual landscape that provide a pleasant optical balance.

Dynamic visual balance   The human eye is constantly darting about, probing, exploring, and wading through a vague and luminous flux of evolving visual impressions. These are sensed subconsciously. At intervals the mind permits, or directs, the eye to bring out of optical limbo and into conscious focus certain visual images. This is a creative effort. For the mind demands that the eye "compose" a visual image that is complete and in equilibrium. This is a joint mind-eye effort, for the acceptable equilibrium is not one of form-balance, value-balance, or color-balance alone, but one of associative-balance as well. The mind-eye team may give little weight to a massive object that has no associative value, but may give much weight to that which has strong associative value or immediate interest. A ripe apple swaying on a branch may thus outweigh the greatest oak tree in the forest, or a chunk of rose quartz outweigh the mountain from which it was broken, or a solitary sun bather outweigh a seemingly limitless seascape.

Thus no two mind-eye combinations scanning a scene could ever bring into register an identical visual image or combination of images. For a scene has no limits, and the possibilities of selective composition are endless. But, by a vastly complicated series of instantaneous subconscious adjustments, each individual "creates" out of optical impressions visual images that are for him in equilibrium and that are therefore, for him, complete. The more sensitive and perceptive the mind-eye team has become through instinct or through training, the richer, the more delightful, and more wondrous is the visible world it reveals.

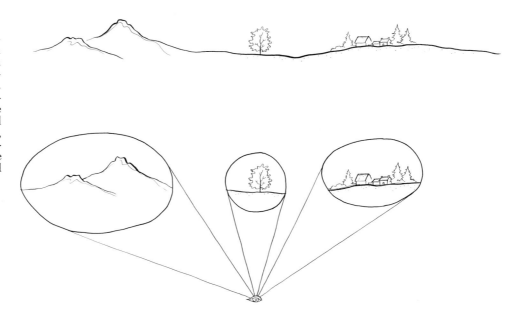

Occult balance: The eye, in scanning the landscape, extracts and composes visual entities — each forming a mind-eye image in equilibrium and complete within itself. It is through a series of such fleeting mind-eye compositions that we come to comprehend, in a visual sense, the object, the relationship, the order or lack of order, the harmony or lack of harmony, and the very nature of our environment and everything within it.

Balance may also consist in a disposition of objects not similar nor similarly placed, but still so chosen and arranged that the sum of the attractions on one side of the vertical axis is equalled by the sum of the attractions on the other side. This kind of balance is called unsymmetrical or occult balance.

HENRY V. HUBBARD

The natural landscape is an indeterminate object; it almost always contains enough diversity to allow the eye a great liberty in selecting, emphasizing and grouping its elememts, and it is furthermore rich in suggestion and in vague emotional stimulus. A landscape to be seen has to be composed . . .

GEORGE SANTAYANA

The eye, especially, demands completeness.

GOETHE

The child or the primitive perceives only *objects* in space. Sophisticated man, with a more highly developed mind and a more selective eye, perceives *relationships*.

It can be seen that only rarely in nature would a sensed composition be balanced symmetrically on either side of a visual axis. But, because equilibrium is required of all visual images, it must be possible to have balance without bilateral symmetry. This is indeed the case. Such asymmetrical or "occult" balance is the norm. Except in those exceptional cases where bilateral symmetry has for some reason been contrived, it is by occult balance that man composes and comprehends the world about him.

Asymmetric planning   Asymmetric planning brings man into closest harmony with nature. Freed of the rigidity of the symmetrical plan, each area may be developed with a fuller regard for its natural landscape qualities. Circulation is more free. Views are of infinite variety. Each object in the landscape may be seen and enjoyed for itself or its relationship to other landscape elements, rather than for its relationship to a prescribed plan pattern. Such plan asymmetry is more subtle, casual, refreshing, interesting, and human. We are not led step by step along or through a rigid composition. We are, rather, set free to explore for ourselves and to discover in the landscape that which is beautiful, pleasant or useful.

Asymmetric planning requires less disturbance of nature and the natural or man-made landscape. Because it is developed in sympathy with the site, it normally requires less grading, retaining walls, screening, and construction. It is therefore more economical. It is also, as a rule, less disruptive and better integrated with the total extensional landscape.

Organic planning is usually asymmetric. The jackpine growing on the mountain slope sends out its probing roots in search of soil pockets and moisture. Its trunk and limbs are braced against the winds, its needle clusters are held up and extended as a living mesh, to best soak

139

Confronted with a complex optical field, one will reduce it to basic interrelationships. Just as in nature there is a tendency to find the most economic surface unity in every formation, so in the visual organization there is a tendency to find the most economic spacial unity in the ordering of optical differences. Facing the turmoil of optical impacts, one's first reaction is to form in the shortest time interval the greatest possible spatial span.

. . .

We cannot bear chaos — the disturbance of equilibrium in the field of experience. Consequently, we must immediately form light-impacts into shapes and figures. Exposed to a visual field that in its light-quality is to the slightest degree heterogeneous, one organizes that field at once into two opposing elements; into a figure against a background. One speaks of white with inevitable implied reference to black, grey or other colors. To convey the meaning of "yes," one implies a latent understanding of "no." A unified whole is thus created. Every image is based upon this dynamic dualism, the unity of opposites. Certain impulses are tied together in a stable visual whole, while other impulses are left in their unorganized fluid state and serve only as background and are perceived as intervals. This organization of figures and backgrounds is repeated progressively until the whole visual field is perceived as a formed, ordered unity — the plastic image.

. . .

Forces of organization driving toward spatial order, toward stability, tend to shape optical units into closed compact wholes. Confronted with a complex optical situation, the beholder searches for the form with the most stable unity, or with the least disturbed relationship to the environment.

. . .

We live in the midst of a whirlwind of light qualities. From this whirling confusion we build unified entities, those forms of experience called visual images. To perceive an image is to participate in a forming process; it is a creative act.

GYORGY KEPES

The term "organic design" need not be an empty platitude. Biology has many valuable hints to offer the designer, if he will but observe closely — and then use what he has learned. Indeed, there is much that could be said in support of a biological approach to the entire process of design, mainly in the sense that one broad biological field, known as ecology, undertakes to investigate the dynamic relations of all the organisms — both fauna and flora — in natural association with each other and with the other forces of the total environment in a given area of the surface of the earth.

NORMAN NEWTON

. . . architecture is not an art, it is a natural function. It grows on the soil like animals and plants. It is a function of the social order. Don't forget that.

FERNAND LEGER

The basic law — in all fields of creation workers are striving today to find purely functional solutions of a technological-biological kind: that is, to build up each piece of work solely from the elements which are required for its function. But "function" means here not a pure mechanical service. It includes also the psychological, social, and economical conditions of a given period. It might be better to use the term "organic (functional) design." Such design must even serve functions which could not be foreseen during the process of designing.

MOHOLY-NAGY

. . . let me remind you of a famous passage in which Samuel Taylor Coleridge defined organic form. In a lecture on Shakespeare, given in 1818, he made a distinction between what he called mechanic form and organic form. "Form is mechanic," he said "when on any given material we impress a predetermined form, not necessarily arising out of the properties of the material." Organic form, on the other hand, is innate; shaping itself from within, as it develops, so that "the fullness of its development is one and the same with the perfection of its outward form."

J. BRONOWSKI

in the cool, drifting morning fogs and to absorb the utmost of vitality from the light and warmth of the sun. It shapes itself to its patch of ground — the furrow and ridge, the rivulet, the stump, the fallen log, the boulder. It responds to the encroachment and to the protection of its neighbors. Where a tip is broken or bent, a new tip is formed. Where the branch is smashed or torn away, the wound is healed and the gaping void is filled with new wood or with fresh twigs and needles. All positive qualities of the environment are utilized. All negative factors are overcome to the limits of possibility. The form of the pine is expressive of its development in harmony with its environment. This age-old process we know to be the process of *organic growth.*

Organic planning, so widely ballyhooed and so seldom practiced in our country, is fundamentally no more nor any less than the organic growth of plan areas, volumes, and forms.

Man-made symmetrical plan forms can never be organic in this sense, except in those rare instances where the essential quality of the use is such that, given unrestrained freedom and conditions of growth, its most logical plan expression would be some type of symmetry. It can be seen that, even in such a case, the impact of natural or man-made landscape features would tend to disrupt the symmetry.

It is abundantly apparent that, in the great preponderance of cases, the logical site-structure or site-project diagram will be asymmetrical. If the diagram expresses a use or complex of uses well suited and related to a total and specific site, and if, in plan refinement, each function is allowed to develop in best relationship to other functions and to all positive and negative factors of the site, then such planning is truly organic. Such a plan, evolved from use best related to total site, is expressive of function, is sympathetic to the site, and achieves a maximum of plan-site harmony. In most mature cultures, such organic planning has been the great ideal.

An asymmetric plan emphasizes the plastic qualities of structures and the landscape. Most things in nature, as well as most structures, are best appreciated when seen "in the round." The asymmetric plan best provides such viewing. The approach of the observer to each plan element is meandering, rather than fixed, giving a sense of modelling and third dimension. This plastic (sculptural) quality of an object, which best reveals its shape, nature, and detail, can be appreciated only if the observer moves around or past the object or sees it on the sweep. Even the pictorial quality of a landscape is imbued with more richness and interest when observed from a constantly changing (in direction as well as distance) line of observation.

An axis may be developed asymmetrically. Such a treatment preserves the good features of the axis, yet allows more plan flexibility and relieves the monotony. It does preclude the controlled, measured cadence and hypnotic induction of bilateral symmetry — qualities which, we have found, are, in some few cases, highly desirable. But the asymmetrically treated axis has much more universal application. It is always appropriate where direction, orientation, or a dominant idea or theme are to be expressed and where plan freedom and interest are desired and where the landscape character of an area is to be preserved or accentuated.

141

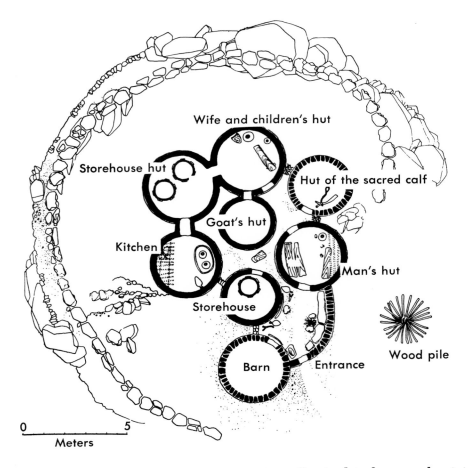

Organic planning. Functional room arrangement of family dwelling, Cameroon.

The use of asymmetry   Asymmetry is well suited to large-scale civic planning. The most pleasant squares of Europe are asymmetrical. What a sad day it would be for San Marco in Venice if the piazza were to be reconstructed in rigid symmetry. The wonder and charm of such towns as Sienna, Verona, or Florence would surely be lost to a symmetrical handling of their streets and buildings and spaces.

The most magnificent garden of history, the Yuan Ming Yuan or "Garden of Perfect Brightness," which today lies in ruin to the west of Peking, was scrupulously asymmetric in plan, as attested to by Attiret, a French priest who, two centuries ago, found his way to the Court of Emperor Ch'ien Lung. In 1743, he wrote to a friend in France describing the fabulous wonders of the Emperor's summer palace in the Yuan Ming Yuan:

"One quits a valley, not by fine straight allees as in Europe, but by zigzag and circuitous routes — and on leaving one finds oneself in a second valley entirely different from the first as regards the form of the land and the structure of the buildings. All the mountains and hills are covered with trees, especially with flowering trees, which are very common here. It is a veritable paradise on earth."

"Each valley . . . has its pleasance, small in comparison with the whole enclosure, but in itself large enough to house the greatest of our European lords with all his retinue. But how many of these palaces would you think there are in the different valleys of this vast enclosure? There are more than two hundred of them."

"In Europe, uniformity and symmetry are desired everywhere. We

142

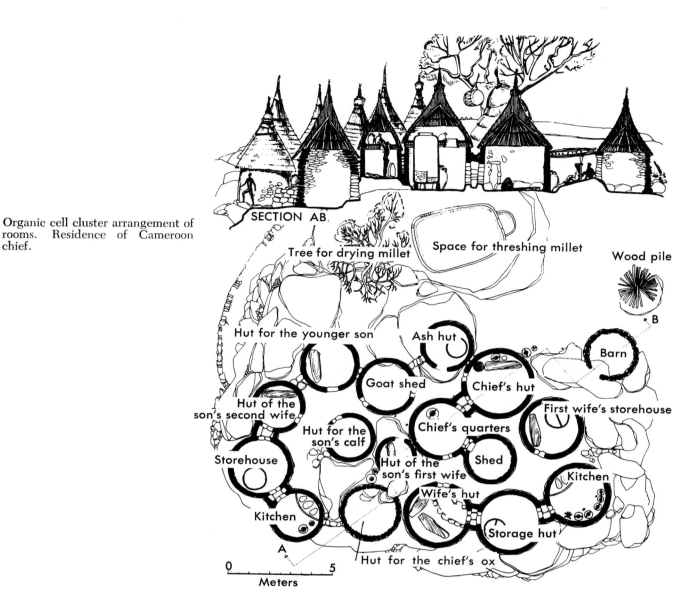

Organic cell cluster arrangement of rooms. Residence of Cameroon chief.

SECTION AB

Tree for drying millet

Space for threshing millet

Wood pile

Hut for the younger son

Ash hut

Barn

Goat shed

Chief's hut

Hut of the son's second wife

Chief's quarters

First wife's storehouse

Hut for the son's calf

Storehouse

Hut of the son's first wife

Shed

Kitchen

Wife's hut

Kitchen

Storage hut

Hut for the chief's ox

0   5

Meters

wish that there should be nothing odd, nothing misplaced, that one part should correspond exactly with the part facing it; in China also they love this symmetry, this fine order. The palace in Peking . . . is in this style . . . But in the pleasances there reigns almost everywhere a graceful disorder, an anti-symmetry is desired almost everywhere. Everything is based on this principle. . . . When one hears this, one would think it to be ridiculous, that it must strike the eye disagreeably; but when one sees them one thinks differently and admires the art with which the irregularity is planned."

"I am tempted to believe that we (in Renaissance France) are poor and sterile in comparison."*

The rash of symmetrical planning that marked the Renaissance in Europe had little planning logic. Far too often, it was symmetry solely for symmetry's sake, a senseless forcing of the natural and man-made landscape into geometric patterns. No wonder our friend Attiret, like many others to follow, found this planning, by comparison with the freedom and rich variety of asymmetry, to be but "poor and sterile." **143**

* As quoted by Hope Danby, in *The Garden of Perfect Brightness.*

The broad loading decks and sail-like shells of this arresting structure give the
opera house a lyric, floating quality that befits both its use and its site.

CIRCULATION

MOST MAN-MADE structures or places have meaning only to man, and only as he experiences them. <u>They are revealed to man by lines or patterns of circulation that lead him to, through, over, under, or around them — on foot or horseback, by plane, train, automobile, or any other means of locomotion or conveyance</u>. We thus realize that the circulation pattern is a major function of any project, because it establishes the rate, sequence, and nature of its sensed experience or visual unfolding.

Every object as a perceptible entity exists in time as well as in space. This is to say that an object cannot be comprehended in its entirety at any one instant or from any one point of observation. It is perceived, rather, through a flow of impressions. When in motion, one sees a series of images blending into one expanding visual realization of an object, space, or scene. Perception, of course, is not a matter of sight alone. All the senses may be involved — sight, taste, smell, touch, and hearing. The rate, order, type, and degree of perception is a matter of design control. Much of this control is effected by planned patterns of circulation.

Experience is rarely static; almost always, there is motion involved, in the person or in the thing experienced. A structure is seldom seen from a fixed point of view or in direct elevation, but usually by man on the move. Therefore, its three dimensional form and modeling are more important than its facade. A plan pattern is seldom seen from a fixed focal point, but is, rather, realized from an infinite number of viewing points by people moving through it. The more fluid the circulation pattern, the more points of view and, therefore, the more interest. It can be seen that the most important visual aspects of a project are those revealed to the moving observer. The most important functional aspects are also those experienced by men in motion or in induced repose.

Motion impelled by form and concept   One afternoon, some time ago, the author entered the National Gallery in Washington to join a group of sightseers who were starting out with a guide. The group stood in the great rotunda, at the base of the towering black marble columns that support the lofty dome. "Do you know," asked the guide, "what the architect of this great building is doing to you now? He has directed you here to give you the theme — the magnificence of all his-

We are living a mobile exist-ence. The earth is rotating; the sun is moving; trees are growing; flowers are opening and closing; clouds are merging, dissolving, coming and going; light and shadow are hunting each other in an indefatigable play; forms are appearing and disappearing; and man, who is experiencing all this, is himself subject to all kinetic change. The perception of physical reality cannot escape the quality of movement. The very under-standing of spatial facts, the meaning of extension or dis-tances, involves the notion of time — a fusion of space-time which is movement. "Nobody has ever noticed a place except at a time or a time except at a place," said Minkowsky in his Principles of Relativity.

GYORGY KEPES

145

The reorganization of our visual habits so that we perceive not isolated "things" in "space," but structure, order, and the relatedness of events in space-time, is perhaps the most profound kind of a revolution possible — a revolution that is long overdue not only in art, but in all our experience.

S. I. HAYAKAWA

tory — to make you feel splinter-high and insignificant before all the greatness that lies behind and ahead. You are shocked by new, strange shapes and sizes and their richness and opulence. But the architect doesn't want to scare you away, as most of us are by strange and unfamiliar things. So, as we approach the Mercury fountain at the rotunda's center, he wants to make us feel at ease. And how does he accomplish this? By the size of things, by scale.

"The figure of Mercury is less than life size. The steps leading up to the fountain are broad and low, rather than high and forbidding. The water play is subdued to a splash and trickle, rather than a rush. The architect gives us also a concept with which we are familiar; not a terrible war god, but one of the more kindly gods, Mercury, who speeds and flashes about on errands of kindness. We, who know the legends, want to walk closer to this figure of whom we have heard so much good. Here in this vast dome of light and space is held out to us that with which we are familiar. All this makes us want to come near, makes us feel relaxed and pleased.

"And so the architect has shocked us, impressed us, and humbled us. He has pleased us. Now he wants to get us moving out into the exhibit rooms. How? You will notice that he starts a centrifugal movement with a dominant spiral theme. The lines of the figure of Mercury are spiral in diagram. The subject of the sculpture, appropriately, is 'flight.' Motion is further suggested by the movement of the water as it ripples toward the fountain brim. All lines move outward. Above us, even the

Line of approach

Abstract variables in line of approach to a given point, area, or space

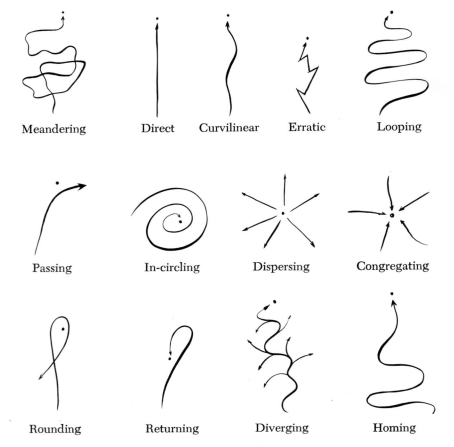

Meandering   Direct   Curvilinear   Erratic   Looping

Passing   In-circling   Dispersing   Congregating

Rounding   Returning   Diverging   Homing

carved eagles on the architrave seem ready to soar away. Even the coffers of the tremendous dome sweep in a great spiral pattern. By sound, motion, and induced idea, by strong urging of architectural form and line, we are compelled to outward motion. . . ."

The planner of an exhibition attempts to foresee people's behavior and predict where they will hurry, stop, look, or drift on. His aim is to control the flow and arrest it where he wants; but controlling the flow does not mean that people are to be moved along predestinate grooves like trams or shuffled around hurdles like sheep. Ideally the planner is aiming to direct people's movement in such a way that they see what there is to see with ease and in their own time. He must also ensure that the public does not get lost, tired, or bored with the whole affair.

JAMES GARDNER

CAROLINE HELLER

The kinematics of motion   Without reference to the cause of movement, it is interesting to dwell for a few moments on the various characteristics of pure motion. By design, the line or trajectory of induced movement may be meandering, discursive, circuitous, looping, zigzagging, ricocheting, ascending, descending, hyperbolic, centrifugal, centripetal, an arc, or a direct straight shot. In speed, the motion may range from the creeping-crawling to the whizzing-whistling. The nature of induced motion may be soothing, startling, shocking, baffling, confusing, exploratory, logical, sequential, progressive, hieratic, linear, wavelike, flowing, branching, diverging, converging, timorous, forceful, expanding, contracting, and so on, *ad infinitum*.

Obviously, the alignment, speed, and nature of motion produce in a moving subject a predictable emotional and intellectual response, and must, therefore, be carefully considered and controlled. The abstract qualities of the path or line by which an object or space is approached must also be considered and controlled with care. Motion that is induced must be accommodated and satisfactorily resolved. This fact is also obvious, but, like so many obvious things, it is too often overlooked in our planning.

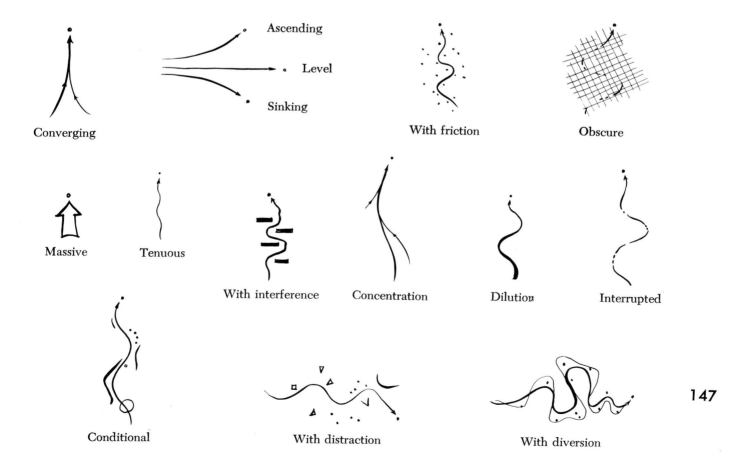

Converging

Ascending

Level

Sinking

With friction

Obscure

Massive   Tenuous

With interference   Concentration   Dilution   Interrupted

Conditional

With distraction

With diversion

147

Impelling factors   Man tends to move:

In logical sequences of progression
In lines of least resistance
Along easiest grades
In lines suggested by directional forms, signs, or symbols
Toward that which pleases
Toward that which is fitting
Toward things wanted
Toward things that have use
Toward change — from cold to warm, from sun to shade, from shade
    to sun
Toward that which has interest
Toward that which excites his curiosity
Toward points of entry
Toward the receptive
Toward points of highest contrast
Toward points of richest texture or color
To attain a goal
By pride of height attained, distance travelled, friction overcome
In haste, via the direct; with leisure, via the indirect
In harmony with circulation patterns
In harmony with abstract design forms
Toward the beautiful, the picturesque
For the pleasurable sensation of motion
For the experience of space modulation
Toward exposure, if adventurous
Toward protection, if threatened
Toward and through pleasant areas and spaces
Toward order, if tired of confusion
Toward confusion, if bored with order
Toward objects, areas, and spaces that suit his mood or need.

Repelling factors   Man is repelled by:

Obstacles   The uninspiring
Steep grades   The forbidding
The unpleasant   The demanding
The monotonous   Danger
The uninteresting   Friction
The dull   Disorder
The obvious   The ugly
The undesirable   The unsuitable

Motion directors   Man is directed or guided by:

Arrangement of natural or structural forms
Implied patterns of circulation
Baffles, screens, space dividers
Dynamic plan lines
Signs
Symbols
Mechanical controls, such as gates, curbs, barriers
Spatial shapes
Suggested progressions, such as violet to red, Hole No. 1 to Hole No. 2.

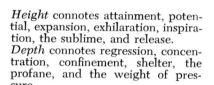

Repose inducers   Man is induced to repose by:

Conditions of comfort, enjoyment, or rest
Opportunity for privacy
Opportunity for fuller appreciation of view, object, or detail
Opportunity for concentration
Restriction of movement
Inability to proceed
Imposed indecision
Pleasant arrangements of forms and space
Functions related to rest and repose
Plan elements suggesting or requiring repose
Attainment of optimum position.

Height connotes attainment, potential, expansion, exhilaration, inspiration, the sublime, and release.
Depth connotes regression, concentration, confinement, shelter, the profane, and the weight of pressure.

Horizontal motion   Man is affected by horizontal motion in the following ways:

Movement is easier, freer, and more efficient in horizontal planes
Movement is safer
Change of direction is easier
Choice of direction is greater
Most functions are better suited to horizontal surfaces
Movement is more stable, in equilibrium with gravitational force
Movement is easier to control
Vision of moving object is easier to control
Vision from moving object is easier to control
Monotony results
Visual interest is in the vertical planes.

Downward motion, or decline   Man is affected by downward motion in the following ways:

Effort is minimized, but elevation must be regained
Safety depends on checks and on texture
Gives sense of refuge, hiding, "digging in"
Regression, return to the primitive
A coasting, swooping sense of being in harmony with the forces of gravity
Sense of increased confinement, protection, and privacy
The coal pit, the swamp, the fertile valley connotation
The rathskeller concept
The bargain basement concept
Downward movement and depth accentuated by deep earthy colors, solidity and simplicity of form, natural materials, and falling or quiet water
Vision is oriented to the base plane
Interest increased in things of the earth — in plants, water, and minerals
Relatively effortless movement, most welcome in the "home stretch" when energies flag.

149

Man is attracted toward:

The unusual

Things at "pix"

Pattern

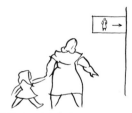

That which is necessary

The restful when weary

Upward motion, rise, or climb   Man is affected by upward motion in the following ways:

Upward motion requires force of lift to overcome gravity

Adds a new dimension to motion

Is exhilarating

Gives sense of accomplishment, conquest of gravity

Gives sense of built-up potential

Gives sense of "going up in life"

Detachment from things of the earth

Imparts a moral implication of exaltation, of being closer to God

Gives sense of being closer to sun, rarefied

Detachment from the crowd, supremacy, command

Implication of military advantage

Attainment of the pinnacle

Expanding views and vistas

Concept of man against the sky

Increased concern for safety and stability, and for texture of the base plane to provide necessary traction and grip

Visual interest in overhead planes and the sky; using sun and sky to full effect

All the above are increased in proportion to angle of inclination.

Induced response   Man responds by:

Relaxing in the familiar, becoming aroused or excited by the unfamiliar

Finding pleasure in unity, variety, and that which is fitting

Finding security in order

Finding amusement and divertissement in the strange, the lively, and in change

Ossifying and decaying physically, mentally, and spiritually amidst the rigid and the fixed.

On the street, in crowded shopping districts and perhaps even more particularly in exhibition areas men (and women, teenagers, kids, dogs, and cats) are cajoled, badgered, seduced, preached to, begged, teased, blasted at, or otherwise attracted by an overwhelming and constantly evolving, rolling barrage of visual persuaders. Sometimes falteringly, sometimes surely, but almost inevitably they (the men, women, teenagers, kiddies, dogs, and cats) follow their eye-mind impellers toward that which is:

Meaningful	Gay
Animated	Lively
Contrasting	Shocking
Unusual	Bright
Beautiful	Familiar, amidst much that is strange
Varied	
Near pix, or eye level	In motion against a fixed background
Decorative	
Necessary	Charming
Desirable	Subdued, when one is weary of the bright
Colorful	

The admirable

The superlative

That which inspires

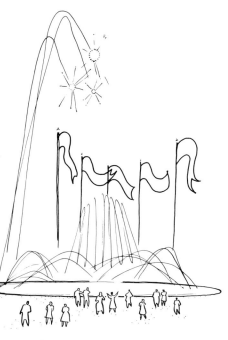

That which is impressive

Restful, when one is weary of the tumult
Startling
Vigorous
Bold
Interesting
Exciting
Dominant
Spectacular
Subtle
Associative
New in concept
Inspiring
Strange, amidst the familiar
New
Pleasing in pattern
Pleasing in form
Pleasing in scale
Pleasing in texture
Pleasing in color
Safe
Stable
Suitable
Convenient
"On course"
Dramatic
Simple
Clean
Natural
Weird
Plausible
Distinguished

Abstract
Select
Successful
Sophisticated
Comprehensible
Superlative
Supreme
Impressive
Surprising
Ingenious
Useful
Logical
Sequential
Progressive
Human
Appealing
Educational
Curious
Exotic
Startling
Appropriate
Stimulating
Admirable
True
Diverting
Amusing
Suggestive
Satisfying
Awesome
Symbolic
Fresh
Excellent

Our senses of taste, smell, odor and feeling are often compelling factors in the subconscious plotting of our courses and the determination of our actions. Physical comfort is a powerful factor too.

Distance as friction   In the various fields of transportation particularly, distance is considered an obstacle to be overcome — area that must be traversed and space that must be bridged. Where speed and economy are factors, it is incumbent upon the planner to select or devise a route that is as direct as practicable and that provides a minimum of frictions.

Such a route would be of optimum grade and alignment. The speed and volume of traffic would be accommodated. Traffic of various types and velocities would be classified and separated. All obstacles would be removed. Grade crossings would be eliminated. Safety would in all ways possible be assured. All objects and elements along the route would facilitate and express a freedom of movement; because, when workmen, passengers, or public relations are involved, such traffic-ways must not only be efficient and free, but must also give the impression of efficiency and freedom. Ideally, the right of way would be of variable and sufficient width to prevent encroachment and contain all foreseeable functions of the route — facilities, views, nuisances, screening, storage,

151

Man is attracted toward:

The exotic

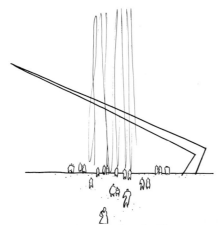

That which is bold

The weird

The elegant

The subtle

expansion, and strategic land reserves. It can be seen that, in many ways, distance may be a negative factor. In such cases, the actual and apparent distances must be reduced and minimized by all means at the planner's command.

Positive qualities of distance   Distance is a function of area, and area is a function of space, and both area and space are usually at a premium. In our world of expansion and increasing pressures, we often yearn for more room and seek to extend our constricting boundaries. Where boundaries are fixed, as is usually the case, we attempt to expand them by some plan device. We expand and increase *apparent* distances. This high art was long ago mastered by the planners in those cultures that lived in compression — on the fortified island or hilltop, or within the city wall. It is an art that we, in the increased planning concentrations and population densities of the near future, must relearn and develop.

Space modulation   It is an established planning fact that we seek in an area or space that quality of harmony, oneness, or unity that is the mark of any well-conceived work of science or art. We are attracted to such places, and rebel at the intrusion of the incongruous element — as, for example, a claptrap hotdog stand in a beautiful natural gorge.

In addition, we seek a harmonious or unified sequence of transition from one space to another like or unlike space. For a man going from his club terrace to the swimming pool below, a detour through the parking lot would be disturbing. When driving his family from their home to a picnic spot he would avoid the business districts and prefer a parkway route, river road, or country lane, to sustain or heighten the anticipated mood, and provide a pleasantly evolving transition from home to picnic site. He seeks, in all such cases, an experience of unified sequential transition, an experience of space modulation.

Man in motion takes great pleasure in the sensation of change — change of texture, light, quality, temperature, scent, visual patterns, expanding or contracting vistas, and the fluid design modulations of objects, spaces, and views.

He takes pleasure in an *area* arranged in shape, line, color, and texture to accommodate and express the use for which it was planned. We have learned also that man's pleasure is increased when the area is further developed into a volume or series of volumes that, by degree and type of enclosure, further articulate the planned uses or use. Man enjoys moving to and through a space and around or past an object. Man also enjoys moving from one space to another, the experience of sequential space-to-space transition.

Sometimes the transition is subtle. One may be so led through a sequence of varying spaces that provide a complete change in use and mood, that the transition is almost imperceptible. Sometimes it is powerful. One may, by planned intent, be so compressed into a low, tight, dark space, that release into a lofty, dazzling, free space is startling and dramatic. But, in any event, the skilled planner, by spatial manipulation, can play upon the human emotions, reflexes, and responses as surely as the skilled musician does with the harp or flute or drum.

In one of the summer palace groups near the Jade Fountain, to the

The spectacular

The familiar

Movement

The appealing

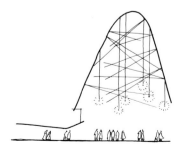

That which is dramatic

west of Peking, is a courtyard that now lies half in ruin. This closely walled space is still known as "The Court of the Concubine." Here lived, many years ago, the favorite concubine of one of the imperial princes. At one end of the courtyard stood her handsome residence of lacquered wood, tile, soft mats, and woven screens, and, at the other end, a light airy pavilion, where she and her maids whiled away the summer afternoons. By legend, she had been brought from the open plains of Szechwan province, and she longed for its lakes, woods, meadows and, far mountains, and for the wide spaces and the freedoms she had known there. And here, in the summer palace, this cramped and constricted courtyard had now become her whole world.

The prince and his planners, wishing to please her, set out to achieve, within the limits of this space, an expansive paradise of freedom and delight. From her residence, to give the illusion of distance, the walls of the courtyard were tapered both inward and down, to vastly increase the perspective toward the facing pavilion; furthermore, to reduce the effect of rigid enclosure, the far plantings extended on either side of, and beyond, the lines of the converging walls. Even the lines of the paving slabs tapered. Moving outward, all textures changed imperceptibly from the rough to the refined, and colors varied from the warm scarlets, reds, oranges, and yellows to the soft, cool, muted greens and lavenders and evanescent greys. Trees and plants in the foreground were bold in outline and foliage; those near the fragile pavilion were dwarfed and delicate. Water in the near fountain gurgled and splashed, while in the far ponds it lay mirrorlike and still. By such manipulations of perspective alone, the views from the concubine's quarters were made to seem expansive and the pavilion was made to appear remote.

As the mistress left the terrace of her residence, to move out in the courtyard, she passed through a pungently aromatic clump of twisted junipers to come upon a curiously contorted "mountain stone" that rose serenely from a bed of moss. On the stone wall behind it was incised a pattern of stylized cloud forms with the poetic inscription, "Above the green plains of Szechwan the clouds rest lightly on the lofty mountain peaks." Here, ten steps from her terrace, yet hidden from view, she could be, in her thoughts, again among her mountains.

Just beyond, and angling temptingly out of sight, was a wall of emerald tile, with a raised tile dragon of flashing red and gold that seemed to writhe in splendid fury toward an open gateway. Inside the gate was a low stone bin spilling over with blooming peonies that laced the sunlit space with fresh bright color and delicious spicy fragrance. The sound of trickling water was meant to lead her eye to a cool and shadowy recess where a teakwood bench was placed near the light spray of a waterfall. From overhead, the branches of a weeping willow cascaded down until the tips dipped into the water where gold and silver fantails drifted languidly among the floating willow leaves. A meandering line of stepping stones led across the pond to disappear into the tracery of a bamboo grove where swaying finches trilled and filled the light air with soft and tremulous melody. The thin pathway led out beyond to a ferny opening beside the farthermost lobe of the pool, which here lay deep and silent. At its edge, a carved soapstone table and cushioned seats were arranged in the shade of a feathery smoke pine near the steps of the pavilion.

153

From the raised pavilion platform, looking back, a surprising new vista met the eye. For, by forced perspective, the residence seemed startlingly near. The path that had led from it was ingeniously concealed, and a new route of return invited one to new features and spaces, or the same courtyard objects and areas viewed in a fresh and different way.

Within this masterful courtyard space we may discover an evolving complex of spaces, each designed to contain and express its usage best. And each transition, space to space, and element to element, is contrived, with a deft assurance of long centuries of practice, as a harmonious, sequential progression.

Space modulation! We in America have yet to learn the meaning of the words. But we *will* learn it in the crowded years ahead, for indeed we *must;* and we will develop it, without a doubt, to new heights of artistry.

Conditioned perception   Experience has taught us that what a thing is, is often of less importance than our relationship to the thing. The tree unseen or unremembered for us does not exist. The tree on the distant hilltop may be for the moment only an object that marks our path. As we approach we see it to be a pear tree with many pleasant connotations. Coming close, we may be tempted to pick its lush fruit. Or perhaps in the noontime heat of an August day we may welcome the chance to lie in its shade or hang a child's swing from one of its lower branches, or place a picnic table at its base. The tree in every case is the same, but our impression of the tree changes each time as our sensed relationship changes. This being so, it would seem that should we place a tree or any other object in a space we must consider not only the relationship of the object to the space, but also the relationship of the object to all who will use the space. We must program the user's perception of the object by a sequence of planned relationships that will best reveal the most appealing qualities of the object.

Our impressions of an object or a space are conditioned by those objects or spaces we have already experienced or that we anticipate. A bright, sunlit court is the more pleasant because we have just left the leafy coolness of an arbor. The splash and spray of a fountain is the more appreciated when we have approached it by way of the hot, dry, sun-baked court. The birch clumps have more meaning when we sense that the river lies just ahead. The wide free space is wider and freer to us when we realize that behind or ahead we have known or will know the compression of the space that is tightly confined.

We plan, then, not a single experience alone, but rather a sequence of conditioned experiences that will heighten the interacting pleasurable impact of each. The Chinese epicure would well understand this procedure, for to him the well-designed banquet is a well-balanced sequence of sensory delights. The thin bland, sharkfin soup, the brittle wafer of salt sea weed, the glutinous richness of jellied egg, mealy water chestnuts, chunky almonds, the sweet astringent bite of wine, light fluffy fried rice, steaming sweet-sour fish in persimmon sauce, bitter tea, crisp vegetables in light peanut oil, tender chewy bits of meat and mushrooms, soft noodles in broth with floating pigeon eggs, the rich custard of ripe durian, mouth-cleansing tea, then cool acidulous mango and more tea — and finally the lightest and dryest of wines. Each such meal is "designed" as an artistically balanced sequence of gustatory, tactile, visual — and intellectual — experiences. Should we be satisfied with less artistry in the planning of the places and spaces of our living environment?

Experience, we may see, is compounded of that which we have perceived, that which we are perceiving, and that which we expect to perceive.

As we move through a space or complex of spaces we subconsciously remember that which we have passed or sensed. We thus orient backwards in time and space, as well as forwards and find that each orientation gives meaning to the other and to all.

Sequence   Sequence, in terms of planning, may be defined as a succession of perceptions or experiences having continuity. Sequences have no meaning except to man as he experiences them. Conversely, most of man's experiences are those of planned or unplanned sequence.

In nature, sequences are casual and free. Sometimes, but not always, they are progressive. Such a progression may be one of ascent, as in the experience of climbing from lowland to mountain peak; or directional, as westward from the central plains, across the desert, over the mountains, through the valleys, and to the sea; or inward, from the sunlit edges of a forest to its deep shadowy interior; or progressions of enclosure, complexity, intensity, convenience, or comprehension.

Sometimes the sequences of nature are revealed with no more order than in the haphazard impressions of a man or child wandering lackadaisically through the landscape, along a lonely stretch of seashore, or among the shallow pools of a tidal flat.

The planned sequence may be casual or disciplined. It may be rambling and intentionally devil-may-care, or it may, to achieve a purpose, be contrived with a high degree of order. The planned sequence is an extremely effective design device. It may induce motion, give direction, create cadence, instill a mood, reveal or "explain" an object or series of objects in space, and develop a concept.

A planned sequence is a conscious arrangement or organization of elements or spaces. It has a beginning and an end that is usually, but not always, the climax. Indeed, there may be several or many climaxes. Each must be supported by, and must satisfy, its sequence. Through its suggestion of motion, one feels compelled to move from the start of a sequence to its completion. Once initiated, sequence and induced movement must be brought to a logical, or at least satisfying, conclusion.

It can be seen that all planned areas and spaces are really experienced almost solely by sequence and climax, by an order of events or perceptions in time. It can also be appreciated that such sequences must be designed and controlled. A good plan controls not only the position of the climaxes, but also their nature, their intensity, and the transitions by which they are evolved.

A sequence may be simple, complicated, or compound. It may be sustained, interrupted, varied, or modulated. It may be focal or diversifying; minute or extensive; and it may be subtle or powerful.

155

Sequence

Abstract representation of various types of plan sequence. Arrows indicate line of progression.

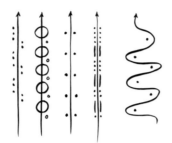

Development of cadence

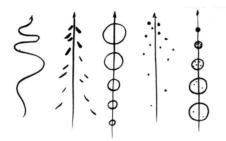

Sequence of intensification

Casual   Asymmetrical   Symmetrical

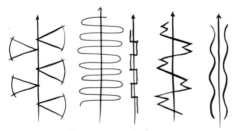

Sequence of alternation

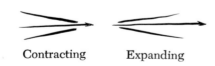

Contracting   Expanding

156

Stepping stones in Kiyozumi Garden, Tokyo, Japan. A planned sequence of high design quality, from beginning to end.

A sequence should interpret, express, or dramatize the elements, areas, or spaces used or traversed. Each sequence, like a distinctive rhythm or refrain, has its own character, and evokes an emotional response that may be fairly well predetermined.

A sequence in its simplest abstract meter may, like the varied rhythms of a jungle drum, instill a feeling of excitement, warning, fear, frenzy, mystery, wonder, awe, pleasure, happiness, exultation, power, anger, belligerence, challenge, temptation, regret, sadness, uncontrollable grief, and comfort.

Woe be to that designer who, by plan sequence, induces in the observer a mood or expectation that is not in keeping with, or satisfied by, the functions of the plan. On the contrary; how superbly effective is that sequential order of forms or spaces that develops and accentuates an induced response in consonance with the plan.

If a space sequence is marked with a rhythmic recurrence of one or more spatial qualities — size, shape, color, lighting, or texture — a cadence immediately becomes evident. Depending upon its nature, intensity, and rate of incidence, such a cadence has a slight to very considerable emotional impact upon the moving observer. Sometimes the effect is desirable, sometimes disastrous. Suffice it to note that in the planning of any spaces through which people are to move, on foot or by vehicle, an understanding of both spatial modulation and space cadence is essential.

The ordered approach   A man in motion is acted upon by the physical environment through which he passes. It would seem, therefore, that a man moving toward a goal could be prepared, by design,

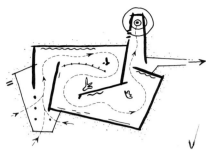

Planned sequential development of
a predetermined experience

for that goal — or moving toward an anticipated experience, could be prepared for that experience. This is, in fact, the case.

As an example of the reverse effect, let us consider a family on their way to a city church that fronts on a busy highway. As they drive along they feel hurried, and then perhaps a little alarmed when they must swing sharply out of the rushing traffic into the tight entrance of the church drive. It is narrow and jammed with idling cars that are waiting to let out passengers. After a lurching and nervous advance, the driver finally discharges his wife and children near the entrance door, only to find soon after that the church parking lot is filled. He frantically crosses the highway to park in the lot of a nearby supermarket, then jogs back up the hill to the church, where he squeezes into the pew beside his family just as the service begins. He and his wife and children are ruffled and tense, and the service is over before they regain their composure. Obviously, for these people, and for great multitudes like them, a pleasant experience of "going to church" has never been properly planned.

In the same community, let us say, another church has been planned to front on a quiet and beautiful residential parkway. On Sunday mornings, as the families make their way to church by car or along the pleasant approach walks, the church is seen set back, framed by trees, and seems serenely inviting. Driveways and parking areas are easily reached and are adequate. A shaded connecting walk leads back to a wide and spacious entrance court, from which the entrance doors open. Here, as he pauses before entry, one is prepared by form, by symbol, by the very quality of the space, for the services inside. Here, after service, families and friends can meet and visit in appropriate surroundings. The approaching, attending, and leaving of this church are all planned as conducive, meaningful aspects of worship.

In the orient such approaches are designed with admirable sensitivity. As one moves, for example, down the roadway toward the entrance gate of a temple grounds, the very street assumes an air of reverent

Progressive sequential realization of a concept or conditioned attainment of a goal

Analogy
The stream and the pedestrian traffic way

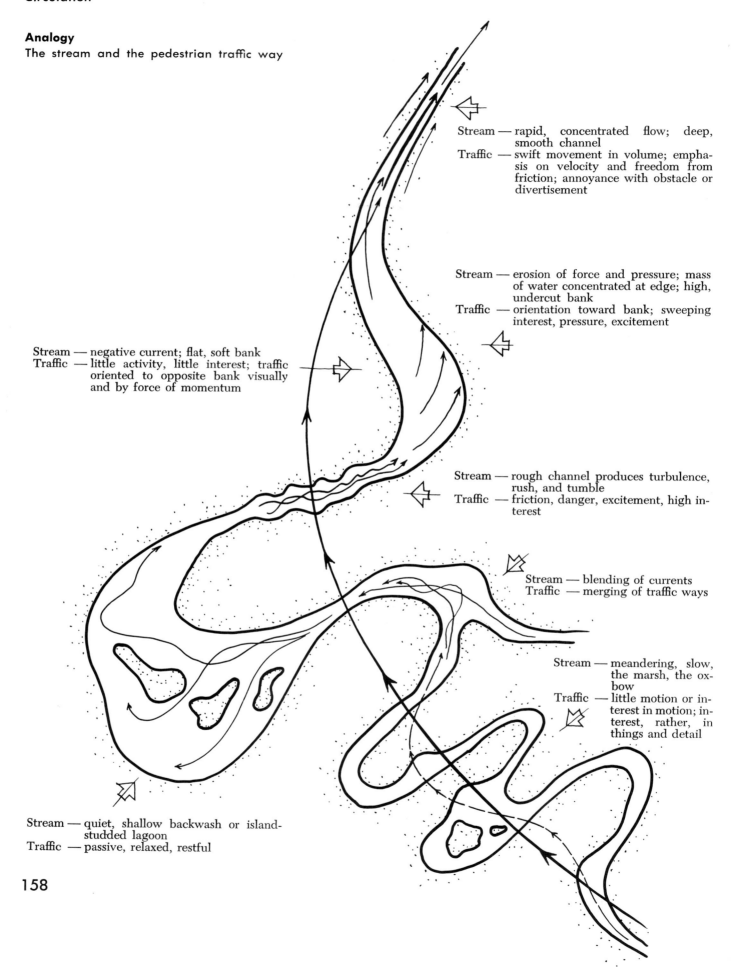

Stream — rapid, concentrated flow; deep, smooth channel
Traffic — swift movement in volume; emphasis on velocity and freedom from friction; annoyance with obstacle or divertisement

Stream — erosion of force and pressure; mass of water concentrated at edge; high, undercut bank
Traffic — orientation toward bank; sweeping interest, pressure, excitement

Stream — negative current; flat, soft bank
Traffic — little activity, little interest; traffic oriented to opposite bank visually and by force of momentum

Stream — rough channel produces turbulence, rush, and tumble
Traffic — friction, danger, excitement, high interest

Stream — blending of currents
Traffic — merging of traffic ways

Stream — meandering, slow, the marsh, the oxbow
Traffic — little motion or interest in motion; interest, rather, in things and detail

Stream — quiet, shallow backwash or island-studded lagoon
Traffic — passive, relaxed, restful

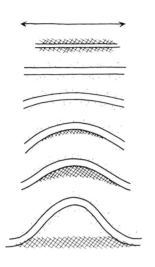

A straight channel of sufficient width accommodates pedestrian traffic flow without erosion at edges — as does a channel with easy curvature. As the degree of curvature increases, erosion at the inner edge increases until finally a short-cut is effected.

Widening of bends in traffic ways expresses and accommodates traffic flow.

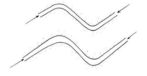

dignity. The temple gates and walls by tradition close out the temporal world and enclose a garden space of tranquil peace, a symbolic paradise. From far down the road to innermost altar, the approach is designed as a superbly modulated transition — from the crude to the refined, from the crass to the rich, from the expansive to the introspective, from confusion to sublimity. By every device of his science and art the planner thus transforms the raucous, strident man of the world into the humble petitioner who kneels before the sacred altar in an attitude of prayer.

By similar means, man may be conditioned for any planned human experience. And, by all odds, he should be.

PEDESTRIAN TRAFFIC

The characteristics of pedestrian traffic can best be understood by comparing them with those of a stream or river. Foot traffic, like flowing water, follows a course of least resistance. It tends toward the shortest distance, point to point. It has a pressure of momentum. It has force. It erodes. Swift movement requires a straight smooth channel with increased width at the curves. If not provided, such a channel will be forced. As in the swift river jutting points are worn away, rock ledges are undercut, and the oxbow is "strung," just so does the force of pedestrian traffic grind away at impinging or constricting forms, or leap its channel to shape a new and freer course.

Just as a man-made canal establishes the route, rate, and maximum volume of its traffic, so man-made walks can fix the path and control the movement of pedestrian traffic. Again, as with the intermittent stream on a level plain, the course of such traffic may be governed by unpredictable variables. Often, in campus planning particularly, where momentums and lines of pedestrian force are so difficult to predetermine, only the major walks are constructed with the buildings, and the crosswalks or meandering walkways are laid down later along those unconscious and natural lines of movement worn thin in the campus turf.

An obstacle in a traffic stream, as in a stream of water, produces turbulence. Turbulence is friction. Where directional traffic or rapid flow is desirable, islands in the path or walkway are best streamlined or shaped to divert and direct flowing traffic in a sweep or glide.

Intersections are points of maximum turbulence. In planning, such turbulence is often a positive quality, as in those places where excitement, activity, or high interest is desirable, or where the flow of traffic is to be perforce decelerated, or where, by plan intent, people are made to mill and churn and jostle about. The degree and nature of such ebullient hurly-burly may be planned, as in the market place, the trade show, the amusement park, or the country fair. Where two or more intersecting streams of traffic are to be merged into one fast, free-flowing stream, the area of juncture must be widened and shaped to provide a smoothly swelling transition and uninterrupted flow.

An intersection must express the functions induced by the fact of intersection. Geographically, the place of the meeting of streams or rivers is strategically important. For here not only the watersheds of

159

two valley systems are merged, but also the life and trade and culture that flow down with the streams. In Pittsburgh, for example, the Golden Triangle is centered for good reason at the point where the Allegheny and Monongahela rivers meet to form the start of the Ohio. Here, as in most such instances, many powerful forces, factors, and requirements are engendered by the fact of convergence. Here is proof of a Gestalt hypothesis, that the whole may be greater than the sum of its parts. In planning, the merging or converging of two or more streams of like or dissimilar nature — whether they are streams of water, trade, culture, transportation, motor traffic, or even pedestrian walkways — induces both negative and positive factors that must be resolved or developed.

Wide pools of pedestrian traffic are often formed at the head or the base of a drop, such as a ramp or a flight of stairs. Casual foot traffic, like a quiet stream, takes a meandering course. Traffic that, by nature or preference, is passive is found where quiet water on a river would be found, in the lagoon or island-studded backwash, and out of the mainstream or current. This sheltered quiet lagoon character, with all its design implications, is germane to those many plan functions that are related to, yet out of, main pedestrian traffic streams. In the same way, the swift freedom of the channel or the sweeping interest of the bend are clearly analogous to many planned places and spaces.

Things seen   Most visual aspects of most projects are seen by the pedestrian as he circulates, and from eye level. Walking is still the most frequent and, in some instances, the only possible means of movement. As we have learned, the line and rate of movement may be, for a specific reason, precisely fixed or directed. Or it may be completely free, allowing a maximum number of alternate routes and a maximum variety of experiences. In any case, the man on foot, as he moves about or comes to rest, is of prime concern to the planner. Indeed, he is usually the sole reason for, and his induced response the sole objective of, the plan.

Slow movement engenders interest in detail. A man in a hurry tolerates no obstruction, but a man moving leisurely welcomes deflection and distraction. He has little interest in motion, and takes more pleasure instead in the things he can see or experience. He explores with his senses, delights in relationships, and is pleased by subtle transitions.

The base plane   Pedestrian traffic moving directly on the base plane is sensitive to its textures. Texture, as much as any design factor, determines the type and speed of foot traffic. A given texture not only accommodates a certain classification of traffic, but may attract it as well, as in the following examples:

Texture	*Traffic*
Natural granite, rough sandstone	The hobnailed boot
Packed earth, the field, the forest duff	The hiking shoe
Water	The bare foot, the wader
Snow	The ski, the snowshoe
Ice	The skate, the crampon
Sand	The clog, the bare toes

Turf	The spiked golf shoe, the crepe-soled sport shoe, the cleated football boot
Bituminous paving	The tennis shoe, the sneaker
Flagstone	The loafer
Cutstone, concrete, paving brick	The business shoe
Terrazzo, polished marble	The dancing pump

Distance and grade   Moving under our own power, we are most conscious of the friction of distance and the effort of climbing a grade. Where actual distance and grade are negative factors, they are reduced insofar as possible by the arrangement of the plan. Apparent distances and grades are further reduced to a minimum by screening, space modulation, and the alignment of traffic ways. Paths, for instance, can loop up or down a long steep grade, to reduce the apparent height and length of climb; for the straight, unbroken climb to the hilltop is in all ways more tiresome than a gradual ascent from station to station along a path that angles up the contours.

Often, as we have noted, within a limited plan complex, it becomes desirable to *increase* apparent distances and heights. This again may be achieved in large measure by the manipulation of traffic ways and sightlines, or by the viewing of a peak from a pit, a pit from a peak, and a far corner from the longest diagonal.

Traffic flow   Pedestrian traffic, being earthbound, is more of a *flow* than a trajectory. This *flow* may be induced, accelerated, divided, pooled, channelled, directed, diverted, or arrested, as the planned functions demand.

RAIL, AIR, AND WATER TRAFFIC

The railroad has changed the landscape. In the early days of our country railroads were driven through centers of resource, productivity, or industry by routes of least resistance. It was almost as simple as that; the railroads were built to "open up" and "develop" the land, and this they did. But their tremendous impact on the landscape was never foreseen, and certainly never planned or controlled. Even today it is not controlled, and this must seem incredible to any man of logical mind.

Travel by rail   From a map, it is easily seen that towns, cities, counties, states, highway systems, and even ocean-spanning shipping lines have been oriented like iron filings to the magnetic field of our railroad systems. These seemingly innocuous lines of gleaming rails and telegraph poles have magnetized the whole of our land and set, in broad terms, the entire plan pattern of our country. To their credit, the railroads have provided the transportation so essential to our growth and strength and economy. On the debit side, they have done violence to the natural landscape, split our cities, generated countless frictions, and irreparably destroyed the natural potential of great land areas by attracting developments that are not consistent with the best use of the land. These infractions against our land and our society have long gone unchecked and must now be stopped and regulated by comprehensive regional and national resource planning.

The planned revisions or extensions of lines or facilities should be considered exactly as for any other planning project. They should be developed through site-use diagrams, fulfilling their functions in fullest possible harmony with the natural and man-made landscape. Such planning will not cripple the railroads. It will rather, in time, reduce their frictions and promote their growth in conformity with the highest potential development of all land areas, and thus increase their usefulness and revenues.

The fleeting landscape   The landscape seen from the train is a landscape in motion. It is observed from an almost level plane, since railroad beds seldom exceed a grade of five per cent. Eye level is approximately eight feet above the rails over which we glide at speeds of up to ninety miles an hour. Nearby forms or objects streaking past have little meaning in themselves. They may effectively serve as screening either as a blur of loose foliage or as a solid wall, earthbank, or structure. They often develop cadences, sometimes pleasurable, sometimes annoying. They usually distract and disturb by their flicker and by the fact that one strains to distinguish and identify them. And, by their jittery insistence, they often destroy the pleasant scenic qualities inherent in the landscape. Railway travel cn many lines would be made much more pleasant if foreground forms and objects were removed or simplified.

Visual interest, from a moving train, is centered in the middle distance or on the distant view. The far view changes imperceptibly and soon becomes monotonous, unless given variety by middle ground interest. To be enjoyable to the viewer, the middle ground interest or action must be consistent with the background and with the modulating foreground enframement. This is well known to the artist who draws and paints the background scenes for animated cartoons. He is concerned with *producing* unfolding relationships of foreground, middleground, and background that work together in harmony. The passenger on the speeding train is interested in *realizing* such relationships.

The passing scene is sensed as a continuing flow of impressions. Just as in a static composition we take pleasure in harmonious relationships, so it is that in the blending emerging compositions of the passing landscape we seek harmonious transitions. That which is fitting we find to be agreeable. That which is inappropriate we find to be disagreeable. If, as passengers on our contemporary railroads, we seek a rapid frictionless passage from point to point through an attractive landscape of variety and interest, we are, in the main, doomed to disappointment. Though the efficiency of the train as a machine has made notable advances, the efficacy of the train as a means of pleasurable travel has not. True, much attention has been lavished on the passenger's physical comfort. But railroad management, wondering at the decline in passenger traffic, would do well to consider the fact that they now provide the most extensive slumming excursions extant. By established railroad custom, the public must ride the same tracks as the tank cars, scrap iron, and livestock; and the passengers, together with the rancid oils, rusty bales, and bawling calves, are routed past the rear doors of the soap factory, the junkyard, and the slaughterhouse. At the time of the railroads' beginning this was accepted practice, but it is no longer acceptable to a public now free to make other choices. If the railroad is to survive as a passenger carrier, it must classify and separate its functions.

The railway potential   Movement by rail, on grade or overhead along a fixed course, has many manifest advantages, including predictability, control, and safety. There are many who believe that the era of the railway is past. But there are many other men of vision who hold that travel by rail has no more than passed through an early stage, and is now on the threshold of an even greater era. This new era will come:

> When the alignment of the railway is planned with the express purpose of developing a region's resources and optimum potential
> And when classified transportation and travel are conceived in terms of pure motion
> And when the railway is envisioned as a group of functions operating in frictionless relation to adjacent functions
> And when the proper development of the land areas contiguous to the railway can be realized by adequate right-of-way widths, restrictions, and zoning
> And when the visual aspects of railway passenger travel have received the same emphasis as have comfort and efficiency
> And when the good features of the landscape have been preserved and accentuated, and when the unsightly or incongruous features have been eliminated or judiciously screened
> And when planners have come to realize that much of our landscape and cityscape is revealed to the world through the eyes of passengers riding by on rail, and when, in such cases, they have planned *to* the railway.

Then travel by rail will become generally what it already is in many instances — an experience of satisfaction, and sometimes sheer delight.

Travel by plane   Travel by plane unfolds a modelled and checkered landscape of towns, hills, lakes, rivers, valleys, farmland, field, and forest moving slowly under the wings. We are impressed with the *continuity* of the landscape. We sense, perhaps for the first time, that every object in the landscape is a related part of the whole. Sight distances are great. Visible areas are enormous. Objects, to be seen, must be simple, bold, and contrasting in colors or textures. They are most often read from the air by their shadows. All essential plan forms or objects requiring recognition from the air must be so emphasized.

Travel by plane is "flight" and is seemingly effortless while one is airborne. This smooth, flashing speed accentuates the frictions and delays of the airport and cross-country travel beyond it. The frictions of port transfer and the frictions of port-to-city distance must be drastically reduced. It seems somehow puzzlingly and annoyingly inconsistent to the airline passenger to have spent longer in getting from the door of his Park Forest home to the door of the plane, and from the New York airport to a Manhattan office, than in spanning the 713 air miles between Chicago and New York. The competitive port of the future will have fast and easy access to other transportation centers and to central discharge points. In many municipalities the helicopter is pioneering in rapid airborne taxi service. There are other improvements just ahead that will soon make even this fascinating "whirlybird" as obsolete as the dodo. The deafening din at the airport aprons is mounting, decibel by decibel, to the point where it will soon become unbearable. Sometime before that critical point, or very shortly after, the pressure of economics and the advance of science will have reduced the earshattering rocket roar to a pleasant whistling hum.

From the dawn of time, man has moved on the ground in two dimensions; only recently has he taken to the air. This new venture in three dimensions has been, in effect, simply two-dimensional travel elevated above the surface of the earth. It has been, in the main, group movement in a fixed trajectory.

An airport should rightly be planned as a *port*. Here, in this air harbor, the land meets an opposite — the air. This meeting and all induced transitions must be analyzed and expressed. All current or forseeable requirements and characteristics of planes, at rest or in flight, must be designed for. From the surrounding towns and cities new exclusive or classified approach roads will be necessary, as will a system of strategically placed air taxi stations. In this light, we can consider an airport primarily in terms of a continuing and ultimate experience of travel — where passengers might arrive by car, park, check baggage, and emplane; or arrive by plane, pick up baggage, and leave by car, limousine, helicopter, or taxi in one swift, pleasant, uninterrupted swoop. There are, of course, many other considerations in the planning of an airport.

Airports require large areas of flat topography, or land that can be readily modified to give long level runways. Because such areas are often of necessity remote, the tendency of airports is to bring to the spot as many port facilities as possible. Hotels, theaters, conference rooms, libraries, and even shopping centers are often planned as an integral part of the airport, right from its inception. Airports long ago established themselves as major recreation centers. On weekends particularly, they are inundated by wave on wave of spectators. Either the sightseeing public must be restricted, or its impact must be anticipated and provided for.

A municipal airport is no longer a landing strip, a dolly-sock, and a ticket booth. The modern airport is an extremely involved complex of myriad related functions, demanding proximity to cities or transportation centers and requiring vast areas of land. An airport and all its functions must be studied as to optimum relationship to the cities and region that it serves. It must be studied, as must all projects planned in the landscape, in terms of minimum frictions and maximum harmonies.

Travel by water   When we think of a boat in motion we think of a smoothly gliding hull, a curving wake of tumbling water, and dancing light. The course of a boat, like the water through which it foams and bubbles, is fluid and undulating. Having no fixed track or roadway, it curves in wide arcs and must be given ample space for maneuvering.

Even at rest at its mooring, it seems mobile. All plan lines relating to boats at rest or in motion should suggest this streamlined fluid mobility. In every way possible, smooth flow should be encouraged and obstructions eliminated. The heavy, the rough, the jagged, and the sharp are out of place. They are destructive and impeding in fact, and disturbing by connotation.

Travel by boat seems almost frictionless. All things and places are left, passed, and approached on the glide. Movement is slow. Change of direction is seldom abrupt. The middle and far distances become, visually, a panoramic background for the objects and details seen more closely at hand. With the sky for the overhead plane, and water for the base, interest is centered on the vertical plane. On this vertical plane the point and the bay give variations in depth. If increased variety of view is desirable, the point may, by design, be given more prominence and the bay be made more recessive; or the passing scene and objects may be given heightened interest by other means.

Being exposed to the elements, the currents, and the tides, a boat requires for its mooring a sheltered harbor or protective pier. Harbor and pier logically provide such shelter by topography, structure, or a combination of both. They are points of transition between the water and the land, where the mobile and free meet the solid and static. The fact of this meeting might well be developed and expressed in all plan forms. Indeed, no great stretch of the imagination is required to understand that *any* structure related to water and boatways gains when the full drama of the relationship is exploited.

A summer cottage on a lake or cove, for example, is not merely a box propped haphazardly along the sandy or rocky shoreline. Together with its landscape forms, it is a planned transition from land to water, solid to fluid, mineral to aqueous, confined to expansive, and strong cast shadow to shimmering light; and often from car to yacht, yawl, canoe, or rowboat. It is terraced down; it overhangs, overlooks; it screens off and then subtly or dramatically reveals; it embraces, ramps or steps into, invites view or movement from land to water and water to land. It accentuates, by lucid structural relationships, the highest qualities of land and lake. At the land approach, it is of the land. It is devised to attract, receive, and accommodate the hiker, the horse, or the motorcar. At the water's edge, it is of the water. It is shaped to attract, receive, and accommodate the bather, the swimmer, or the boat.

A riverside restaurant, if worthy of its site, will orient to the river and its traffic and display it in all its motion and color. On the landward side, it will take its form from the features of the land and from the passing walk or street or highway. On the riverside, it will be shaped to the line of the river's flow and to the curve of the approaching craft. It is a rewarding experience to dine in such a waterside restaurant, with its glass-walled dining room projected and elevated to catch the sweeping river view; or at shaded tables set on a terrace or deck beside the river wall, or even spaced out on the pier beside the bobbing boats and lapping water. In the same way, with the seaside hotel, the water- front park, the bridge, the pier, the harbor, and the lighthouse, our plan forms and structures must best express the meeting of land and water. They must capture and blend the highest native qualities of each.

A structure that dramatizes its relation to the river

When the horse was discarded, the winding roads and streets over which he jogged were not discarded with him. The automobile inherited them. Some of them have been "improved" from time to time, but their basic features have remained unchanged. The result of pushing motor cars out over these old roads was at first simply a mild havoc and runaway horses, but later, "the traffic problem." Today we are still rebuilding old roads that were constructed for another vehicle, instead of special roads for the special needs of the automobile. This simple fact is the key to the whole present-day traffic problem.

NORMAN BEL GEDDES

Boatways and waterways, when properly planned, have few detrimental characteristics and many attractive features. Large bodies of water ameliorate the climate, enliven the landscape, and provide a direct and inexpensive means of travel and transportation. Rivers follow the valley floors. Usually their easy gradient encourages travel along their banks as well as upon their surface. They, together with their feeding streams and rivulets, promote a lush growth of vegetation and the most agreeable landscape environment of the regions through which they pass. All waterways attract industrial, commercial, and residential development. How can they all be accommodated? Which should have preference? The solution here is not usually one of blanket prohibition, for such prohibitions tend to dam up overwhelming pressures, but is rather one of planned relationships. Lucky is the region or city that is empathetically and wisely related to its rivers, lakes, canals, or waterfront.

AUTOMOBILE TRAFFIC

Highways, streets, and even driveways, as plan elements, must be considered as *lethal lines of force*. These lines and their intersections are lines and points of smashups, crippling accidents, and death. If a high tension line crossed a community with its wires stretched low or sagging within reach of children, there would be a storm of citizen protest. Yet unprotected highways slice freely through the landscape, and our cities and our suburbs are cut into senseless squares by murderous boulevards and streets. Why? In the name of all reason, *why?*

There is, in the light of unprejudiced analysis, not one valid reason for our present checkerboard system of streets, except for the obvious ease of laying them out. This seems a sorry excuse indeed. Our street and property patterns were, in fact, devised in the era of the horse and buggy, and for the convenience of the surveyor. Because they so profoundly affect the pattern, quality, and very safety of our daily life, it is high time for a change.

Man in his automobile has found traffic friction increased from mere annoyance to a deadly phenomenon. In self sefense he has devised wider roads, separated roads, segregated traffic, the overpass and underpass, freeways, skyways, and skyline drives. Engineers, in solving the very practical problem of moving man and his automobile through space, have created sweeping forms of tremendous grandeur. Yet new forms, new concepts, and new diagrams must be devised, if man is even to keep pace with the roaring, fuming, four-wheeled monster that he has created.

In the planning of our highways and streets, we must think of them also, and equally, as *friction-free paths of vehicular movement.* This clearly is their primary purpose. Yet, if we were to plot a typical street or highway as a force diagram, we would wonder how a more friction-studded, danger-loaded, chaotic trafficway could possibly be conceived. We know, for instance, that each point at which the paths of two vehicles merge is a point of friction, and each point at which they cross is a point of hazard. Obviously, the fewer such points, the better. Yet, with rare exceptions, our present trafficways are so laced and interlaced with mergings and crossings that their very function is precluded. How blind we have become in our conditioned complacency!

In our trafficways of the future, the grade intersection will be eliminated in every possible instance. Roads will be planned for fast, safe, uninterrupted traffic *flow.* Turning radii will be greatly increased. Rights of way will be widened and shaped to accommodate and contain all foreseeable roadway functions. Vehicular traffic of various types and speeds will be segregated and given separate and specially planned routes. Marginal frictions will be eliminated. Imaginative safety controls and devices will be planned with and built into the highways. High-speed transcontinental motorways will weave through the open country *between* our towns and cities rather than threading them center-to-center. Our residential, commercial, and industrial districts will be off to the side — protected and entered by widely spaced, free-flowing access ways. Alignments will be diagrammed for ideal traffic movement to and through the region, the city, and its satellite communities.

A highway, road, or driveway is a unified whole in itself. It must be complete and useful. It must be safe. It must be economical. It must function well. It must provide a pleasant experience of movement from point to point throught the landscape. This useful and pleasurable quality is most possible when, and perhaps only possible if, the road's right of way is aligned in harmony with the landscape and is wide enough to accommodate and contain all of its physical and visual functions. How pleasant is the parkway with limits that extend to the rim of the valley through which it winds, or the parkway with a right of way that has been intelligently widened to preserve the sight lines from a sloping grade or ridge top!

Highways, roads, and driveways will continue to be designed as a major, and usually *the* major, means of access to an area or project. Each project or landscape area will be considered in relation to its access way — and conversely, each line of access will be conceived as an integral and related part of the thing or place toward which, or away from which, it leads. In planning them, we will think in terms of sight lines, transitions, deceleration patterns, visual guides, and angles of approach.

The street system of our cities and the road system of the region follow archaic patterns which go back to a time of beast drawn vehicles. The needs and practices that created the old thoroughfares are entirely alien to the auto. The old road necessarily ran through the villages, which provided resting places for passengers, a stage where horses could be fed and exchanged. Today those old regional routes – have become highways, and motor vehicles speeding along them carry traffic danger into every village and town.

LUDWIG HILBERSEIMER

Have you ever conceived of a road which would allow no car to approach your own — which would hold you to your course without the danger of being struck or striking any object — where you could decide in advance how fast you would like to drive, and by maintaining that constant, effortless pace, arrive at your destination on scheduled time? It sounds impossible? But you can have such a road. The means of bringing it about are available. The idea is thoroughly practical. It can be built to work in conjunction with an automatic control installed in your car. The highway you use can be made as safe and pleasant at all times as it would be if your car were the only automobile upon it.

NORMAN BEL GEDDES

The eyes of a person riding in a car sweep along a plane of sight about four feet above the road. All things observed move toward or past this point of "pix." Whole landscape systems, if they are to be seen mainly from the automobile, must be oriented to, and focused upon, the lens of the eye that is moving at this level. Eyes flashing past objects at fifty miles per hour cannot perceive intricate detail, or much more than the first blurred words of text on those countless historical markers that are set inexplicably along the berms of our nation's high-speed highways. Things that will be seen or experienced from a moving car must, by all logic, be planned or designed for this specific and highly specialized impact. The moving eye finds interest in evolutions and transitions of form, color, and pattern, for which planned sequences and space modulations are highly effective.

The modern highway with its adjunct bridges, cloverleafs, and structures is not only the most dominant feature of our landscape, it is also the most salient factor in our land and community planning. Once established in any landscape, a roadway becomes a potent landscape feature, and immediately changes the character of the land areas through which it makes its way. In most site-structure diagrams the roadway is the most dynamic line to which use-areas can be related. Before we can plan effectively this fact must be understood.

Without doubt, the most telling advances in our planning in the near future will be the diagramming of safer and more reasonable relationships between man and the automobile and, more specifically, between trafficways and our cities, communities, and the surrounding landscape. The automobile has rendered obsolete the traditional planning concepts. The new concepts should be better; for this much cannot be denied the automobile, it has given us new and exhilarating freedoms of distance and time. We move today more freely than man has ever moved before. However, the automobile has also imposed a new and distressing double scale. Far too much of our present landscape is experienced from the viewpoint of both the speeding automobile and the pedestrian. In terms of frictions and visual scale, these two experiences are clearly incompatible. This omnipresent modern dilemma has hardly been recognized as yet, let alone resolved. If ignoring it made it a constant problem, perhaps studying and resolving it will bring the first plan forms and patterns fully expressive of our promising motor age. In the new environment, motor and pedestrian traffic will be segregated. Our living and working areas will be readily approached and serviced by the automobile, but they will be oriented to, and interspersed with, attractive, refreshing pedestrian spaces unpenetrated by roadways. Walking will again be a pleasure, when it is freed from the sound and sight and danger of rushing traffic, and when it leads us through places and spaces that were designed for walking. And our motorways, designed solely and specifically for free vehicular movement, will seem a dream on wheels.

THE APPROACH DRIVE

In locating a project or structure on any site, a factor of first importance is the line of traffic approach. This line will not only dictate or influence the best position of the structural elements, but will probably also determine the position and relationships of the site use-areas as well.

Assuming that an approach drive is to be developed between a proposed structure and an existing highway or street, let us consider the ideal design requirements, all else being equal:

A driveway should approach from the right. In America a car moves in the right lane of traffic with its wheels to the curb. We have here an "Alight, Queen" instinct that tells us, as we near a destination, to chart a course that will bring the right side of our car to the curb, the marquee, or the entrance door, where our "Queen" is handed out or handed in again. This right curb approach is valid mainly because of two way streets, which make pulling to the left curb dangerous, illegal, or inconvenient, and usually all three.

Approach from the left is often more logical and, sometimes, the only way possible. If such an approach is to be planned, we might try to arrange sufficient depth to permit the drive to swing past the entrance and circle back from the right — all within the property limits. If, however, the driveway must perforce lead in from the left, we do what we can to make this seem feasible by making the point of discharge obvious, by providing a landing platform on the right hand side, or planning discharge from the left into an entrance court.

One-way traffic at a building entrance is always preferable. It is safer. There is also a psychological advantage, for the driver with his right wheels to the curb feels superior and, for some strange reason, very, very clever.

We design the drive to make the first impression of the structures or property attractive. A building is usually more interesting if seen from a sweeping drive approach, to show its form and extent before attention is centered upon its detail. Much of the nature of a building or any other structure is thus revealed by a planned exposition of its plastic qualities from a drive that leads past or around it. We open "shots" to the structure; each shot from the proper distance and position, and with the best possible enframement for displaying the element viewed.

The driveway should be so aligned as to reveal the sculptural qualities not only of the structure, but also of the site — the pleasantly undulating edge of a woodlot or planting, the modeling of topographic forms, the counterplay of tree trunk against trunk, mass against mass, texture against texture, color against color, as one sweeps along.

Highways are best planned, as in this example, as free-flowing streams of vehicular traffic.

We design for an attractive space and theme modulation, from drive entrance to building entrance, to parking court, and return.

We devise a transition from the character of the highway to the character of the structure; from the large scale of the open landscape to the scale of the entrance court; from the unorganized to the organized, or vice versa; from high velocity to repose. At one instant, a person may be whistling along in his automobile at seventy miles an hour; two minutes later, he may be standing contemplatively at the building entrance. Between the two conditions are telling changes in scale and attitude that must somehow be agreeably resolved. We must somehow, in the design of the driveway, prepare the visitor for the experience of arrival.

We strive in all ways to keep the drive in character with the structure or the project. They must give the appearance of having been planned together as one continuing sequence of visual expression and use.

The driveway should never appear to collide with a structure, but rather it should sweep toward it and past.

We do not violate the landscape.

We design, of course, to take full advantage of the site — its topography, its cover, its vistas, views, and other landscape features, and its native character.

The alignment of the driveway presents perhaps our best opportunity for the planned visual unfolding or realization of the site, or the "discovery" of any feature within it. It should focus attention on desirable elements.

We plan the alignment to eliminate or screen out the unfortunate features of the site or the less desirable features of the structure.

We should plan the driveway to prevent the splitting of the site. Rather, we would in all ways possible preserve the best site areas and landscape features.

We flow with the contours of the land.

We move from hollow to ridge, from dense cover to open sweep, maximize in all ways possible the pleasurable impact of the site.

Because a driveway and its gutters or swales often provide the natural drainageway for large areas of a property, the grades, where possible, should be such as to permit surface water flow without ponding, or without undue erosion.

We avoid the long shot across paving toward the structure or any significant feature.

We avoid the direct shot through or into the parking area, for parking is a service function and is usually best screened. The parking area is normally best convenient but incidental to, and secluded from, the structure. Ideally the driver would pass the entrance on his right, discharge his passengers, continue, park, and find his way back easily and pleasantly to the entrance door. Ideally, too, he would be able to circle back with the entrance on his right again as he picked up his passengers and departed.

We design with a full understanding of the mechanics and maneuverability of the car. These dictate to a large degree the texture, width, grade, and radii of the paving. Pavement textures may change to differentiate between areas of movement and areas in which to stop or park. Road widths may vary — swelling at the entrance throat, at the curves, and at the forecourt — always suggesting traffic *flow*.

Traffic tends to the right, but also to the easier fork and to the easier grade.

We set the driveway entrance, whenever possible, at the point of most logical penetration or highest visual interest along the highway property line. It should be well marked. It should invite one in. It should give the theme and set up the sign or symbol that explains. Perhaps by recalling the materials or forms of the main structure, it may "expand" the structure from highway to building site.

We consider the advertising and public relations values of site and structure relationship to highway.

We consider the position of the throat entry in relation to those adjacent and other features of the extensional landscape.

The driveway entrance must also be set at a point of safe sight distance up and down the passing highway. It must never be set below the crest of a highway's steep vertical curve. It must permit of ample deceleration width and distance from the main traffic stream. A right-angle entrance alignment is best for two-way sighting.

Provide a "glide-in" entrance, where possible, in harmony with traffic flow.

Study ways by which to facilitate left hand turns — by reduced speed, wide sweep, positioning, alerting, and explaining.

A driveway should be short, for economy and ease of maintenance. We plan it for all weather and for all conditions of darkness or light. Consider sun position at all times.

Paving is hot in the summer, cold in the winter. Avoid making the structure an island in a sea of paving.

A driveway approach should be logical. It should present the driver with a minimum number of decisions.

A driveway must be planned as a study in movement, transition, and connection. It must be planned as an *experience* of arrival and departure.

A driveway should be obvious and, at the same time, restrained. This is to say that it must read clearly to the driver, but should intrude as little as possible on the natural landscape.

Consider the drive approach in terms of contracting and expanding volumes.

A driveway should be safe. Avoid, where possible, all crossing of pedestrian walkways or areas of children's play. Avoid backing into any areas where children might be about.

And once again, as with all landscape features, we develop the drive or driveway itself as a complete and satisfying element of design.

STRUCTURES IN THE LANDSCAPE 6

THE FORECOURT, OR AREA immediately in front of a structure or group of structures, is best planned at the same time and as an integral part of the structure, at least in diagram. It is designed to attract and accommodate the types of approaching traffic. It receives guests and directs services. It focuses attention on the entrances, it prepares one for entry, and establishes the appropriate atmosphere.

The psychology of arrival is more important than you think. If it is not obvious where to park, if there is no room to park when you get there, if you stumble into the back door looking for the front entrance, or if the entrance is badly lighted, you will have subjected your guests to a series of annoyances which will linger long in their subconscious. No matter how warm your hearth or how beautiful your view, the overall effect will be dimmed by these first irritations.

THOMAS D. CHURCH

To be successful visually, a forecourt must absolutely have a receptive *cove* or *harbor* quality. Those who have sailed will remember that the long uninterrupted shoreline has little of visual magnetism, while the point or jutting promontory has an outward thrust, and tends to direct interest and motion away from the land. But what sailor can resist the pull of the harbor? No matter what, he must change his course to enter the inviting cove. The forecourt, or some element of the forecourt, must be a planned cove in abstract form; and, along its periphery, the richest, "hottest", most interesting point should be the project or building entrance.

The approach court should "read" from the lines of passing or converging traffic. From far up and down the canyon that is New York's Fifth Avenue one can see and sense the open, sunlit, tree-lined space that is the forecourt of the Public Library. And on the avenue, blocks away, one feels that one is moving not "down the street" or "up the street" but rather, "toward the Library." From this telling masterpiece of planning we may learn that, somewhere along the traffic lines, the forecourt or its planned extensions must place the visual sign, symbol, thing, or space that alerts and then explains the structure or feature toward which it provides direction.

The defined open space is activated by moving sun and shadow, and by changing sky and passing cloud.

Our forecourt will be conceived as a use-area or series of use-areas. It may extend the functions of the street or highway by providing a turning circle, parking space, or merely a widened unloading strip. It may extend the approaching sidewalks by including paved courts or terraces. It may extend the function of a building by providing outdoor spaces or levels into which and onto which the interior uses and users may flow. The forecourt may even concentrate or focalize the functions of a building, the way, for example, the small cafes along many a bustling street in Rome serve as little more than kitchens and wine cellars for the crowded tables on the piazzissima "out front."

The pull of the harbor

Lack of interest—monotony

Outward thrust—repulsion

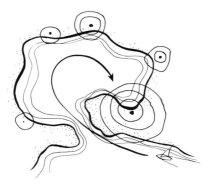

Inward pull—attraction

A superb handling of exterior solids and voids

A forecourt may be selective, attracting some visitors or uses and repelling others. The kindergarten forecourt, for instance, with its tiny candy-pink gate and its low painted tables and "kiddie" toys, might be irresistible to one youngster while his brother, two years older, "wouldn't be caught dead" in the place. Some approach courts are planned to permit deliveries; some, very obviously, are not. Others may, within their limits, classify and accommodate traffic of several varying types.

A forecourt is a volume or series of volumes encompassing the required plan functions and focusing attention from the approaches to a building feature or entrance. Our approach volumes and forms should develop a logical sequence of progression. We should experience pleasant transitions from exterior to interior spaces. As we near or move through the forecourt we should sense a feeling of "homing in."

A forecourt is a foreground. It complements or enhances by contrast the feature or the structure. It develops and accentuates the character or the mood. A well-conceived forecourt will marry a project or structure to its near and distant approaches, and will serve to integrate it with adjacent structures and with the total landscape.

THE DEFINED OPEN SPACE

Open spaces assume an architectural character when they are enclosed in full or in part by a structure or structural elements. Often such a space is an extension of a building. Sometimes it is confined within the limits of a single building, or enclosed by a group of buildings. Sometimes such a space surrounds a structure or serves as its foreground, or as a foil, or as a focal point. Each such defined open space is an entity. It is complete within itself. But more, it is an inseparable part of each adjacent space or structure. It can be seen that such related spaces and structures are best conceived and developed together as a meaningful complex of solids and voids.

A defined outdoor volume is a well of space. Its very hollowness is its essential quality. Without the corresponding void a solid has no meaning. Is it not then quite evident that the size, shape, and quality of the negative space will have a powerful retroactive effect upon the adjacent positive masses? Each structure requires for its fullest effective expression a satisfying balance of mass and void. The same void may not only satisfy two or more solids and relate them to each other, it may also relate them as a group to some further structures or spaces beyond.

Whatever its function, where the hollowness of such a volume is a quality to be desired, this concavity is meticulously preserved and emphasized — by letting the shell read clearly; by revealing enclosing members and planes; by incurving, or belling out the sides; by the use of recessive colors and forms; by letting the bottom fall away; by terracing or sloping down into and up out of this base; by digging the pit; by depressing a water basin or reflective pool and thus extending apparent depth to infinity. A cleanly shaped space is not to be choked or clogged with trees or other standing elements. This is not to infer that the volume should be kept empty, but rather that its *hollowness* should be in all ways maintained. A well-placed arrangement of elements or even

175

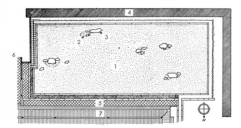

(1) Sanded ground, (2) Moss, (3) Stone, (4) Earth wall, (5) Tile pavement, (6) Ornamental gate, (7) Verandah.

The Garden of Ryoan-ji, surely one of the ten outstanding gardens of all time, is an abstract composition of stones and moss in a bed of raked gravel simulating the sea; this walled garden space extends the limits of the monastery refectory and terrace. Designed as a garden for contemplation, its distinction lies in its simplicity, its perfection of detail, its suggestion of vast spaces, and its power to set free the human mind and spirit.

a grove of high-crowned trees might well increase this sense of shell-like hollowness.

The defined open space, unlike the roofed space, is open to the sky, with the obvious advantages of flooding sunlight, shadow patterns, airiness, rain, sky color, and the beauty of moving clouds. It has disadvantages, too, but we need only plan to minimize them and capitalize on every beneficial aspect of the openness to the sky. Let us not waste one precious yard of azure blue, one glorious burst of sunshine, or one puff of welcome summer breeze that can be caught and made to animate, illuminate, or aerate this hollow vessel that we plan.

If the volume defined by a structure is open to the side, it becomes the focal orb or prism of transition between the structure and the landscape. If open to the view, it is usually developed as the best possible viewing station, and the best possible enframement for the view seen from the various viewing points within the structure.

The defined open space is normally developed for some use. It may extend the function of a structure, as the motor court extends the entrance hall, or as the dining court extends the dining room or kitchen. It may serve as a separate function in itself, as a recreation court at the center of a dormitory, or a military parade ground flanked by barracks. But whether or not it is directly related to its structure in *use,* in character and quality it must be. Such spaces — patios, courts, quads, plazas, public squares — become so dominant and focal in most building groups that the very essence of the structure is distilled and captured there.

THE COMPOSITION OF STRUCTURES

We physical planners like to think of ourselves as masters of space organization, yet, in truth, we are often baffled by the simplest problems of space arrangement and structural composition. What, for instance, is the ideal relationship of a building to its surrounding sea of space; or a building to its fronting approaches; or two buildings facing each other across an intervening mall; or a group of structures to each other and the spaces they enclose? Our predecessors had their theories on these matters and developed their sound principles. Many superb examples of their art are still to be seen — the Parthenon, Rome's Capitoline Piazza by Michelangelo, LeNotre's Garden of Versailles, Villa Lante, the Alhambra. Yet we contemporaries proceed in blithe ignorance or disregard of the truths and lessons of history. If we, proud spirits that we are, must learn our truth first-hand, there need be no problem; for we are surrounded by examples of the good and the bad, and need only develop a discerning eye to distinguish art from error, and evolve our own guiding axioms.

Structures and spaces   What can we say of the composition of structures and spaces? Let us start from the beginning. If we were to place a building or any other structure on a ground plane, for instance, how much space should we allow around it? First, we want to see it well from its approaches. The spaces about it should not only be large enough *or small enough,* but also of the right shape and spatial quality

A winter scene in the Abby Aldrich Rockefeller Sculpture Garden of the Museum of Modern Art.

This magnificent urban space extends the limits and function of the museum and serves in all seasons as an exhilarating exhibition area.

We need desperately to re-learn the art of disposing of buildings to create different kinds of space: the quiet, enclosed, isolated, shaded space; the hustling, bustling space pungent with vitality; the paved, dignified, vast, sumptuous, even awe-inspiring space; the mysterious space; the transition space which defines, separates and yet joins juxtaposed spaces of contrasting character.

We need sequences of space which arouse one's curiosity, give a sense of anticipation, which beckon and impel us to rush forward to find that releasing space which dominates, which climaxes and acts as a magnet, and gives direction.

PAUL RUDOLPH

This rage for isolating everything is truly a modern sickness.

CAMILLO SITTE

An isolated city dwelling, suspended as it were in space, is but a Utopian dream. City dwellings should always be considered as the component parts of groups of structures, or districts.

JOSE LUIS SERT

For as there cannot be a socially healthy population consisting only of egotistic individualists having no common spirit, so there cannot be an architecturally healthy community consisting of self-sufficient buildings.

ELIEL SAARINEN

to compose with the structure and best display it. We want to be sure that enough room is allowed to accommodate all the building's exterior functions, including approaches, parking and service areas, courts, patios, terraces, recreation areas, or gardens. Such spaces can be volumetric expressions of the ideal site-structure diagram. We want to be certain that the structure and its surrounding spaces are *in toto* a complete and balanced composition of functional and visual elements. Just as all buildings have purpose, so do the open spaces that they interrupt, enclose, or define. Such spaces must clearly be related to the character and the mass and function of such structures.

Often the form of a structure itself is not as important as the exterior space patterns that it creates or develops. The portrait painter knows that the outline of a figure or the profile of a head is sometimes secondary to the shape of the spaces created between figure or head and the surrounding pictorial elements or enframement. Often it is the relationship of the figure to the surrounding shapes that gives the figure its essential meaning, and so it is with buildings. Our structures can be spaced out in the landscape in such a way as to permit full and meaningful integration with other man-made structures and spaces, and with the natural landscape itself.

Groups of structures   When two or more buildings are related, the buildings as a group, together with the interrelated spaces, become an architectural entity. In such a situation, each structure, aside from its primary function as a building, has many secondary functions in relation to the group. The buildings as units are grouped to shape and define exterior volumes in the best way possible. They may be placed:

As enclosing elements
As screening elements
As backdrop elements
To dominate the landscape
To organize the landscape
To command the landscape
To embrace the landscape
To enframe the landscape
To best preserve, modify, or accentuate landscape forces, features, or forms
To create a new and controlled landscape
To orient the new landscape outward or inward
To dramatize a function
To dramatize the enclosing structures
To dramatize the enclosed space
To dramatize some feature or features within the space.

They are placed, in short, to create closed or semienclosed spaces that best express and accommodate their function; that best reveal the structural form, the facade, or other features of the surrounding structures; and that best relate the group as a whole to the total extensional landscape.

We have seen too often in our day a building rising on its site in proud and utter disdain of its neighbors or its position. We search in

Composition of structures

Where a structure is to be related to a given area or space, both the shape and the character of the area or space will be affected by the positioning of the structure.

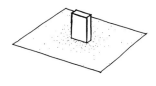

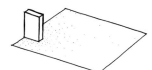

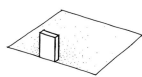

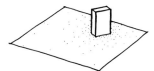

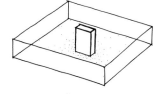

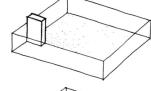

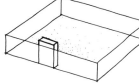

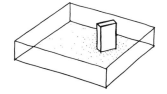

vain for any of those relationships of form, material, or treatment that would bring it into harmony with the surrounding forms or spaces, that would compose it with the existing elements of the local scene. Such insensitive planning would have been incomprehensible to the ancient Greeks or Romans, who conceived each new structure as a compositional element of the street, forum, or square. They did not simply erect a new temple, a new fountain, or even a new lantern; they consciously made an addition to their street, their square, or their city. Each new structure and each new space was contrived as an integral and balanced part of the immediate and extensional environment. These planners knew no other way. And in truth, there can be no other way,

This handsome cluster of street lights was, in the best tradition, designed as an integral part of its city and its square.

179

Composition of structures

Often the form of the structures themselves is not as important as that of the spaces they enclose.

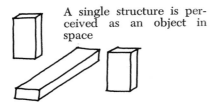

A single structure is perceived as an object in space

Two or more structures are perceived not alone as objects, but also as related objects, and they gain or lose much of their significance in the relationship.

Static

Dynamic

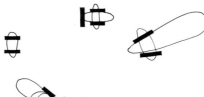

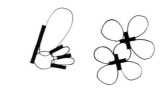

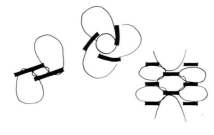

Opposing structures generate a field of dynamic tension

if our buildings and our cities are again to please and satisfy us.

We have said that each building or structure as a solid requires for its fullest expression a satisfying counterbalance of negative open space. This truth, of all planning truths, is perhaps the most difficult to comprehend fully. It has been comprehended and mastered in many periods and places — by the builders of the Karnac Temple, Kyoto's Imperial Palace, or the Gardens of Soochow, for example. We still find their groupings of buildings and interrelated spaces of supremely satisfying harmony and balance; each solid has its void, each building has its satisfying measure of space, and each interior function has its exterior extension, generation, or resolution of that function.

What do we modern planners know of this art, or its principles, that have been evolved through centuries of trial and error, modification, reappraisal, and patient refinement? The Orientals have a highly developed planning discipline that deals with such matters in terms of "tension and repose." Though its tenets are heavily veiled in religious mysticism, its plan applications are clear. It is a conscious effort in all systems of composition to attain a sense of repose through the occult balance of all plan elements — whether viewed as in a pictorial composition or experienced in three dimensions:

The near balanced against the far
The solid against the void
The light against the dark
The bright against the dull
The familiar against the strange
The dominant against the recessive
The active against the passive
The fluid against the fixed.

And, in each instance, the most telling dynamic tensions are sought out or arranged to give maximum meaning to all opposing elements and the total scheme. Though repose through equilibrium must be the end result, it is the *relationship* of the plan elements through which repose is achieved that is of utmost interest. It is the contrived opposition of elements, the studied interplay of tensions, and the sensed resolution of these tensions that are, when fully comprehended, most keenly enjoyed.

A group of structures may be planned in opposition to both each other and the landscape in which they rise, so that, as one moves through or about them, one experiences an evolving composition of opposing elements, a resolution of tensions, and a sense of dynamic repose. A single tree may be so placed and trained as to hold a distant forest or a group of smaller trees in balanced opposition and give them richer meaning. A lake shining deep and still in the natural bowl of a valley may, by its area and contour and other qualities, real or associative, hold in balanced repose the opposing hills that surround it. A plume of falling water at the lake's far end may balance its placid surface in the same way. And to achieve a satisfying equilibrium, the lake or falls may need to be modified or reinforced; perhaps other elements will have to be added.

Walter Beck, long a student of oriental art and composition, has said

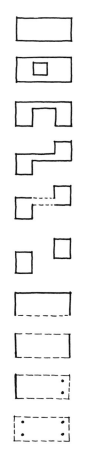

Spatial penetration of structure

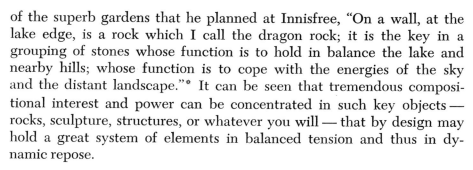

of the superb gardens that he planned at Innisfree, "On a wall, at the lake edge, is a rock which I call the dragon rock; it is the key in a grouping of stones whose function is to hold in balance the lake and nearby hills; whose function is to cope with the energies of the sky and the distant landscape."* It can be seen that tremendous compositional interest and power can be concentrated in such key objects — rocks, sculpture, structures, or whatever you will — that by design may hold a great system of elements in balanced tension and thus in dynamic repose.

It would seem, from a comparison of the European and oriental systems of planning, that the Western mind is traditionally concerned primarily with the object or structure as it appears in space, while the Eastern mind tends to think of structure primarily as a means of defining and articulating a space or a meaningful complex of spaces.

In this light, Rasmussen, in his book *Towns and Buildings* has made a revealing graphic comparison of two Imperial Parks, that of King Louis XIV at Versailles, and that of the Chinese Emperor in Peking. Both were completed in the early 1700's, both made use of huge artificial bodies of water, and both were immense; but there the similarity ends. A close study of these two diametrically opposed planning approaches, illustrated here, will lead one to a fuller understanding of the philosophy of both Occidental and Oriental planning in this period of history.

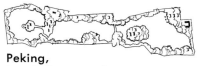

**Peking,
Sea Palace gardens**

A close study of the two diametrically opposed planning approaches here demonstrated will lead one to a fuller understanding of the philosophy of both occidental and oriental planning.

Too often when placing or composing structures in space we revert to cold geometry. Our architectural libraries are bulging with building plans and diagrams laid out in crisp, abstract patterns of black and white that have little meaning except in the flat. It is small wonder that buildings that take their substance from such plans are destined to failure, for they were never conceived in terms of form in space, or spaces within form. The world is cluttered with such unfortunate travesties. The proper planning of buildings, parks, and cities is a far cry from such geometric doodling. A logical plan in two dimensions is a record of logical thinking in three dimensions. The enlightened planner is thinking always of what will be experienced as one moves to, through, and around a space-structure composition. His concern is not with the plan forms and spaces as they appear on the drawings, but rather with these forms and spaces as they will be experienced in actuality.

Versailles Park

Many Renaissance squares, parks, and palaces are little more than dull geometry seen in the round. One clear strong voice crying out against such puerile planning was that of Camillo Sitte, a Viennese architect whose writings on city building first appeared in 1889 and whose ideas are today still valid and compelling.

It was Sitte who pointed out that the ancients *used* their public spaces, and that these spaces and the buildings around them were planned together to satisfy the use. There were market squares, religious squares, ducal squares, civic squares, and others of many varieties; and each, from inception through the numerous changes of time, maintained its own distinctive quality. These public places were never geometrical,

181

* From *Painting with Starch*

Fifteen plans from Camillo Sitte, all at uniform scale

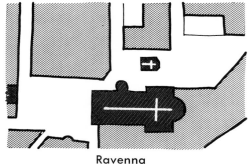

Ravenna

Pistoia

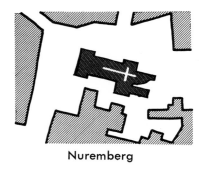

Nuremberg

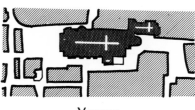

Verona

In designing a building, the architect is always led to imagine the work as it is intended to look when finished, placing himself mentally in the position of a visitor who is examining it carefully and critically. Thus it is that he feels the future impressions that his design may make, the surprises that certain new and original solutions may reserve, the architectonic subtleties that the most sensitive will seek out and comprehend. And in the course of this effort of the imagination, the architect reviews the architectonic elements that he considers essential, endeavoring to ascertain whether his reasoning is sound, whether the material he proposes to use is suitable, whether the colors are harmonious, and whether the forms created are handsome and true. For this purpose he takes up an imaginary position in places where drawings are liable to be inexpressive, and strives to feel the volumes he is designing, in all their grandeur and proportion.

OSCAR NIEMEYER

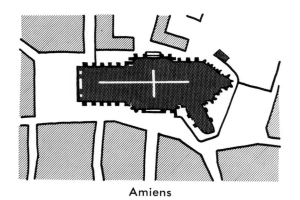

Amiens

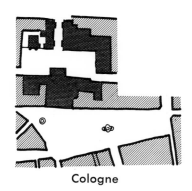

Cologne

nor were they entered by wide axial streets that would have destroyed their essential attribute of enclosure. Rather, they were asymmetrical; they were entered by narrow winding streets that penetrated at or near the corners. Each building or object within the space was planned *to* and *for* the space and the streams of pedestrian traffic that would converge and merge there. The centers of such spaces were left open; the monuments, fountains, and sculpture that were so much a part of these spaces were placed on islands in the traffic pattern, off building corners, against blank walls, and beside the entry ways — each positioned with

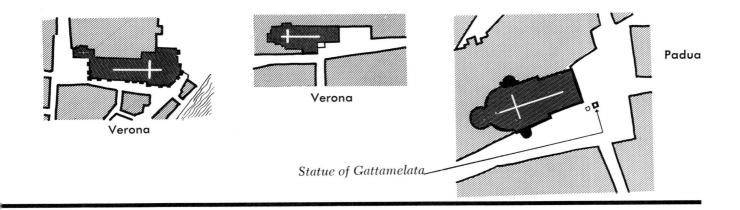

Verona

Verona

Padua

Statue of Gattamelata

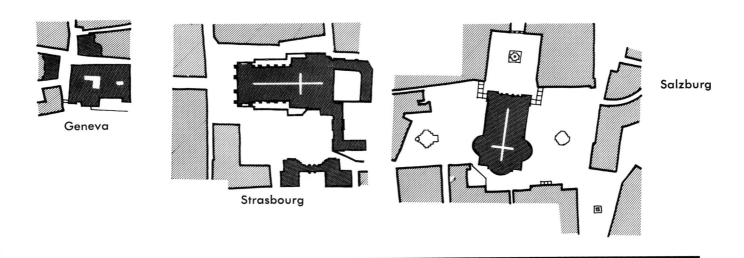

Geneva

Strasbourg

Salzburg

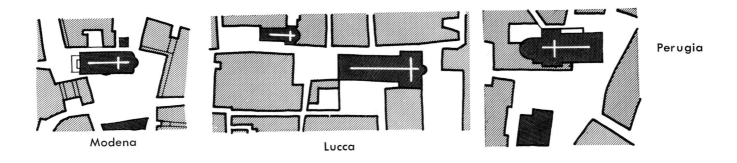

Modena

Lucca

Perugia

infinite care in relation to surfaces, masses, and space. Seldom were such objects set on axis with the approach to a building or its entrance, for it was felt that such objects detracted from the full appreciation of the building as one moved toward it, and, conversely, that the axis of such a building was seldom a proper background for a work of art.

Sitte discovered that such important buildings as cathedrals were rarely placed at the center of an open space, as we almost invariably place them today. Instead they were set back against other buildings, or off to the side, to give a better view of facade, spires, or portals,

183

and to give the best impression from within the square or from its meandering approaches.

Rules of composition   Down through the centuries, much thought has been given to the establishment of fixed formulas or rules that might govern building proportions, or the relationship of one building to another, or of a building to its fronting or surrounding space.

There have long been those who believe that mathematics is the all-pervading basis of our world of matter, growth, and order. To them it has followed naturally that order, beauty, and even truth are functions of mathematical law and proportion. The "golden rectangle," for example, has long been a favorite of mathematicians, perhaps because of the fact that, if a unit square is subtracted from each ever-diminishing rectangle, a golden rectangle remains each time. This "ideal" rectilinear shape (whose sides have a ratio of $1:1.618$, or roughly $3:5$) has appeared again and again, in plan and in elevation, in the structures and formed spaces of the Western world.

M. Borissavlievitch, in his absorbing work, *The Golden Number*, has explored its application to architectural composition. He proposes that, although the Golden Rectangle *considered by itself* is, both philosophically and esthetically, the most beautiful amongst all horizontal rectangles, "when considered *as a part of a whole,* it is neither more beautiful nor more ugly than any other rectangle. Because a whole is ruled by the laws of harmony, by the ratios between the parts and not by a single part considered by itself." He notes that "*Order* is indeed the greatest and most general of esthetic laws," and then suggests that there are only two laws of architectural harmony — the *Law of the Similar* and the *Law of the Same.**

The Law of the Same   Architectural harmony may be perceived or created in a structure or composition of structures that attains order through the repetition of the *same* elements, forms, or spaces.

The Law of the Similar   Architectural harmony may be perceived or created in a composition that attains order through the repetition of *similar* elements, forms, or spaces.

Borissavlievitch notes that "whilst the *Law of the Same* represents unity (or harmony) in uniformity, the *Law of the Similar* represents unity in variety." He wisely notes also that ". . . an artist will create beautiful works only in obeying unconsciously one of these two laws, that is without even knowing them, otherwise they would not be true. Whilst we create, we do not think about them, and we follow only our imagination and our artistic feeling. But when our sketch is made, we look at it and examine it as if we were its first spectator and not its creator, and if it is successful we shall know, because of our knowledge of these laws *why* it is successful; if it is not, we shall know the reason of that failure."

"The beautiful," said Borissavlievitch, "is felt and not calculated."

Fibonacci, an Italian mathematician of Renaissance times, discovered a progression that was soon widely adapted to all phases of planning

---

* Though Borissavlievitch is speaking here only of *proportions,* it is to be noted that the Laws of the *Same* and the *Similar* apply as well to materials, colors, textures, and symbols.

The location of the equestrian statue of Gattamelata by Donatello in front of Saint Anthony of Padua is most instructive. First we may be astonished at its great variance from our rigid modern system, but it is quickly and strikingly seen that the monument in this place produces a majestic effect. Finally we become convinced that removed to the center of the square its effect would be greatly diminished. We cease to wonder at its orientation and other locational advantages once this principle becomes familiar.

The ancient Egyptians understood this principle, for as Gattamelata and the little column stand beside the entrance to the Cathedral of Padua, the obelisks and the statues of the Pharaohs are aligned beside the temple doors. There is the entire secret that we refuse to decipher today.

CAMILLO SITTE

The most obvious place to put the house is not always the right one. If there is only a small area of flat land, you'll be tempted to use it for the house. It probably should be saved for arrival, parking or garden.

Houses can be built on a slope, but it means a lot of grading and walls later when you try to get enough flat land for the areas you need around the house.

Is there one particular spot on the property that seems just right in every way? Have you picknicked there and found it idyllic? Have you spent long winter evenings planning a house there? Has it occurred to you that if you build your house there the spot will be gone? Maybe that's where your garden should be.

THOMAS D. CHURCH

Composition of structures

The number of polar relationships increases arithmetically with the addition of each unit to a complex of structures. Since each new unit modifies the composition, its relationship to all other units is a matter of design and planning concern.

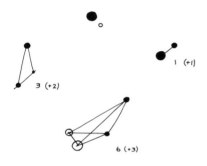

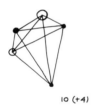

Architectural harmony created through the repetition of the *same* elements

— starting with units 1 and 2, if each new digit is the sum of the previous two, a progression of 1,2,3,5,8,13,21,34, and so forth will result, which, translated into plan forms and rhythms, is visually pleasing. It was later discovered that this progression approximated the growth sequence of plants and other organisms, which added, of course, to its interest, and confirmed in the minds of planners the notion that this progression was "natural" and "organic."

Vitruvius, a Roman architect and scholar who lived in the first century before Christ, set about to discover a system of proportion that he could apply to his plans and structures. In his search he undertook

185

Architectural harmony created through the repetition of *similar* elements.

The Vitruvian figure inscribed in a circle and square became a symbol of the mathematical sympathy between macrocosm and microcosm.

R. WITTKOWER

an exhaustive study of the architecture and planning of ancient Greece. In the course of his work he produced a book setting forth his findings and expounding his theories on the anthropomorphic module, a unit of measurement based on the proportions of the human body, that was to have a profound effect on the thinking and planning of the Renaissance. In this book he included the following passage, containing the crux of his proposition:

"The plan of a temple must have an exact proportion worked out after the fashion of the members of a finely proportioned human body. For nature has so planned the human body that the face from the chin to the top of the forehead and root of the hair is ¹⁄₁₀ part; also the palm of the hand from the wrist to the top of the middle finger is as much; the head from the chin to the crown is ⅛ part; from the top of the breast with the bottom of the neck to the roots, ⅙ part; from the middle of the breast to the crown, ¼ part; ⅓ part of the height of the face is from the bottom of the chin to the bottom of the nostrils; the nose from the bottom of the nostrils to the line between the brows, as much; from that line to the roots of the hair, the forehead is given ⅓ part. The foot is ⅙ the height of the body; the cubit ¼; the breast also ¼. The other limbs also have their own proportionate measurements. And by using these, ancient painters and famous sculptors have attained great and unbounded distinction.

"In like fashion the members of the temples ought to have dimensions of their several parts answering suitably to the general sum of their whole magnitude. Now the navel is naturally the exact center of the body. For if a man lies on his back with his hands and feet outspread, and the center of a circle is placed on his navel, his fingers and toes will be touched by the circumference. Also a square will be found described within the figure in the same way that a round figure is produced. For if we measure from the sole of the foot to the top of the head, and apply the measure to the outstretched hands, the breadth will be found equal to the height, just like sites which are squared by rule.

"Therefore if nature has planned the human body so that the members correspond in their proportions to its complete configuration, the ancients seem to have had reason in determining that in the execution of their works they should observe an exact adjustment of their several members to the general pattern of the plan."*

The Renaissance masters pored over these Vitruvian theories and developed them further in detail and in depth. They revived the Greek mathematical interpretation of God and the world, and adapted to their

* From *Vitruvius on Architecture*, translated by Granger.

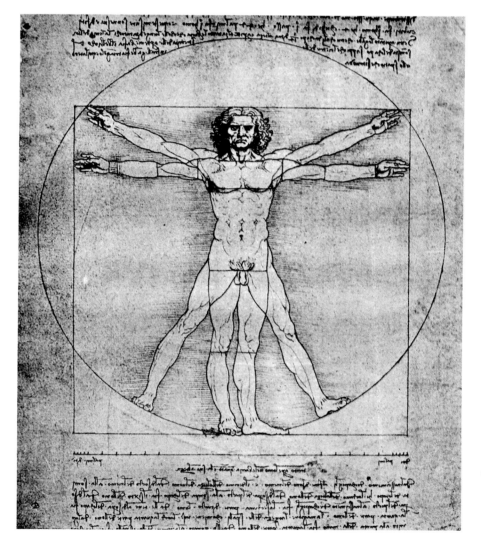

A study by Leonardo da Vinci from one of his notebooks illustrating his principle that "the span of a man's outstanding arms is equal to his height."

thinking the Christian belief that man, as the image of God, embodies the harmonies of the universe.

Leonardo da Vinci, a creative giant of the Renaissance, analyzed and tabulated his own system of mean proportions of the component parts of the human figure in relation to its total height, and then derived a table of classic proportions and ratios from which he developed for each project a suitable modular system. As architect–engineer–sculptor–painter, he translated his findings into all his works and through them demonstrated to posterity his conviction that, to achieve order and beautiful proportion in any work, the major masses or lines and the smallest detail must have a consistent mathematical relationship.

"The conviction that architecture is a science and that each part of a building has to be integrated into one and the same system of mathematical ratios may be called the basic axiom of Renaissance architects," Granger tells us. And yet physical planners today are still searching for the module or system of modules most applicable to their work, though it is apparent to most that the significant module must be derived from some function of the human body or being.

It was long ago discovered that the ratio of height to width, structure to space, or element to element should not appear to be exactly one to one, one to two, one to three, or one to four. A proof of the general validity of this tacit rule was brought home to the author vividly on an occasion when he visited, with several friends, the studio of Hiroshi Yoshida, the late distinguished Japanese woodblock artist. The old master was leafing through a stack of prints that represented many years of his work. In one pile he would place those prints he particularly liked, and in another pile he would put those that had less appeal for him. A philosopher who was present suggested that much could be learned if the artist told us what elements were common to those he preferred and those he had discarded. Yoshida thoughtfully noted the qualities of harmonious color, expressive form, and composition in what he termed his better work, but he was at a loss to discover the root of his displeasure in the lesser prints.

"I have noticed," said one of the other visitors, "that each of the compositions you dislike is split by some line or form into two, three, or four equal parts. In Western composition this is usually avoided."

"Ah so!" replied Yoshida after some moments of quiet reflection. "In Japan I have never learned of such a rule, but it must be, I perceive, a valid one." After a few moments he continued, "I shall not violate this rule again, at least without intention."

"Without intention?" someone queried.

"Yes," continued the artist, "we have observed that this compositional phenomenon has its unfortunate effects. It must also have its proper applications — and one might so split a composition if, by subject, one should wish to convey a subtle sense of monotony, schism, or tension."

This preceding principle of composition does not imply that a modular treatment of structures or spaces is not desirable. One of the highest qualities of Japanese planning is their insistence, in every structure or plan, upon a fundamental order or mathematical relationship of the

188

elements. This stems from the use of the *tatami* or woven grass mat (approximately 3 × 6 ft.) as a standardized unit of measurement. Traditionally, a modular grid system based upon this unit has been the basis of all building plans and elevations and the surrounding spaces. Doors are 3 × 6 ft., ceilings are 9 ft. high; a room is a given number of mats in length and width; a building plan is so many mats in area. In their planning the Japanese make use also of the 12-ft. dimension, which is divisible by 1,2,3,4, and 6.

If a unit such as a closet or case requires less than the full module it is not distorted to fill the module, it is rather set free within the module and *composed* within the modular framework. The fact that an object is smaller or larger than the module is not concealed, but is artistically revealed and elucidated. This system of order differs significantly from the rigid geometric planning of Europe's Renaissance, which worshipped insistent symmetry rather than such a free and flexible system of modular organization.

According to Messrs. Hegeman and Peets, in their definitive treatise *Civic Art,* "It appears that the human eye is so organized as best to see the detail of an object if separated from it by a distance equal to just about the largest dimension (height or width) of the object." In an object such as a building, height, rather than breadth, is of predominant importance, because the viewer exercises more freedom in shifting his glance laterally than up and down. "A distance between observer and building equal to about the height of the building is identical with his seeing the building within an angle of 45 degrees. This angle is measured between a line from the eye to the horizon and a line from the eye to the object's highest point . . . In order to see at its best a building as a whole (i.e. leaving aside the detailing) the observer should be separated from the building by a distance equalling about twice its height, which means that he should see it at an angle of 27 degrees. In this latter case the building will fill the entire field of vision of an observer who holds his head motionless. If the observer wants to see more than just one building, if for instance he wants to see this building as part of a group . . . he should see it at an angle of about 18 degrees, which means he should be separated from the building by a distance equal to about three times its height . . . if the distance between the observer and building increases further, that is if the angle between the top of the building and line of sight to the horizon becomes less than 18 degrees, the building begins to lose its predominance in the field of vision . . . A plaza longer or wider than three times the height of the surrounding buildings is therefore in danger of being of imperfect value as a setting for monumental buildings. The proportions of such a plaza will change if the most important points from which the architect wants his main building to be seen do not lie at the circumference of the plaza but somewhat inside the plaza. . . . In such cases it is advantageous to accentuate that area of the plaza which may be considered the most favored and from which one gains the best view of the principal building."

Along the same line of thought Camillo Sitte has stated, "It is difficult to determine the exact relationship that ought to exist between the magnitude of a square and the buildings which enclose it, but clearly it should be an harmonious balance. An excessively small square

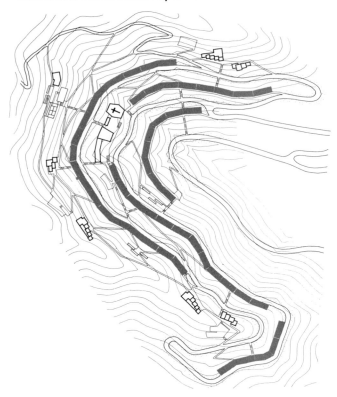

Various compositional arrangements of apartment structures

Ribbon pattern in free alignment, to flow with the topography. Site-structure harmony is pleasantly evident.

Ribbons of structure arranged architecturally produce a cohesive unity and sense of discipline.

is worthless for a monumental structure. A square that is too big is even worse, for it will have the effect of reducing its dimensions however colossal they may actually be. This has been observed thousands of times at Saint Peter's in Rome. . . . Experience shows that the minimum dimension of a square or plaza ought to be equal to the height of the principal building in it, and that its maximum dimension ought not to exceed twice that height unless the form, the purpose, and the design of the building will support greater dimensions . . . The average dimensions of the great squares of the old European cities are 465 by 190 ft."*

Arrangements of buildings　　Individual buildings are sometimes spaced out as deployed units of a greater architectural composition. It can be seen that such structures and the spaces they control combine to give a more impressive or imposing impact than would be possible for any single structure of the group. Sometimes this is desirable, sometimes it is not. Such a grouping of structures seems most valid when each building not only *appears* as a part of, but also *functions* as a part of, the total complex. The buildings may be arranged in rigid symmetry with the consequent attributes of idealism, order, perfection, and permanence. Or they may, for even better reasons, be arranged asymmetrically. But, in every case where a building serves as a unit of an architectural group, the entire group is treated as a co-

* In *The Art of Building Cities.*

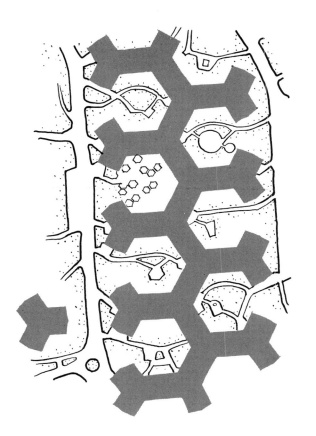

Attenuated structures arranged in geometric pattern. Interest and variety are achieved mainly through variation in site development and approach.

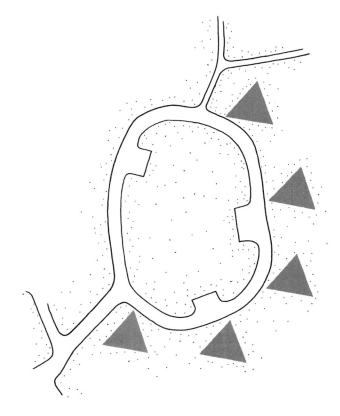

Free-standing buildings with order of spacing and orientation only. Such a grouping achieves a spirit of sculptural monumentality.

hesive and unified composition, and each structure within the group owes architectural allegiance to the whole.

Buildings may be arranged freely in the landscape as individual units. Because such structures need not be planned as part of a group, they and the spaces around them may be planned with much more freedom. Their relationship is not one of building to building, but rather of building to landscape, with all that this implies.

Buildings of similar character or form may be spaced out, even at great distance, in such a manner as to dominate a landscape and give it unification. Such an arrangement may be architectonic, or it may be casual. By such a treatment a civic, campus, carnival, or any other character may be given to an extensive landscape. Though a great variety of uses may be given to the intervening landscape areas, each element within the visual field of the total group must be compatible by association. A quiet chapel within the exuberant atmosphere of Disneyland would lose much of its meaning, as would a faro concession within the visual limits of a theological seminary.

Structures are often composed in relation to natural or man-made forms and forces, such as the highway, the railroad, the river, the lake, and the valley. In such cases, the buildings, singly or in groups, may be given their form and spacing to best achieve the most desirable **191** relationships. A resort group and its fronting lake are in effect composed as a harmoniously interrelated unit, in which the lake adds much to the resort and the resort, in turn, to the lake. A factory and its sidings

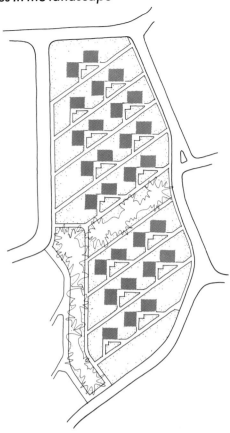

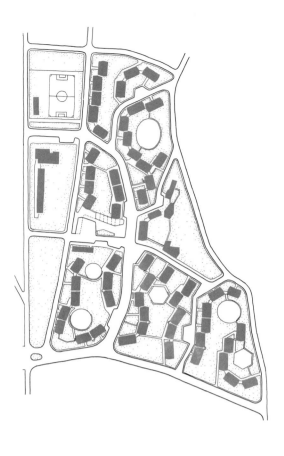

Ordered arrangement of structures producing a strong and harmonious architectural relationship of all units to the whole. Even on an irregular site, however, a quality of monotony is evident.

Buildings arranged in free compositional pattern. Note pleasant variety of defined spaces and building relationships. Such groupings provide a more relaxed and pleasant environment for living.

are designed *to* and *with* the railroad. A roadside restaurant is planned "as one" with the highway in terms of landscape character, sight distances, approaches, resolution of momentums, and the composition of spaces and forms.

It is always to be remembered that a building complex, as much as a natural wooded grove or open meadow, has its own distinctive landscape character that must be recognized and understood, so it can be accentuated or consciously modified.

Some building compositions are static. They are complete in themselves. They require no change and, in fact, admit of little change, if any. Where the qualities of monumentality, permanence, and established order are intended, this may be desirable.

Other building groupings are fluid, flexible, and seem by their very nature to express change and growth. Where such change or growth is intended, where freedom, experimentation, or development are desirable qualities, a static composition is to be avoided. It can be seen that not only the structures themselves but also their abstract arrangement in space determines to a large degree their character and the character of the total landscape area that they influence or embrace.

Often scattered buildings may be brought into a more workable and more visually pleasant relationship by connecting them with paved areas or well defined lines of circulation. Again, this integration may be accomplished by the addition of structural elements such as walls,

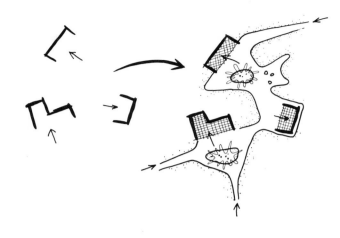

Diverse plan elements related by well-defined patterns of circulation.

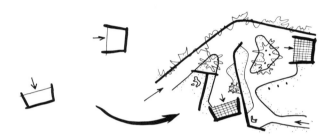

Classification by the addition of structural elements plus definition of circulation patterns.

Integration of structures

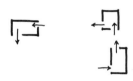

Three disconnected plan elements

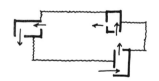

Addition of connective linkage

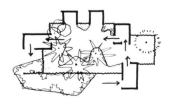

Further articulation of plan circulation

fences, screens, or even tree rows or hedges that bind them together. Perhaps the very elements that unite such structures may at the same time segregate or classify.

Many structures are so composed as to give their maximum visual impact from one or more fixed viewing stations or prescribed lines of approach. In such cases, where a feeling of monumentality is desired, the composition offered must clearly approach perfection. Far more often, and far more wisely, buildings and their related spaces are composed to read from fluid lines of movement; for people most often like freedom of movement and freedom of choice. They prefer change in compositions and a variety of experiences. And the best arrangements of buildings and spaces are those that accommodate and express their purpose and, from all viewing lines and stations, within and without, are compositionally pleasing. This, if there be a law, is the law of grouping structures. Compositional perfection of plan diagrams means nothing until the plan has been tested by section, by perspective or model in three dimensions, and finally, upon completion, by the supreme test of human experience.

In the study of building arrangement, it is revealing to note that in the construction of Peking the purpose of its planners was not to build parks within the city, but rather to build their city within a park. Perhaps this idea of structures composed in space has been best expressed by the late John Knox Shear who said, "Ideally, all the world would be a garden with structures beautifully interspersed."

193

PLANNING THE REGION 7

It sometimes seems that our contemporary planning is an unholy game of piling as much structure or as much city as possible in one spot. The urban areas to which we point with pride are often merely the highest, widest, and densest piles of architecture. Where, in these heaps and stacks of masonry, is forgotten, stifled man? Is he refreshed, inspired, and stimulated by his urban environment? Hardly; for in our times, too often, a city is a desert.

THE CITYSCAPE

To be bluntly truthful, our new American cities, squared off and cut into uncompromising geometric blocks by unrelieved, unterminated trafficways, have more of this arid desert quality than the mature cities of either Europe or the Orient.

If we compare a map of Rome as it was in 1748 with an aerial photograph of New York as it is today, we marvel at the infinite variety of pleasant spaces that occurred throughout the Eternal City. Of course, as Rasmussen has pointed out, "Great artists formed the city, and the inhabitants, themselves, were artists enough to know how to live in it." We wonder why such spaces are missing in our contemporary city plans.

The urban spaces of America are mostly corridors. Our streets, our boulevards, and our walks are always leading past or through to something or somewhere beyond. Our cities, our suburbs, and our home-sites are laced and interlaced with these corridors, and we seek in vain to find those places or spaces that attract and hold us and satisfy. We do not like to live in corridors; we like to live in rooms. The cities of history are full of such rooms, planned and furnished with as much concern as were the surrounding structures. If we would have such places, we must plan our corridors not as channels trying to be places as well, but channels planned as channels. And we must plan our places as places.

The old cities had, and still have to their credit and memorable

Large cities seen from an altitude of several hundred feet do not present, as a whole, an orderly facade. Their vastness is their most striking feature; whatever quality they possess is lost in sheer quantity. Areas that give evidence of planning occupy but a small surface. Disorder predominates. Buildings are piled up near the center and scattered haphazardly toward the outskirts. The few green spots and other places of beauty known to the tourist, seem hidden in a maze of grey and shapeless masses that stretch toward the surrounding country in tentacular form. The very borders of the city are undefined, junk and refuse belts merging with the countryside. If on beholding this sight we pause to contemplate modern cities and consider what they could have been if planned, we must admit in the end that, in spite of their magnificent vitality, they represent one of man's greatest failures.

JOSE LUIS SERT

The corridor-canyons, which are New York City's streets, stretch on interminably without relief, without focal point, or without the welcome interruption of useful or meaningful space.

195

Nolli's map of Rome.

A city should be built to give its inhabitants security and happiness.

ARISTOTLE

The essential thing of both room and square is the quality of enclosed space.

CAMILLO SITTE

Town and country must be married and out of the union will spring a new life, a new hope, a new civilization.

EBENEZER HOWARD

The problem of the landscape architect — even as of the architect, the town planner, the engineer, and indeed all men of good will — is now, and will be more acutely every day, the development of ways and means for bridging the gap between town and country, the antithesis between urban and rural life — more specifically between the masonry, the asphalt, and the dingbat construction of the town and the quiet greenery of meadow, forest, and shore. How to open up the town to the country, how to bring the town culturally to the country — that is our primary problem, and it will be expressed and measured in terms of quantity and quality of vegetation.

GARRETT ECKBO

charm, their plazas, piazzas, courts, squares, and fountains — and their distinctive, undefinable, uplifting spirit of civic monumentality (a word much maligned in current planning circles). These cities were conceived in terms of human experiences; in terms of civic art; and in terms of meaningful patterns of structures and open spaces. Our cities, with few exceptions, are oriented to the noise, fumes, and frictions of our traffic-glutted streets.

Whom are we to blame for this? Aristotle, in his *Rhetoric*, states, ". . . truth and justice are by nature better than their opposites, and therefore if decisions are made wrongly, it must be the speakers who (through lack of effective powers of persuasion) are to blame for the defeat." For our purpose, this passage might well be paraphrased as:

"Facility, interest, and beauty are by nature better than chaos, the dull, and the ugly, and therefore, if decisions are made wrongly, it must be we planners who, through lack of effective powers of persuasion (or more compelling concepts of planning), are to blame for the defeat."

In searching for a more enlightened approach to urban planning we must look back and reappraise the old values. While recognizing the fallacies of the old "City Beautiful" approach in its narrowest sense, we must rediscover the age-old, yet ever-vital and essential, art of building cities that inspire, satisfy, and work. And surely we will; for already we are disturbed and alarmed at the vapid, soulless nature of the cities we have planned — or worse, have allowed to grow unplanned in sporadic, senseless confusion.

We, in contemporary times, have lost the art and feeling of over-all plan organization. Our cities are lacking in coherent relationship and plan continuity. We, with our automobiles as the symbol and most important planning factor of our times, have found the meandering streets, places, and plan forms of the ancient cities to be unsuitable. We have rejected (with good reason) the synthesizing device of the inexorable "grand plan," but have found, as yet, no substitutes, save the pitiful grid and other pathetic patterns of uninspired geometry. The transit, the protractor, and the compasses have demarked for us a wholly artificial and mechanistic system of living areas and spaces. We must, and will, develop a new plan organization, a new plan diagram, that is better suited to our life. In such a plan organization the signifi-cant space is bound to return, and we will have new cities where again the spaces are as important as the structures.

The desert character of our cities is concentrated in the downtown city core. Here the average cityscape is a conglomerate aggregation of metal, glass, and masonry cubes set on a dreary base plane of oil-spattered concrete and asphalt. It is bleak, chill, and gusty in winter-time, and in the summertime it shimmers and weaves with its stored-up, radiating heat. Within view of its naked towers, the open countryside beyond is often 12° warmer in winter and 20° cooler in summer.

Such an oppressive and barren cityscape falls far short of the mark. Our cities must be opened up, refreshed, revitalized. Our straining traffic arteries must be realigned and widened, to pass under or around the perimeter of great city parks or business squares in which the stores and restaurants and office buildings stand and breathe. In contrast with sharp building profiles and the hard surface and dull hues of pave-ment, building stone, and brick, the open park spaces must give the welcome relief of foliage, shade, splashing water, flowers, and bright color. Like oases, such urban spaces will transform the city into a new landscape of pure delight, that will be, in truth, an inviting refreshing environment.

Misguided efforts   A common error in our city planning and our zoning ordinances is the assumption that the more space there is be-tween buildings and the greater is the setback from the street, the better. Thus, by regulation, is foreordained a city that resembles a sieve — open, vacuous, where most outdoor activity is visible from the streets, and where walled outdoor privacy is often not even permitted.

The house on the city lot

Present

No fence or wall permitted

Side yard required

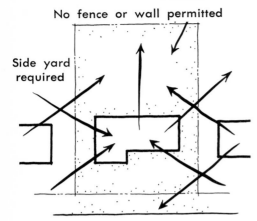

Advanced

Wall for privacy

Too narrow for use

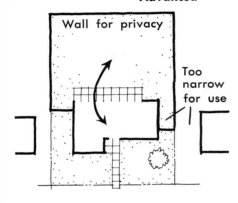

Ultimate

Relaxation of side-yard, setback, and exclosure restrictions will permit full use of lot, privacy, and indoor-outdoor transitions

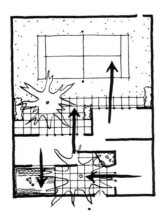

Most of the city's myriad sideyard or buffer spaces might better be consolidated for some significant use. Air, sunlight, and open space are highly desirable features, but their distribution and treatment are as important as their extensity.

People enjoy compression. Georgetown, in Washington, D.C., surely one of the most delightful residential areas of our country, has narrow brick structures set wall to wall along its narrow, shaded streets. Its brick walk pavements, often extending from curb to facade, are opened here around the smooth trunk of a basswood tree, or punched out there to receive a holly, a boxwood, a figtree, or a bed of myrtle or pink geraniums. In this compact community, where space is at such a premium, the open areas are artfully enclosed by fences, walls, or building wings to give privacy and to create a cool and pleasant well of garden space into which the whole house opens.

The great estates of Europe and this country, with their vast expanses of turf and sweeping vistas, are grand and impressive, but one soon becomes bored and finds little in them that would make one wish to linger. They prove that spaciousness in itself is not always a desirable thing. The author, in working long with public housing, has discovered that the very openness of a project is at first the thing that has the most appeal to families who move in from older neighborhoods or from the cramped and aching slums. But soon they become dissatisfied with the severe buildings, the wide grass areas, and the play equipment set out on flat sheets of pavement. One hears the officials ask, "What's wrong with these people? Why aren't they happy? What did they expect? What more do they want?"

What they want, what they miss, what they unconsciously long for, are such congregating places as the carved and whittled storefront bench, the rear porch stoops, the packed-clay, sun-drenched boccie courts, the crates and boxes set in the cool shade of a propped-up grape arbor or in the spattered shadow of a spreading ailanthus tree. They miss the meandering alleys, dim and pungent, the leaking hydrants, the hot bright places against the moist dark places, the cellar doors, the leaning board fences, the sagging gates, the maze of rickety outside stairs. They miss the torn circus posters, the rusting enamelled tobacco signs, the blatant billboards, the splotchy patches of weathered

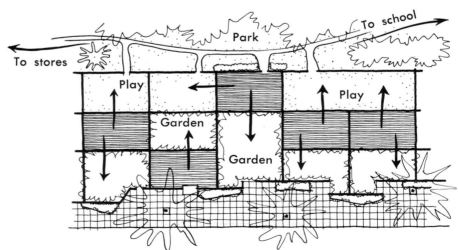

Minimum homes for maximum living

The best features of townhouse living are exemplified in this handsome residence.

There are, certainly, ample reasons for redoing downtown — falling retail sales, tax bases in jeopardy, stagnant real-estate values, impossible traffic and parking conditions, failing mass transit, encirclement by slums. But with no intent to minimize these serious matters, it is more to the point to consider what makes a city center magnetic, what can inject gaiety, the wonder, the cheerful hurly-burly that make people want to come into the city and to linger there. For magnetism is the crux of the problem. All downtown's values are its byproducts. To create in it an atmosphere of urbanity and exuberance is not a frivolous aim.

JANE JACOBS

paint. They miss the bakery smells of hot raisin bread and warm, sugared lunchrolls, the fishmarket smells, the clean raw smell of gasoline, the smell of vulcanizing rubber. They miss the strident neighborhood sounds, the intermittent calls and chatter, the baby squalls, the supper shouts, the whistles, the "allee, allee oxen," the pound of the stone hammer, the ring of the tire iron, the rumbling delivery truck, the huckster's cart, the dripping, creaking ice wagon. They miss the shape, the pattern, the smells, the sounds, and the pulsing feel of life.

What they miss, what they *need,* is the compression, the interest, the variety, the surprises, and the casual, indefinable charm of the slum that they left behind. This, in essence, is the charm of the left bank of Paris, of San Francisco's Chinatown, of Beacon Hill in Boston. This same charm of both tight and expansive spaces, of delightful variety, of delicious contrast, of the happy accident, is an essential quality of planning that we must constantly strive for. And one of the chief ingredients of charm, when we find it, is a sense of the diminutive, a feeling of pleasant compression. Private or community "living spaces" become a reality only if they and the life within them are kept within the scale of pleasurable human response and sympathetic understanding.

199

Evolution of a way of life

Primitive
Shelter is main consideration.

Greco-Roman
Protection and privacy are of prime value.

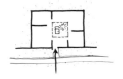

Renaissance
Each structure an idealized object in space.

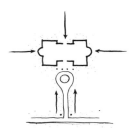

Oriental
Nature revered, privacy demanded. Structures related to lot and total landscape.

200

A further error of our current master city plans stems from the compulsion of their authors to force our cities into blocks and areas of consistent lot sizes and use. Such "ideal" cities of monotonous conformity are "grey" in tone. If we examine almost any recent city plan, we find that one zone is for single family houses, another zone for rowhouses, and another for highrise apartments; an isolated patch is for stores, a green area will someday be a park. May we place in this residential area an artists studio? It is not allowed! An office for an architect? A florist shop? A bookstall? A pastryshop? No! In a residential area such uses are not permitted! That would be spot zoning, the sin of all planning sins! These are the rules, and thus the rich complexities that are the very essence of the most pleasant urban areas of the world are at present regulated out of our "grey" cities. London, after the blitz, was replanned and rebuilt substantially according to this new and antiseptic planning order. The new London areas were spacious, clean, and orderly, and all was perfect, except for one salient feature — these areas were incredibly dull, and nobody seemed to like them. Our zoning ordinances, which, to a large degree, control our city patterns, are rather new to us. They have great promise as an effective tool, and are perhaps the key to achieving an urban environment of great vitality, efficiency, beauty, and charm — when we have learned to so use our zoning powers as to insure these qualities, rather than to preclude them.

The human scale The needs of the human beings who would dwell and work and live in our cities must come to have precedence — over the insistent requirements of traffic, over the despoiling demands of industry, and over the callous public acceptance of rigid economy as the most consistent criterion for our street and utility layouts and for the development of our boulevards, plazas, parks, and other public works.

What are the human needs of which we speak? Some have been so long ignored or forgotten in terms of city planning and growth that they may seem now almost quaint or archaic. Yet they are *basic*. The human being *needs* and must have once again in his cities a rich variety of *spaces,* each planned with sensitivity to best express and accommodate its function; spaces through which he may move with safety and with pleasure, and in which he may congregate. He must truly have *health* and *convenience* on a hitherto undreamed of plane. He must also have *order*. Not an antiseptic, stilted, or grandiose order of contrived geometric dullness or sweeping emptiness, but a functional order that will hold the city together and make it work — an order as organic as that of the living cell, leaf, and tree. A sensed cohesive and satisfying order, that permits of the happy accident, is flexible, and combines the best of the old with the best of the new. An order that is sympathetic to those structures, things, and activities that afford interest, variety, surprise, and contrast, and that have the power to charm the heart. The human being needs in his cities *sources of inspiration, stimulation, refreshment, beauty, and delight*. He needs and must have, in short, a *salubrious urban environment*, conducive to the living of the whole, full life.

Such a city will not ignore nature. It will be, rather, planned in harmony with nature. And it will invite nature back into its confines in the form of clean air, sunshine, water, foliage, breeze, and refreshing gardens and parks.

THE CITY AND THE REGION

Present American showcase (Vestigial renaissance)

Nature ignored. Outward orientation. Privacy is lost. Little use of property. A product of side-yard, setback, and no-fence restrictions.

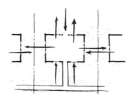

Future American-trend home

Total use of site as living space. Privacy regained. Indoor-outdoor integration. Natural elements introduced. Compact home-garden units grouped amidst open park and recreation areas which preserve natural landscape features.

In every historical epoch except our own, the cultivated and influential person, the civilized, polite and urbane citizen, inevitably lived within the city. . . . Indeed, the classical names for the city express these very virtues: civis — *city, civilized, civilization;* urbs — *urbane;* polis — *polite and elegant.*

IAN L. McHARG

The city has been considered for too long as a circumscribed entity. We have thought in terms of the city versus the farmland, the city versus the suburbs, the city versus the counties or townships in which the city lies. Many serious and often needless frictions and tensions have developed through lack of coordination of the planned development of these units or areas. There have been stupendously costly duplications of administration and facilities. Scathing animosities have been generated that will preclude for years intelligent cooperation on even the simplest interarea issues or plans. There is, however, a wise and growing tendency among planners to consider the development of the city and its contiguous areas in terms of an economic or cultural *region*. The advantages of such regional studies and planning are obvious in terms of economy and effectiveness.

Concurrent with the tendency to broaden the scope of planning from an urban to regional basis is a marked tendency to decrease the emphasis on planning the total city as a whole, and concentrate more attention on the planning of self-contained neighborhoods — neighborhoods with a population of 1,000 to 1,500 families, approximately the number required to support an elementary school, its own neighborhood shops and services, and its own neighborhood social center, playgrounds, and parks. These revitalized, replanned neighborhoods, surrounded by greenbelts and connected by freeways to the manufacturing or industrial complexes, the city core, and the region, give promise of a more humanized and organic new metropolis.

A community, as differentiated from the neighborhood, would comprise two or more neighborhoods separated by open or greenbelt spaces, but connected with secondary streets oriented to elements of vital communal interest — usually to a high school community center and two or more junior high school facilities. Such communities need not be contained within the city limits, but, simply for the easing of traffic pressures, may well be spaced out into the surrounding region as satellite communities of perhaps 30,000 to 40,000 population, with their own industrial–manufacturing complex, and with their own business, shopping, and communal facilities, including schools, playfields, churches, playhouse or theatre, and community hospital.

The central city, with its core, would serve such satellite communities on more of a regional basis, as the dominant center of commerce, finance, government, culture, and higher education. Here would be the federal, state, and regional office centers, the corporation offices, the banking houses, the stock exchange, and the board of trade. Here would be the great churches and universities and the regional hospitals. Here would be the auditorium, stadium, ballpark, library, zoo, aquarium, planetarium, and public gardens. And here would be the restaurants, theatres, symphony, and ballet, and the urban shops, all of which would draw upon and now better serve the region.

Such things of course don't just happen. They must be planned — with such detail and with such breadth of scale as have never before been attempted in the planning of man's environment. In this process, the applied knowledge of all the arts, sciences, and humanities must, and will, be brought to bear.

Will the city reassert itself as a good place to live? It will not, unless there is a decided shift in the thinking of those who would remake it. The popular image of the city as it is now is bad enough — a place of decay, crime, of fouled streets, and of people who are poor or foreign or odd. But what is the image of the city of the future? In the plans for the huge redevelopment projects to come, we are being shown a new image of the city — and it is sterile and lifeless. Gone are the dirt and noise — and the variety and the excitement and the spirit. That it is an ideal makes it all the worse; these bleak new Utopias are not bleak because they have to be; they are the concrete manifestation — and how literally — of a deep and at times arrogant, misunderstanding of the function of the city.

WILLIAM H. WHYTE, JR.

The unit of measurement for space in urban society is the individual . . .

ARTHUR B. GALLION

The latent longing of man for a life in mutual appreciation should be brought to blossom and fruit by education; but the external conditions needed for its fulfillment must also be created. The architects must be given the task to build for human contact, to build an environment which invites meetings and centers which give these meetings meaning and render them productive.

E. A. GUTKIND

The first step in adequate planning is to make a fresh canvass of human ideals and human purposes.

LEWIS MUMFORD

The mistakes of planning are found in the overcautious concepts — not the bold.

PAUL SCHWEIKHER

Make no little plans; they have no magic to stir men's blood, and probably themselves will not be realized; make big plans, aim high in hope and work, remembering that a noble logical diagram, once recorded, will never die, but long after we are gone will be a living thing, asserting itself with ever growing insistency.

DANIEL BURNHAM

The first stage toward doing something is to know what is wrong.

IAN NAIRN

Any plan is essentially the scheduling of specific means to definite ends . . . Any kind of planning implies conscious purpose . . .

CATHERINE BAUER

Genuine planning is an attempt, not arbitrarily to displace reality, but to clarify it and to grasp firmly all the elements necessary to bring the geographic and economic facts in harmony with human purpose.

LEWIS MUMFORD

We are gradually coming to the realization that the contemporary forces which have led to the development of social techniques express the desire of the human mind to control, not merely its environment, but also, through the latter, itself.

KARL MANNHEIM

Planning is that conceiving faculty which must recommend ways and means of transmuting the possibilities and impossibilities of today into the realities of tomorrow.

ELIEL SAARINEN

Designing is an intricate task. It is the integration of technological, social and economic requirements, biological necessities, and the psychophysical effects of materials, shape, color, volume, and space: thinking in relationships.

MOHOLY-NAGY

For planning of any sort our knowledge must go beyond the state of affairs that actually prevails. To plan we must know what has gone on in the past and what is coming in the future. This is not an invitation to prophecy but a demand for a universal outlook upon the world.

SEIGFRIED GIEDION

We have begun to understand that designing our physical environment does not mean to apply a fixed set of esthetics, but embodies rather a continuous inner growth, a conviction which recreates truth continually in the service of mankind.

. . .

Good planning I conceive to be both a science and an art. As a science, it analyzes human relationships; as an art, it coordinates human activities into a cultural synthesis.

WALTER GROPIUS

To build intelligently today is to lay the foundations for a new civilization.

LEWIS MUMFORD

The family In one of our larger American cities the average family, according to recent census figures, numbers 3.6 persons. Each family yields for public schools (parochial schools not included) approximately 0.1 high school, 0.125 junior high, and 0.3 elementary school student.

In our democratic society, as in the highest cultures of the past, the family is the smallest and yet most significant social unit.

The organization of the region

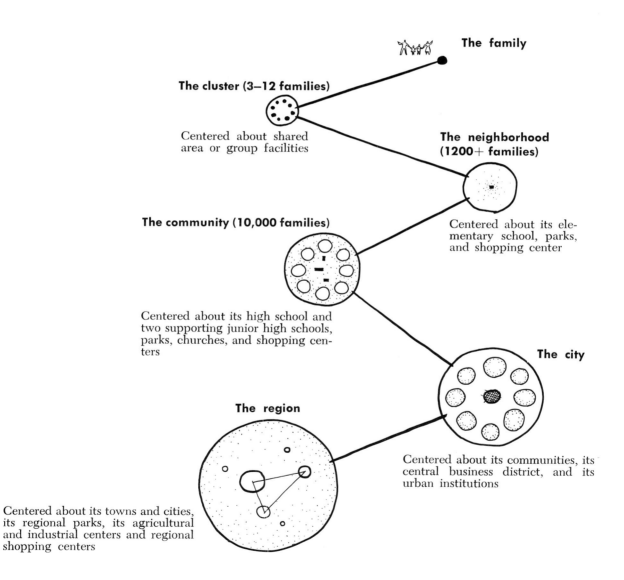

The family

The cluster (3–12 families)
Centered about shared area or group facilities

The neighborhood (1200+ families)
Centered about its elementary school, parks, and shopping center

The community (10,000 families)
Centered about its high school and two supporting junior high schools, parks, churches, and shopping centers

The city
Centered about its communities, its central business district, and its urban institutions

The region
Centered about its towns and cities, its regional parks, its agricultural and industrial centers and regional shopping centers

Five cul-de-sac arrangements that provide a "cluster" of family dwellings

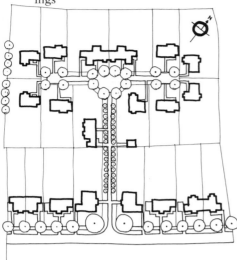

Welwyn Garden City

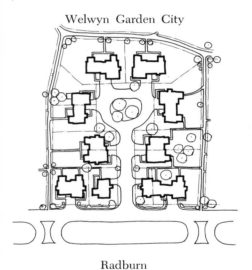

Radburn

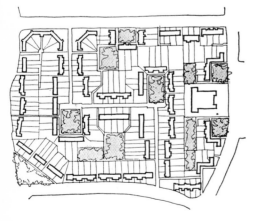

Letchworth

204

Desirable environmental features for the family include:

Access by automobile to within 200 ft. maximum of the front door.
Off-street parking space.
Access by pedestrian walk.
Protection from traffic, danger, friction, and other nuisances.
Fresh air and sunshine.
Privacy for the nurture of body, mind, and spirit.
Outdoor recreation space, preferably enclosed for relaxing, gardening, dining, or play.
Integration of indoor and outdoor living spaces.
Contact with nature — soil, plants, water, rocks, trees — even mosses and lichens.

The cluster   Three to twelve families constitute the optimum interfamily social group. In such a complex, "kaffee-klatches," parties, children's play and games, and "get-togetherness" on a first name basis are natural and spontaneous.

Ideally, the families in such a cluster would have a unity of group goals and standards, but a diversity of individual status and interests.

If more than twelve families are grouped together planwise, they automatically segregate into smaller social units or "clusters."

Desirable environmental features for the cluster are:

Group off-street parking (less penetration of street curbs, less backing, less danger).
Freedom from traffic friction.
Pedestrian interaccess.
Focal area or feature — court, sitting area, children's sandbox, or play equipment.
Design-plan entity.
Harmonious site and architectural character.
Physical separation from adjacent cluster.

The neighborhood   Arthur Gallion has said:

"The neighborhood unit is not some sociological phenomenon; it embraces no particular theories of social science. It is simply a physical environment in which a mother knows that her child will have no traffic streets to cross on his way to school, a school which is an easy walking distance from the home. It is an environment in which the housewife may have an easy walk to the shopping center where she may obtain the daily household goods, and the man of the house may find convenient transportation to and from his work."[*]

The neighborhood should be small enough to encourage participation of all families in common neighborhood concerns, and large enough to support the smallest educational unit — the elementary school with its kindergarten. The optimum neighborhood size will usually be that which will support the optimum elementary school.

[*] From *The Urban Pattern*.

Fort Detrich

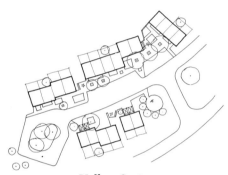

Valley Springs

*Any architect worth his salt
knows that a building is not
designed by putting together
a series of rooms. Any building
that is good has an underlying
design concept that binds all the
parts together into a whole.
Without this it is not architecture. Nor does a designed
neighborhood consist of a series
of "projects" that are strung together. There must be an
underlying design plan that
binds together the pieces and
makes the neighborhood an
entity.*

EDMUND N. BACON

About 1,200 families in the average neighborhood multiplied by 3.6 yields a population of 4,320, of which there are approximately 360 kindergarten and elementary school pupils, requiring 10 to 12 classrooms plus neighborhood facilities.

Desirable environmental features of the neighborhood include:

A neighborhood focal point — usually the elementary school with its recreation area (ideally centered in a park with not more than a half-mile walk through the park to the kindergarten or the elementary school without crossing traffic).

Peripheral access road with connections to a free-flowing parkway.

Elimination of rectangular residential islands surrounded by concrete rivers, with their streaming traffic.

Safe residential streets laid out in short loops and culs-de-sac.

Every home abutting planned park and recreation spaces.

Neighborhood facilities — auditorium, parklets, parks and recreation courts including tot lots, baseball and basketball, "golden age" areas, and nationality games such as boccie and bowling on the green.

A neighborhood shopping center.

Ideally, the neighborhood might be composed of planned tracts of 5–25 acres, grouped around a lobe or lobes of semiprivate park that opens into the larger neighborhood-community park and public school system. Each such tract, developed as an entity, with private or public funds, would be freed of all individual lot restrictions, and would be subject to a review by the public planning agencies based on performance only. Land use patterns and densities, as approved, would then be fixed by contract between owner and municipality.

The community   The size of a community is determined by its greatest need, which is generally the high school and supporting junior high schools.

Approximately 10,000 families in the community multiplied by 3.6 yields a population of 36,000, and approximately 1,000 students for one senior high, plus 625 students each for two junior high schools. (These approximate high school and junior high school enrollments are generally conceded to produce a workable balance of economic and teaching factors).

The theoretically ideal community would be composed of eight to ten neighborhood units, connected by parkway and over-or-underpass to community churches, shopping center, and schools.

A community usually can and should support:

A high school
Two junior high schools
A community hospital
A library
A church or churches
A sportsfield
A community shopping center
A light craft airport–heliport
Light industrial or manufacturing centers.

205

One of the better-planned American neighborhoods of the twentieth century

The physical plan can seldom, if ever, create a "neighborhood" except in the most abstract use of the word. It can, however, very materially assist other forces in fostering a true neighborhood feeling.

HENRY S. CHURCHILL

Every community needs a symbol of its existence. Much of modern community frustration has come into being because a symbol of the visual meaning for its life is missing. Because no symbol is found, there is no center on which to focus life.

RALPH WALKER

206

Since physical forms and patterns can only express and accommodate a prescribed way of life, better communities will follow only when new and better concepts of community life and land ownership and use are evolved. The mark of a good community is an evident sense of community enterprise.

Desirable environmental features of the community include:

A natural periphery demarked by highway, greenbelt, river, ridge, cliff, ravine, or other physical barrier.

Community identity — orientation to a symbol, such as a high school, factory, church, shopping center, country club, or park — that gives it focus and meaning.

Provision for outdoor communal activities in clean, sunlit, and shaded spaces uninterrupted by traffic flow.

Minimum friction and danger in use of the automobile, coupled with maximum convenience, free-flowing trafficways with no grade crossings.

Flexibility in forms and patterns to enable adjustment to new technological and socio-politico-economic development.

Community land reservoirs zoned for temporary agricultural, park, or other use, but to be withdrawn for development as needed.

Carl Koch has made this comment on the community: "There is a Chinese proverb that says, in effect, that by conforming to outward convention, we earn the right to be ourselves inwardly. The most beautiful places to live follow this principle — the old New England town or Louisburg Square in Boston are good examples. In contrast, a walk down the street of most of our subdivisions shows us that merely changing exterior details — the pitch of a roof, the color of the shingles, a porch here, an extra dormer there; all done to conceal a plan identical to the house next door — achieves only the monotony and standardized look that the designer has been at such pains to hide. Both Louisburg Square and the old New England village are in a sense made up of similar but homogeneous elements so assembled as to provide a unique and unified whole. In the proper context repetition of elements does not make for monotony. Nature isn't afraid of standardization. A flock of flying birds, each almost identical, is a thrilling sight. A tree covered with thousands of almost identical leaves is a thing of beauty.

"What makes the old New England town so attractive, and also satisfies us as we walk through Louisburg Square, is the outward conformity of the buildings to each other and the way they relate to each other to form the frame or walls of a common whole. The buildings, though well designed as units, are all part of a larger unified design. The community is the unit of design, not the individual house."

The city The form of a city will be, at best, the studied expression of its varied functions organized harmoniously in time, in nature, and in space. A good city plan must express our times, our technology, and our ideals. It must be an adaptable organic unity, with its roots in the past and its orientation to the future.

A city is a large and densely populated center of economic, social, and political activity, having a relatively fixed geographic position and specific governmental powers granted to it in charter form by the state. It is the center of an urban culture.

Our new cities will be only as good as enlightened public opinion permits or demands them to be. This enlightenment and persuasion toward progress is a vital and often neglected phase of every planning effort.

The city core should be as compact as possible and should function as the nerve center of the city and its region. The city plan is best conceived in terms of systems, interlaced and interlocking, each system designed for optimum performance, and all systems organized for optimum relationships.

Here are the governmental and business centers, offices, department stores, theatres, the opera, the symphony, the museums, and cathedrals. Many large areas of high population density cannot in the fullest sense be called cities, because they lack many of the important urban characteristics.

The city must be a growing, functioning organism, requiring and capable of providing light, air, water, food, circulation, elimination of waste, forming, and regeneration — or else it will decay and die. It must have a workable social, economic, and political structure, expressed and accommodated in flexible, three-dimensional form.

Desirable environmental features of the city include:

All good planning must begin with a survey of actual resources: the landscape, the people, the work-a-day activities in a community. Good planning does not begin with an abstract and arbitrary scheme that it seeks to impose on a community; it begins with a knowledge of existing conditions and opportunities.

. . .

The final test of an economic system is not the tons of iron, the tanks of oil, or the miles of textiles it produces: The final test lies in its ultimate products — the sort of men and women it nurtures and the order and beauty and sanity of their communities.

LEWIS MUMFORD

A city plan is the expression of the collective purpose of the people who live in it, or it is nothing.

HENRY S. CHURCHILL

207

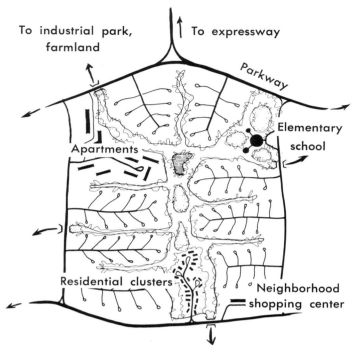

Neighborhood Plan Diagram number one: approximately 1200 families (1/3 in multifamily).

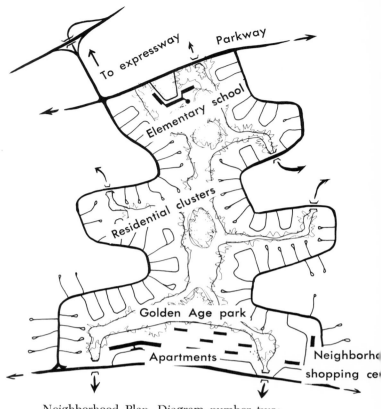

Neighborhood Plan Diagram number two: approximately 1200 families (1/3 in multifamily).

The first urban function and the efficient cause of the way of life, which is the city's purpose, is livelihood. Therefore, in any city plan the primary point is the selection of the industries. In general, every external activity is planned on the principle of efficiency, the efficiency of means to achieve ends, where means are the more external arrangements and ends are the more internal satisfactions.

PERCIVAL AND PAUL GOODMAN

The most of those high qualities that civilization has attributed to urbanity; the least of those evils that the ages have condemned

Order, efficiency, beauty, stimulation, delight, and a milieu conducive to the development of the full human powers

Significant art forms — architecture, bridges, parks, squares, sculpture, fountains

A cohesive and comprehensible city diagram

Pedestrian ways and places and spaces, and a new pedestrian scale

Tight pedestrian cores or islands, without interior automobile circulation, but surrounded with parking towers and penetrated by rapid transit

Organized sequences and aggregations of spaces in which people may live, work, and play

An expression of the city dweller's gregarious nature — congregating places where people can meet to exchange goods, services, and ideas, such communal open spaces as the marketplace, the shopping mall, the park, the square, the plaza, and the promenade

Classification of traffic with traffic and parking accommodated but made incidental to the higher aspects of city life

Differentiated vehicular trafficways and areas

Trafficways designed as trafficways, and not as building frontage

An order of movement and an order of nonmovement

Planned sequences of forms and spaces

Organic and coordinated systems of traffic, transit, transportation, utilities, parks, structures, and open spaces

A comprehensive organic order — an order of dispersion rather than

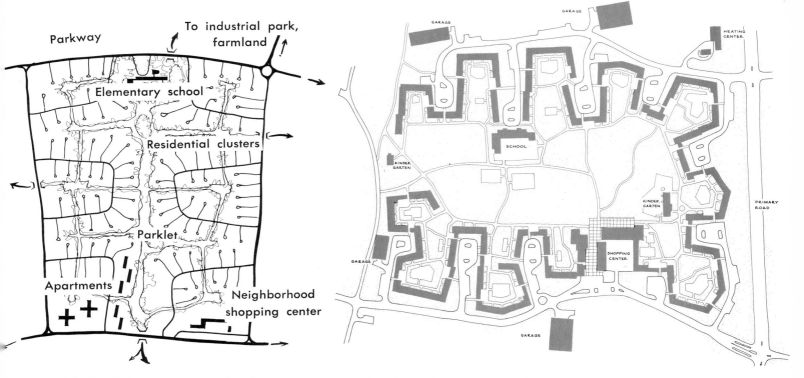

Neighborhood Plan Diagram number three: approximately 1200 families (1/3 in multifamily).

A neighborhood of apartment dwellings, each related to an exterior approach and an interior social court—and to a large central park area. The relatively high density of the apartment groups yields large open space where it counts.

The city in its complete sense, then, is a geographic plexus, an economic organization, an institutional process, a theatre of social action — and an esthetic symbol of collective unity. On the one hand it is a physical frame for the commonplace domestic and economic activities; on the other, it is a consciously dramatic setting for the more significant actions and the more sublimated urges of human culture.

LEWIS MUMFORD

isolation — with planned relationships and unities, as well as planned units

Provision for response to urban stimuli without friction and with pleasure

Opportunities for privacy. Maximum opportunities for social intercourse

A highly developed rapport with nature's forms, forces, and features

Beauty of place and space and form

A rich and satisfying esthetic unity

Human scale, so that man feels himself in harmony with, and in proportion to, that which he sees and hears and feels — a sense of being pleasantly related to his city, and thus to his world

Easy and pleasant transition between urban and regional areas

Individual freedom within a cohesive social organization

A salutary environment.

The region   A region is a large and generally unified, but loosely defined, geographical area that provides the supporting base for one or more centers of population concentration. To simplify the complex problems of regional planning almost to the point of naivety, we might propose that each region should be analyzed, planned, and zoned for its highest and best use in relation to its projected population and inherent resources. Planning on a regional basis, whether in terms of geographic, political, social, or economic regions, provides a more comprehensive and effective frame of reference than the consideration of metropolitan areas alone.

209

Regional planning is the conscious direction and collective integration of all those activities which rest upon the use of earth as site, as resource, as structure, as theatre.

LEWIS MUMFORD

The new regional pattern will be determined by the character of the landscape: its geographical and topographical features, its natural resources, by the use of land, the methods of agriculture and industry, their decentralization and integration; and by human activities, individual and social in all their diversity.

L. HILBERSEIMER

There will be in the future no roads or tracks which must be crossed at grade. Transportation and transit lines will be depressed or buried as free-flowing tubes — or lifted up above the earth that the goods or traffic they carry may glide along swiftly, safely, almost without friction.

PHILIP DOUGLAS SIMONDS

Most evidence points toward the need for a regional form of government that would eliminate the complex and overlapping system of borough, township, county, town, and city governments competing for revenue and power. The proposed new regional governments would tax the entire regional base for the good of the total region.

Desirable environmental features of the region include:

Land use-areas resembling static islands

Circulation channels that are fluid

Wide, free, uninterrupted open spaces — agricultural, recreational, or conservancy districts in the midst of which will be developed the organic "live–work–trade–grow" centers interconnected and nourished as living tissue by a network of veins and arteries providing flow of traffic and goods

Neighborhoods, communities, and cities, and their supporting agricultural, industrial, and commercial complexes, bound together by a free-flowing system of classified and separated traffic routes

For economy and appearance, all "use-forms" and "use-areas" developed in harmony with topographical and ecological patterns.

Traffic patterns and land use-areas   Land use-areas are static. Trafficways are fluid, and should feed and drain these areas and provide them with the maximum opportunities for easy interconnection.

Land use-areas and the trafficways that serve them must be considered simultaneously. The land use-areas defined by the traffic diagram must be of the size and the shape best suited to their optimum use. In the planning of land use-areas, the lines of traffic-flow that they describe and develop must also be considered.

In the interest of flexibility, (because land planning concepts have a way of changing radically and rapidly) it would seem best to serve the specific use-areas of a region with many relatively minor, but free-flowing, trafficways, rather than to carve them up with great, broad traffic swaths. Whenever we plan the feeder routes, expressways, or their termini (and their absorptive capacity) we must consider all at once. A great majority of our traffic problems result from the planning of our freeways and expressways without a full consideration of their function or their impacts.

No study of a proposed trafficway is complete without a study of its effect on the areas it connects and through which it passes.

A superior expressway should not be planned *to* an area, but rather *past* an area, with several opportunities to cut off *toward* the area.

The outer belts should be considered as *circulation* belts, to provide rapid lateral movement. They are classifiers, giving choice of routes to districts or centers. Their sections and interchanges should express rapid and free traffic flow.

The inner ring should be developed as an *interceptor*, to receive and distribute traffic, or to divert it.

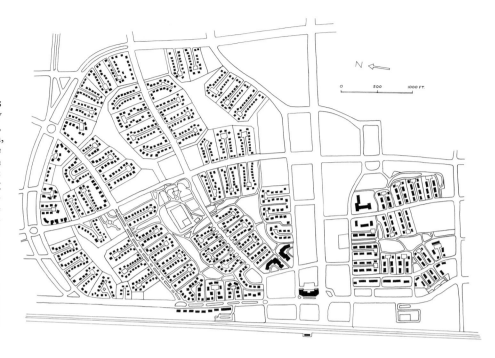

Radburn, New Jersey, 1928. This revolutionary concept of community living was devised by its planners, Henry Wright and Clarence Stein, as an answer to living with the automobile. Homes were grouped in superblocks with automobile access from cul-de-sac streets, precluding high-speed through traffic. Pedestrian walkways, free of automobile crossings, provided access to large central park areas in which, and around which, were grouped the community social, recreational, and shopping centers.

In this plan concept were sown the seeds of ideas that have sprouted in most of the superior neighborhood and community plans of succeeding years.

Harlow, England, 1948. This New Town was so planned as to preserve large areas of the natural landscape as buffers between the various components of the community. Basis of organization was a comparatively small neighborhood unit of 150–400 dwellings, which in the opinion of Frederick Gibberd, the planner, "makes possible more intimate and friendly social groupings than are provided in a neighborhood based on school sizes."

With this latter premise the author does not agree—holding that the elementary school with its recreational and social facilities is the logical neighborhood center, provided that the neighborhood plan arrangement permits of more intimate social clusters of from three to twelve families grouped about their common space.

211

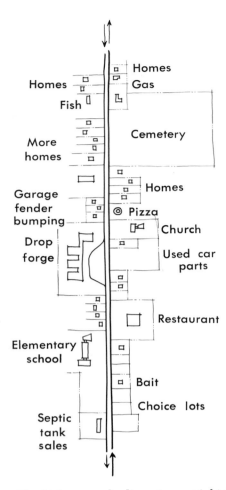

The highway and adjacent uses. A highway most anywhere in most any state: 50 driveway entrances per mile; unplanned, unzoned, unintelligent—a study in friction, confusion, inefficiency, and chaos.

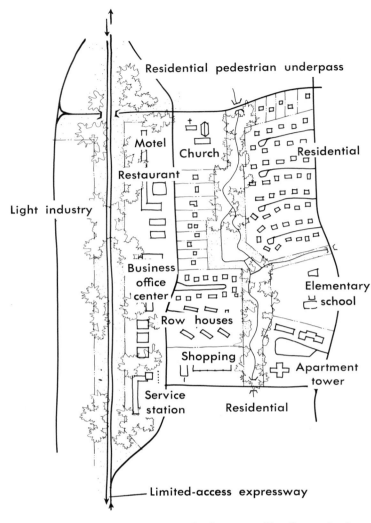

Planned, zoned, intelligent; highway traffic flows freely; functions are grouped; homes orient to park; school, church, and shopping areas have access.

Minimum areas of open space The following are recommended as the minimum usable outdoor areas to be considered in planning, for the social units indicated:

Family (3.6 persons average)

For the single family, duplex, or rowhouse — 300 sq. ft. minimum of usable free space on grade, enclosed or semi-enclosed, and exclusive of parking. For walk-up or highrise units — 100 sq. ft.

Cluster (3 to 12 families, 11–43 persons

Two hundred sq. ft. per dwelling unit of additional group space for paving, benches, trees, sculpture, fountain, shrubs, flowers, lawn, or play equipment.

To see the interdependence of city and country, to realize that the growth and concentration of one is associated with the depletion and impoverishment of the other, to appreciate that there is a just and a harmonious balance between the two – this capacity we have lacked. Before we can build well in any scale we shall, it seems to me, have to develop an art of regional planning, an art which will relate city and countryside in a new pattern from that which was the blind creation of the industrial and territorial pioneer. Instead of regarding the countryside as so much grist doomed to go eventually into the metropolitan mill, we must plan to preserve and develop all our natural resources to the limit.

LEWIS MUMFORD

We spend more and more hundreds of millions of dollars to build more and more super highways to more and more remote distances so that more and more people may drive more and more rapidly until they come to the place where they must stop and wait and wait longer and longer — to get into the district where it is harder and harder and harder to move around at all!

FREDERICK BIGGER

The city in the region

Neighborhood (1,200 families, 4,320 persons)

Community (10,000 families, 36,000 persons)

City

Region

Three acres minimum per 1,000 population reserved for school playgrounds, recreation areas, and parks. This is exclusive of vehicular parkways.

Five acres minimum net public space reserved per 1,000 population for school play grounds, athletic fields, and parks. This includes the neighborhood public space but excludes street and highway rights of way and parkways.

Ten per cent minimum of its total area in public open places, parks, and playgrounds. This includes the public space of the communities but excludes streets and highway rights of way and parkways. This should yield approximately ten acres for every 1,000 of population.

Twenty acres total minimum per 1,000 population reserved for public open places, parks, playgrounds, and recreation areas, including hunting lands, fishing waters, and wildlife preserves. This includes the public open space of the communities, towns, and cities *and* parkway rights of way when, and only when, the parkways are widened to include the natural topographical features of the landscape through which they pass.

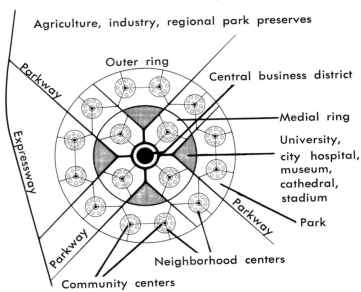

Agriculture, industry, regional park preserves

Outer ring

Parkway

Expressway

Central business district

Medial ring

University, city hospital, museum, cathedral, stadium

Park

Parkway

Parkway

Neighborhood centers

Community centers

213

The sacred temples were set high upon the rock platform to command the city and to inspire its citizens.

ENVIRONMENTAL PLANNING

The essential planning quality of a people or culture, and sometimes even their simplest plans, may often be comprehended only through an understanding of their underlying philosophic orientation.

This may be seen in simple terms in the culture of the Athenians. Philosophically the Greeks understood and believed in the truth of utility and the beauty of function (which, from a close look at our cities, homes, automobiles, furniture, hats, and other artifacts, most present-day Americans do not). And so, for their day-to-day living, they planned their streets, spaces, and structures in harmony with topography, for ease and directness of function, and for pleasurable convenience. Each form, each space, and each structure was planned to express and accommodate its use, and to best relate to adjacent forms and spaces and to the embracing landscape.

Philosophic orientation   Philosophically, the Greeks believed that the family lay at the inward center of their world; and so, with absolute logic, their homes were oriented inward. From the outside, their homes were unostentatious. The entrance, often no more than a simple

214

aperture in the wall that faced the winding street, opened into a private world of serenity and delight — into private spaces where living, conversing, and learning were cultivated as high arts.

Philosophically, the Greeks conceived of their civic buildings and temples in different terms. They were symbols of all that was high and noble, and, as symbols, were set back or held up to be seen in the round. They were planned to embody and connote the ideal and the highest degree of order. They were consciously created focal points to which a whole city was tacitly oriented. To understand the ancient Greek cities, these things must be understood.

Philosophically, the Egyptian saw life as a march down a priestly and unswerving path, to come at last before the judges of the dead. This "destiny idea" controlled his thinking, his art, and even the plan layout of his home. His whole existence was that of compulsive movement in one fixed line — the line of the processional, along which were spaced out vast masonry planes and columns and arches in rhythmic sequence and grandeur. His one aim was to extend himself as far as possible in depth along this line. To understand the Egyptian and his cities, palaces, temples, and tombs, we must understand this central concept that runs through the whole form language of his culture. In contrasting Egyptian with Chinese culture, Oswald Spengler says of the Egyptian:

"But whereas the Egyptian treads to the end a way that is prescribed for him with an inexorable necessity, the Chinaman *wanders* through his world; consequently, he is conducted to his god or his ancestral tomb, not by ravines of stone, between faultless smooth walls, but by friendly Nature herself. Nowhere else has the *landscape* become so genuinely the material of the architecture."

And of the Chinese: "The temple is not a self-contained building but a layout, in which hills, water, trees, flowers, and stones in definite forms and dispositions are just as important as gates, walls, bridges and houses. This culture is the only one in which the art of gardening is a grand religious art. There are gardens that are reflections of particular Buddhist sects. It is the architecture of the landscape, and only that which explains the architecture of the buildings . . ."*

To understand our own American planning we must understand that, although the *way* was the prime symbol of the Egyptian, the *body* or *form* that of the classical age, and *man-nature* that of the Orient, we inherit from northern Europe, as the prime symbol of our culture, the notion of *endless space*. Planned in this endless space, embracing it, and interrelated with it, we must contrive our form world.

We must understand, too, that at the moment our society is hellbent on an exuberant experimental binge. We are slightly tipsy with our heady new technology. We are reappraising and experimenting with all facets of our life. We are young and eager, and we are fired with the pioneering spirit. If we seem to others (and sometimes even to ourselves) to have much energy and action but little direction, it is perhaps that, as yet, we have no cohesive, directional philosophy of our own to serve us as a guide.

215

* *Decline of the West.*

At the dawn of civilization, say 5,000 years ago, the population of the world cannot have numbered much more than 20 million. Today the yearly increase in world population is nearly twice this amount. Self-multiplying, like money at compound interest, world population reached the billion mark in the 1850's and the 2 billion mark in the 1920's. Even more disquieting the rate of increase has also been steadily increasing. At the present rate, today's population will double itself in less than 50 years.

JULIAN HUXLEY

Any consideration of the future of open space, such as exists between our urban centers, requires a thoughtful appraisal of one of our most voracious consumers of land: housing. Man's preference in housing, especially in urban fringe areas, results in the sprawl of single detached units in an awesome continuum across the country-side.
What is the origin of the desire for this type of shelter expression — this compulsion to flee the city and to build cube on cube across the open land? Is it a desire for tax relief? Vested equity? Breathing space? Contact with the land? Or the poetics of "Home Sweet Home"? Regardless, is the solution largely that of better design within the acceptance of this preference? Or change from separated horizontal forms to unified collective density patterns? Perhaps as space between units decreases, space between our urban centers may be preserved, or may increase.

WALTER D. HARRIS

216

A new planning order   Our country has passed, or perhaps is still passing, through a pioneering stage. Until but very recently, one of our rugged pioneering freedoms has been man's freedom to do with his land whatever, yes, just about *whatever* he wanted to do. Under the proud banner of this dubious right, we have voraciously exploited our natural resources and ruthlessly despoiled our land.

We have reduced millions upon millions of acres of forested watershed to eroded gullies and ruin. We have gouged enormous tracts of fertile land into barren wastes in our strip-mining operations. We have watched billions of cubic yards of rich topsoil wash out, irretrievably, into the sea. We have polluted our streams and rivers with sewage and industrial waste. We have plundered and ravished our natural environment to a degree unprecedented in any other civilization of the present or the past. We have erred, and grievously. Now, rather late, but at last, we have come to see the error of our ways.

In seeking a better way, our present planning philosophy has been mainly one of checking and prohibition. It has been, to a large degree, a negative philosophy. No doubt this has been necessary and helpful, but it is not enough. It is high time now, that we reappraise our whole approach to the physical planning process, so that we may devise a *positive* planning approach more in keeping with our era of fantastically stepped-up scientific discovery and population explosion.

Population growth, increasing densities, and relentless expansion are inevitable. Our planning concentrations are bound to further penetrate and infiltrate our remaining areas of natural landscape. This is a normal and, in many ways, desirable process. But in the name of all reason, we must see that this process is wisely guided and controlled. Our efforts as physical planners in relation to this expansion would seem to be threefold.

First, we must seek to *preserve* intact such significant natural areas and features as are necessary to protect our watersheds and maintain our water table; to conserve our forests and mineral reserves; to check erosion; to stabilize and ameliorate our climate; to provide sufficient land reserves for recreation and for wildlife sanctuary; and to preserve areas of notable natural landscape interest or value. Such areas might best be purchased and administered by federal, state, or local park or conservancy commissions.

Secondly, we must ensure the logical *development* of the existing landscape. Such thinking points to a national resource planning authority. Such an authority would be empowered to explore and determine, on a broad scale, the best conceivable use of all land areas and natural resources; to conserve through purchase those that should be so preserved; to encourage, through zoning legislation and federal aid, the best and proper development of these and all remaining areas for the long range good of the nation; to constantly reassess and keep flexible its program and master plans; and to engage for this work the best of the trained physical planners, geographers, geologists, biologists, sociologists, and other related scientists. These people might well be elected to this post of high honor by their respective professional groups.

Thirdly, we must consciously and astutely *continue the evolution* toward a new system of physical order. This order may be one of new ideals or new orientation. It may be one of improved relationships, as man to traffic, man to city, man to man. It may be an order that will integrate our patterns of living, harmoniously, with the landscape. It may be an order of new landscape concepts, forms, and diagrams. It may be an order of new landscape continuity — place to place and space to space.

A need for the visionary   The world is fast changing and the tempo of this change is ever accelerating. We struggle to keep abreast of the times. Experience has taught us that we can no longer base our long-range planning on simple projection. New concepts burst upon us, disrupting all established planning criteria. Ideas that seemed implausible yesterday are accepted and applied today, and tomorrow will be already outmoded. As physical planners looking to and arranging the very framework for the future, we must be sensitive to the trends and alert to the signs that presage them. We must accept the fact that many revolutionary ideas, whether we find them personally revolting or appealing, *may* become realities. Such ideas include:

Interplanetary travel
The colonization of outer space
Antigravitational devices
Selective, instantaneous, and unlimited audio-visual communication
New sources and applications of vast power
The tapping of the energies of the tides, the sun, and the earth's molten core
Weather control
Hydroponic culture of food and raw materials
Large-scale mining and harvesting of the sea
Compulsory birth control
Euthanasia
Selective breeding of humans through artificial insemination
Hybridization of humans, as by nuclear radiation of chromosomes
Rapid and marked changes in the human physique and mind
Complete racial integration
Planned ascendance of "advanced types"
The mastery of our technology
Transportation and transit by suction tubes, rockets, and beamed capsules
Disappearance of the automobile and, with it, highways and streets, and thus the emergence of new patterns for living and construction
Low cost, flexible, mobile shelters — blown, woven, or fabricated to size
New statutory provisions for the constant repair, redevelopment, and renewal of the decaying cells of our urban, suburban, and rural bodies
Stringent national resource planning
Leaseholding and controlled use of all property and resources

Man is a sun-roused dreamer, en route to tomorrow, a place he spins out of himself across the emptiness of time from gossamers of his imaginings.

JOHN LEAR

World government, world courts, world taxes, world army, and world
 police force

Radically new political, social, and economic structuring

Revolt against the increasing demands for conformity, and a return to
 individualism

As an alternative, the complete subjugation of the individual to his
 society

Little time spent in the production of *goods;* much time spent in
 the production of *ideas*

A highly developed science of environmental planning

Means of coordinating and bringing to concerted focus on our planning problems the experience and accreting knowledge in all areas
 of our culture

Greater insight into, and knowledge of, the forces that govern the
 cosmos and the development of a life attuned to this power.

In our planning for a better environment, and thus for an ever-
improving way of life, we might well consider these sage bits of advice
gleaned from the writings of Dr. Walter Gropius, the distinguished
architect:

"Discriminate between the essential and the incidental."
"Search for that which unites us rather than divides us."
"Seek always unity in diversity."
"And never forget that beauty is a basic requirement of life."

A planning concept   It is time now that we mature — slowly, if it
must be — to a higher concept of planning that will help us to better
realize to the fullest our human potential, and to seek and find for
man a more keen and perfect relationship with his living, circumam-
bient universe.

Such a new concept will evince a greater respect for man, and will
seek a deeper insight into his true nature, his requirements, and his
latent powers. It will seek, perhaps for the first time, to satisfy the
whole needs of man — the needs of his body, mind, and spirit. It will
seek to persuade and develop his inherent drives and creative impulses,
rather than repress them.

Such a new concept will instill in us a deeper respect for nature,
and seek a better understanding of nature's compelling powers. It will
not seek to conquer or imitate nature, but will rather attempt to conserve and conform, stimulate and guide. It will engender in man a
sense of stewardship for the natural landscape and for each feature and
measure of the land.

It will encourage man to relearn the old truths and discover new
truths of nature's law. Man will again, in time, regain the old instincts,
experience again the glowing animal vitality and spiritual vibrancy
that come from a way of living attuned to nature's way. He will find
his own *tao,* or way of life in equilibrium with, in harmony with, nature.

This new concept will teach us again to plan, to integrate, to coordinate our man-made forms with nature's forms, features, and forces.
It will teach us to search out and apply to our planning the lessons
of history. It will teach us to look to the past for ideas and knowledge,

*To understand life, and to
conceive form to express this
life, is the great art of man.
. . . And I have learned to know
that in order to understand both
art and life one must go down
to the source of all things:
to nature.*

.   .   .

*Natures' laws — the laws of
"beauty," if you will — are
fundamental, and cannot be
shaken by mere esthetic con-
ceitedness. These laws might
not be always consciously
apprehended, but subcon-
sciously one is always under
their influence. Moreover, these
laws as they appear in nature's
form-world have been greatly
amplified, insofar as man's consciousness of their existence is
concerned. Because the micro-
scope and the telescope have
opened new vistas into both the
microscopic and macroscopic
realms, the seeing and sensing
man of today has enriched his
understanding of nature's laws
— the laws of organic order —
to a heretofore unforeseen degree. And behind these laws, the
sensing and seeing man discerns
the pulsing rhythm of
eternal life.*

.   .   .

*The more we study nature's
form-world, the more clearly
it becomes evident how rich in
inventiveness, nuances, and
shiftings nature's form-language
is. And the more deeply we
learn to realize, in nature's
realm, expressiveness is "basic."*

.   .   .

*As for the realm of man,
the same is true.*

ELIEL SAARINEN

218

not to copy its outmoded forms. It will encourage us to advance these ideas and this knowledge, stage by stage and hour by hour, evolving always our own expressive forms. Thus we will learn and live and grow — and thrill to the growing process.

Our new concept of planning will look to the future, to guide us into those areas of most promise and most meaning; to help us sense the obstacles and to preclude or overcome them; to teach us to seek always the higher order and more perfect organic development. Because man is the most highly developed living organism we know of, so far, the continuation of this development must surely be our purpose here. Our philosophers confirm this thinking when they tell us that to best fulfill our purpose is our ultimate destiny.

What is the optimum use that man might make of his terrestrial home? What should be the aim of man as the dominant organic type on earth? The most general answer is that he should aim at the maximum realization of possibilities.

JULIAN HUXLEY

EPILOGUE

LOOKING BACK, I feel exceedingly lucky to have been in the Harvard School of Design during 1936–39, in the tumultuous years of "the rebellion." At the time, I admit, I was somewhat puzzled and disappointed at first, for I had come following the bright Beaux Arts star. Its particular brilliance in those times was perhaps like the last blazing of a meteor ending its orbit, for the Beaux Arts system* was soon to wane. But, blazing or waning, it was gone by the time I arrived there.

Dean Joseph Hudnut, one of the first of the architectural educators to read the signs, soon brought to the school three prophetic and vital spirits, Gropius and Breuer, late of Germany's Bauhaus, and Wagner, a city planner from Berlin. They came as evangelists, preaching a strong, new gospel. To the jaded Beaux Arts student architects, wearied of the hymns in praise of Vignolo, beginning to question the very morality of the pilaster applied, and stuffed to their uppers with pagan Acanthus leaves, the words of these new professors were both cathartic and tonic. Their vibrant message with its recurring and hypnotic text from Louis Sullivan, "Form must follow function," was strangely compelling. We began to see the glimmer of a beckoning light.

A fervor almost religious in quality seemed to sweep the school. As if cleansing the temple of idols, Dean Hudnut ordered the Hall of Casts cleared of every vestige of the once sacred columns and pediment. The egg and dart frieze was carted away. The holy Corinthian capital was relegated to the cobwebs and mold of the basement. We half expected some sign of God's wrath. But the wrath did not come, and the enlightenment continued.

As the architects sought a new approach to the design of their structures, the landscape architects sought to escape the rigid plan form of the major and minor axis, which diagram, inherited from the Renaissance, had become the hallmark of all polite landscape planning. Inspired by the fervent efforts of our architectural colleagues, we assiduously sought a new and parallel approach in the field of landscape planning.

Through the resources of Harvard's great library of planning we

The Piazza of San Marco, Venice

---

* A system of architectural and design instruction that held almost complete sway over American schools from the beginning of the century to the early 1940's.

peered into history. We pored over ancient charts and maps and descriptions. We scanned the classic works of Europe and the Orient for guidance. We searched for inspiration in the related fields of painting, sculpture, and even music.

Our motives were good, our direction excellent. But, unknowingly, we had made a fatal error. In searching for a better design approach, we sought only to discover new *forms*. The immediate result was a weird new variety of plan geometry, a startling collection of novel clichés. We based plan diagrams on the sawtooth and the spiral, on stylized organisms such as the leafstalk, the wheat sheaf, and the overlapping scales of sturgeon. We sought geometric plan forms in quartz crystals. We adapted "free" plan forms from bacterial cultures magnified to the thousandth power. We sought to borrow and adapt the plan diagrams of ancient Persian courtyards and early Roman forts.

We soon came to realize that new forms in themselves weren't the answer. A form, we decided wisely, is not the essence of the plan; it is rather the shell or body that takes its shape and substance from the plan function. The nautilus shell, for instance, is, in the abstract, a form of great beauty, but its true intrinsic meaning can be comprehended only in terms of the living nautilus. To adapt the lyric lines of this chambered mollusk to a plan parti came to seem to us as false as the recently highly respectable and generally touted practice of adapting the plan diagram of, say, the Villa Medici of Florence to a Long Island Country Club.

We determined that it was not new or borrowed forms we must seek, but a new philosophy of planning. From such a philosophy, we reasoned, our new plan forms would evolve spontaneously. The quest for a new philosophy is no mean quest. It proved as arduous as had been our quest for new forms. My particular path of endeavor led in a search through history for timeless planning principles. I would sift out the common denominators of all great landscape planning. At last, I felt sure, I was on the right track.

In retrospect, I believe this particular pilgrimage in search of the landscape architectural holy grail was not without its rewards, for along the way I met such stalwarts as Le Notre, Repton, Lao-tse, Kublai Khan, Caesar, and fiery Queen Hatshepsut. Some few of their plan-concepts and principles so eagerly rediscovered (and now set forth in simplest terms in this book) have served, if not in their whole as a planning philosophy, at least as a sound and useful standard of measure and a critical guide.

Like the good Christian who, in his day-by-day living, is confronted with a moral problem and wonders, "What would Christ do if he were here?" I often find myself wondering at some obscure crossroads of planning theory, "What would Repton say to that?" or "Kublai Khan, old master, what would you do with this one?"

But back to our landscape classes and our student revolution. Sure that we had found a better way, we had broken with the axis. According to Japanese mythology, when the sacred golden phoenix dies, a young phoenix rises full blown from its ashes. We had killed the golden phoenix, with some attending ceremony, and confidently expected its young to rise strong-winged from the carnage. We had never checked the mythological timing. But we found that, in our own instance, the process was not immediate.

In lieu of the disavowed symmetry we turned to a studied plan asymmetry. Our landscape planning in those months became a series of graphic debates. Our professors moved among our drafting tables with wagging heads and stares of incredulity. We had scholarly reasons for each line and form. We battled theory to theory and axiom to principle. But, truth to tell, our projects lacked the sound ring of reality and we found little satisfaction in the end result of our efforts.

Upon graduation, after seven years' study in Landscape Architecture, a year of roaming abroad, and with a hard-earned Master's degree, I seemed to share the tacit feeling of my fellows that, while we had learned the working techniques and terms of our trade, the indefinable essence had somehow escaped us. The scope of our profession seemed sometimes as infinite as the best relating of all mankind to nature; sometimes as finite as the shaping of a brass tube to achieve varying spouting effects of water. We still sought the poles to which our profession was oriented. For somehow it seemed basic that we could best do the specific job only if we understood its relationship to the total job we were attempting to do. We sought a revealing comprehension of our purpose. In short, what were we, as landscape architects, really trying to do? But even more particularly, I believe, we sought new terms of expression, a new design idiom.

Like the old lama of Kipling's *Kim*, I set out once again to wander in search of fundamentals, this time with a fellow student.* Our journey took us through Japan, Korea, China, Burma, Bali, India, and up into Tibet. From harbor to palace to pagoda we explored, always attempting to reduce to planning basics the marvelous things we saw.

In the contemplative attitude of Buddhist monks, we would sit for hours absorbed in the qualities of a simple courtyard space and its relationship to a structure. We studied an infinite variety of treatments of water, wood, metal, plant material, sunlight, shadow, and stone. We analyzed the function and plan of gardens, national forests, and parks. We observed people in their movement through spaces, singly, in small groups, and in crowds. We watched them linger, intermingle, scatter, and congregate. We noted and listed the factors that seemed to impel them to movement or affected the line of their course.

We talked with taper-fingered artists, with blunt-thumbed carpenters, with ring-bedecked princes, and with weathered gardeners whose calloused fingers bore the stains and wear of working in the soil. We noted with fascination the relationship of sensitive landscape planning to the arc of the sun, the direction and force of the wind, and topographical forms. We observed the development of river systems and the relation of riverside planning to the river character, its currents, its forests and clearings, and the varying slopes of its banks. We sketched simple village squares, and attempted to reduce to diagram the plan of vast and magnificent cities. We tested each city, street, temple group, and marketplace with a series of searching questions. Why is it good? Where

223

* Lester Collins, later Chairman of Harvard's Department of Landscape Architecture.

The Garden of Ryoan-ji: originally the containing wall was capped with straw thatch—far better in scale and spirit for this garden space of great sublety yet great strength.

does it fail? What was the planner attempting? Did he achieve it? By what means? What can we learn here? Discovering some masterpiece of planning, we sought the root of its greatness. Discovering its overall order, we sought the basis of order. Noting unity in order, we sought the true meaning of unity.

This consuming search for the central theme of all great planning was like that of the old lama in his search for truth. Always we felt its presence in some degree, but always somehow the essence seemed to escape us. What were these planners really trying to do? What was the aim of their planning? What was their planning approach? Finally, wiser, humbled, but still unsatisfied, we returned to America to establish our small offices and be about our work.

Years later, one warm and bright October afternoon I was leaning comfortably in the smooth crotch of a fallen tree, hunting grey and fox squirrel, the timeless sport of the dreamer. My outpost commanded a lazy sunlit hollow of white oak and hemlock trees. The motionless air was soft and lightly fragrant with hayfern. Close by, beyond a clump of dogwood still purple with foliage and laced with scarlet seed pips, I could hear the squirrels searching for acorns in the dry, fallen leaves. An old familiar tingling went through me, a sense of supreme well being, and an indefinable something more.

I half recalled that the same sensation had swept through me years ago, when I had first looked across the city of Peking, one dusky evening, from the drumtower at the north gate. It had come again in Kyoto, when I stood in the Silver Pavilion, overhanging the quiet water of its pine-clouded pond. And again I recalled this same sensation when I had moved along the wooden-slatted promenade above the courtyard garden of Ryoan-ji, with its beautifully spaced stone composition in an abstract panel of raked gravel, simulating the sea.

Now what could it be, I wondered, that was common to these faroff places and the woodlot where I sat? And all at once it came to me!

The soul-stirring secret of Ryoan-ji lay not in its plan, or its forms, or its spaces, but in what one *experienced* there. The idyllic charm of the Silver Pavilion was sensed without consciousness of planned forms or shapes. The pleasurable impact of the place was solely in the response it evoked in man. The most stirring impacts of magnificent Peking came often in those places where no plan was evident and no studied form existed.

What must count then is not primarily the plan approach, the designed shapes, spaces, and forms. What counts is the experience!

The fact of this discovery was for me, in a flash, the key to understanding Corbusier's great power as a planning theorist. For he perhaps of all contemporary planners can, in simplest diagram, most powerfully grip the mind and kindle the imagination. He thinks, I could now see, not primarily in terms of lines and masses, but rather in terms of impacts. He designs and shapes and arranges human experiences. Such planning is not *adapted* from the crystal. It is crystalline. It is not *adapted* from the organism. It is truly organic. To me, this simple revelation was like staring up a shaft of sunlight into the blinding incandescence of pure truth.

With time, this lesson of insight seems increasingly clear. One plans not places, or spaces or things — one plans experiences. The places, spaces, and things take their form from the planned experience.

By this criteria, a highway is not best designed as a strip of pavement of given section, alignment, and grade. A highway is properly conceived as an experience of movement. The successful highway is planned, in this light, to provide for the user a pleasant and convenient passage from point to point through well-modulated spaces, with a maximum of harmonies and a minimum of friction. Many of the serious failures of our American roads, highways, and turnpikes stem from the astounding fact that, in their planning, the actual experience of their use was never even considered.

The best community or city, by this test, is that which provides for its citizens the best environment for the experience of living.

A garden, by this standard, is not at best designed as an exercise in geometric acrobatics; it is not a construction of globes, cubes, prisms, and planes within which are contained the garden elements. In such a geometric framework the essential qualities of stone, water, and plant forms are lost. They become but structural elements. Their prime relationship is not to the observer, but to the geometry of the plan. Final plan forms may be, in some rare cases, severely geometric, but to be valid the form must take its shape from the planned experience, rather than the experience from the preconceived form.

225

A garden, perhaps the highest, most difficult art form, is best conceived as a series of planned relationships of human to human, human to structure, and human to some facet or facets of nature, such as the lichen-encrusted tree bole of an ancient ginkgo tree, a sprightly sun-flecked magnolia clump, a trickle of water, a foaming cascade, a pool, a collection of rare tree peonies, or a New Hampshire upland meadow view.

A *garden* is best conceived as an environment in which human life-patterns may be ideally related to natural or man-made elements within the garden space. In such an ideal garden, the user is seldom conscious of the specific plan forms, but rather of the myriad pleasant relation-ships induced by the planned environment.

A *park* is best conceived as an environment in which human life-patterns may be ideally related to natural or man-made elements within the park confines.

A *city* is best conceived as an environment in which human life-patterns may be ideally related to natural or man-made elements within the city space.

The highest aspects of all cities down through history were not de-rived from their plan geometry. Rather, these aspects resulted from the essential fact that, in their planning and growth, the life functions of the citizens were considered and accommodated. The higher concepts of city life and human relationships were the main concern.

To the Athenian, Athens was infinitely more than a pattern of streets and structures, voids and solids. To the Athenian, Athens was first of all a glorious way of life. What was true of Athens should be no less true, and should, in all conscience, be much more true of our "enlight-ened" planning today.

The design approach then is not essentially a search for form, not primarily an application of principles. The true design approach stems from the realization that a plan has meaning only to man, for whom it is planned, and only to the degree to which it brings facility, accom-modation, and delight to his senses, and inspiration to his mind and to his soul. It is a creation of optimum relationships resulting in a total experience.

Down through the ages, and in all corners of our globe, the highest aspects of man's planning are those that bring him into optimum re-lationship with an object, a force, or a concept. Some of these relation-ships, with examples, are given below:

Man to nature	Japanese countryside; rural Great Britain
Man to the landscape	Gardens of Soochow
Man to the sea	Hiroshima, Inland Sea of Japan
Man to tide	Mont Saint Michel
Man to a harbor	Hong Kong; Buenos Aires
Man to a lake	Vale of Shalimar; Lake Como
Man to a natural waterfall	Kegon Falls at Tyuzenzi
Man to manipulated water	Villa d'Este
Man to architectural water panels	Versailles

A garden is best conceived as an environment.

Man to a tree	California's redwood forest; Maruyama Park, Kyoto
Man to a forest	Kyoto
Man to sun's heat	Alhambra
Man to snow	St. Moritz
Man to wind	Sulus of Borneo; mountain villages of Tibet
Man to mountain	Terraced watergardens of Java
Man to a view	Shugakuin — the Emperor's Summer Palace in Japan
Man to a vista	Summer Palace of Peking
Man to a river valley	Rhine
Man to protective ground forms	U.S. Artillery Manual
Man to canal	Bangkok; Venice; Amsterdam
Man to a marketplace	Darjeeling
Man to a city square	St. Mark's Plaza
Man to urban park	Central Park; Sea Palace Gardens; Tuileries

Man to urban life	Paris; Peking
Man to vehicular traffic	Garden State Parkway
Man to a building	Katsura Detached Palace
Man to articulated spaces	Typical Japanese residence
Man to a building complex	Acropolis; Forbidden city
Man to a garden	Abbot's Garden of Nikko
Man to sculpture	Temple of Athena, Athens
Man to bas-relief	Ankor Wat
Man to a symbol	Tori of Japan as at Itsuku-shima Shrine
Man to Diety	Temple of Karnac; Kamakura Buddha
Man to regal magnificence, pomp, and pageantry	Temple of the Sun, Peking
Man to the infinite	Buddhist Shrine of Shri Pada, Ceylon
Man to the eternal	Rome
Man to ideal concept of land ownership	Stockholm
Man to ideal concept of land development	Kyoto
Man to concept of earthly paradise	Yuan Ming Yuan

On review, it is noted that the majority of these examples are oriental. This will come as no surprise to those who have traveled or studied there. In the Orient, through an unbroken tradition of over four thousand years, the art and science of land planning and space organization has been developed to a degree of power and subtlety seldom realized in Europe or, as yet, in the experimental pioneer planning of America.

We make much of this matter of optimum relationships. What then is an optimum relationship between a man and a given thing? It is a relationship that reveals to man the highest inherent qualities of that which is experienced or perceived.

In the final analysis, in even the most highly developed plan areas or details, one can never plan or control the transient nuances, the happy accidents, the minute variables of anything experienced; for most things sensed are unpredictable, and often hold their very interest and value in this quality of unpredictability. As one watches, for instance, an open fire, he senses the licking flame, the glowing coal, the evanescent ash, the spewing gas, the writhing smoke, the soft splutterings, the sharp crackle, and the dancing lights and shadows. One cannot control these myriad perceptions that, in their composite, produce the total experience. One can only, for a given circumstance or for a given function, plan a pattern of harmonious relationships, plan the optimum framework, plan the maximum opportunity.

The perception of relationships produces an experience. If the relationships are unpleasant, the experience is unpleasant. If the relationships sensed are those of fitness, convenience, and order, the experience is one of pleasure, and the degree of pleasure is dependent on the degree of fitness, convenience, and order.

Fitness implies the use of the right shape, the right size, and the right material. *Convenience* implies facility of movement, lack of friction, comfort, and reward. *Order* implies a logical sequence and a rational arrangement of the parts.

The perception of harmonious relationships, we learn, produces for man an experience of pleasure. It also produces an experience of beauty. What is this elusive and magical quality called beauty? By deduction, it becomes evident that beauty is not in itself a thing primarily planned or planned for. Beauty is a result. It is a phenomenon that occurs at a given moment or place when, and only when, all relationships are harmonious.

Plato has told us that happiness is no more than a matter of harmonious sensed relationships. If this is so, then the end result of intelligent planning should be the perfect relationship of man and his works with his natural environment, and *per se*, the creation of a paradise on earth. Unfortunately, this can never be, for humans are, sadly, human. Moreover, because the very nature of Nature is change, such planning would be a continuing process, without possible completion, without end. And so it must be. But we may learn from history this clear truth — that the completion is not the ultimate goal. The goal for all physical planners is an enlightened planning *process*. Again, for instruction on this point, we may turn to the older, wiser cultures of the Orient which have shown us that, because of the dynamic nature of their philosophies, the Taoist and Zen conceptions of perfection lay more stress upon the process through which perfection is sought than upon perfection itself. The Zen and Taoist art of life lies in a constant and studied readjustment to nature and one's surroundings, the art of self-realization, the art of "being in the world."

Plan not in terms of meaningless pattern or cold form. Plan, rather, a human experience. The living, pulsing, vital experience, if conceived as a diagram of harmonious relationships, will develop its own expressive forms. And the forms evolved will be as organic as the shell of the nautilus; and perhaps, if the plan is successful, it may be as beautiful.

For to live, wholly to live, is the manifest consummation of existence.

LOUIS H. SULLIVAN

ILLUSTRATION CREDITS

All drawings not otherwise credited are the work of the author. Position on page is indicated as follows: T = *top,* B = *bottom,* L = *left,* R = *right,* M = *middle.*

PAGE AND
POSITION

233

QUOTATION SOURCES

Adams, Henry *The Education of Henry Adams.* Houghton Mifflin Co., Boston, 1928

Bacon, Edmund N. *Planning.* The American Society of Planning Officials, Chicago, 1958

Beck, Walter *Painting with Starch.* D. Van Nostrand Co., Inc., Princeton, New Jersey, 1956

Bel Geddes *Magic Motorways.* Random House, Inc., New York, 1940

Benet, Stephen Vincent *Western Star.* Farrar & Rinehart, Inc., New York, 1943

Borissavlievitch, M. *The Golden Number.* Alec Tiranti, London, 1958

Bowie, Henry P. *On the Laws of Japanese Painting.* Dover Publications, Inc., New York

Breuer, Marcel *Sun and Shadow.* Dodd, Mead and Company, New York, 1955

Bronowski, Jacob *Arts and Architecture,* February and December, 1957

Carson, Rachel *The Sea Around Us.* Oxford University Press, New York, 1951

Carver, Norman F., Jr. *Form and Space of Japanese Architecture.* Charles E. Tuttle Company, Rutland, Vermont, 1956

Church, Thomas D. *Gardens Are for People.* Reinhold Publishing Corp., New York, 1955

Churchill, Henry S. *The City Is the People.* Harcourt, Brace and Co., Inc., New York, 1945

Crowe, Sylvia *Tomorrow's Landscape.* Architectural Press, London, 1956

Danby, Hope *The Garden of Perfect Brightness.* Henry Regnery Company, Chicago, 1950

Eckbo, Garrett; Kiley, Daniel Urban; and Rose, James C. "Landscape Design in the Urban Environment," *Architectural Record,* May, 1939

Eckbo, Garrett *Landscape for Living.* F. W. Dodge Corporation, New York, 1950

Gallion, Arthur B. *The Urban Pattern.* D. Van Nostrand Co. Inc., New York, 1949

Gardner, James and Heller, Caroline *Exhibition and Display.* F. W. Dodge Corporation, New York, 1960

Giedion, Siegfried *Space, Time and Architecture.* Harvard University Press, Cambridge, 1941

Goodman, Percival and Paul *Communitas.* University of Chicago Press, Chicago, 1947

Granger, Frank Stephen, translator *Vitruvius on Architecture.* G. P. Putnam and Sons, New York, 1931

Gropius, Walter "The Curse of Conformity" *The Saturday Evening Post,* September 6, 1958 (page this book, 202)

Gropius, Walter *Scope of Total Architecture.* Harper and Brothers, New York, 1955 (page this book, 197)

Greenough, Horatio *Form and Function.* University of California Press, 1947

Gutkind, E. A. *Community and Environment.* Watts and Company, London

Hayakawa, S. I. *Language in Thought and Action.* Harcourt, Brace and Co., Inc., New York, 1939

Hilberseimer, Ludwig K. *The New Regional Pattern.* Paul Theobald Publishing Co., Chicago, 1949

Hubbard, H. V., and Kimball, T. *An Introduction to the Study of Landscape Design.* Macmillan Co., 1917

Huxley, Julian "Are There Too Many of Us?" *Horizon,* September, 1958

235

Jacobs, Jane *The Exploding Metropolis*. Doubleday & Company, Inc. New York, 1958

Kakuzo, Okakura *The Book of Tea*. Charles E. Tuttle Co., Rutland, Vermont, 1958

Kepes, Gyorgy *Language of Vision*. Paul Theobald and Company, Chicago, 1944

Lawrence, D. H. *Etruscan Places*. Secker, London, 1932

Maholy-Nagy, Laszlo *The New Vision*. Wittenborn, Schultz, Inc., New York, 1930

Mai-mai Sze *The Tao of Painting*. The Bollingen Foundation, Inc., New York, 1956

Mannheim, Karl *Man and Society in an Age of Reconstruction*. Harcourt, Brace and Co., Inc., New York, 1940

McHarg, Ian *Landscape Architecture* (a quarterly magazine of A.S.L.A.), January, 1958

Mendelsohn, Eric *Perspecta* (the Yale architectural journal), 1957

Michener, James *Return to Paradise*. Random House, Inc., New York, 1951

Mumford, Lewis *The Culture of Cities*. Harcourt, Brace and Co., Inc., New York, 1938 (pages this book, 202 and 209)

Mumford, Lewis *Faith for Living*. Harcourt, Brace and Co., Inc., New York, 1940 (page this book, 207)

Nairn, Ian *Outrage*. The Architectural Press, London, 1956

Neutra, Richard J. *Survival Through Design*. Oxford University Press, New York, 1954

Newton, Norman T. *An Approach to Design*. Addison-Wesley Press, Inc., Cambridge, 1951

Niemeyer, Oscar, *Modulo*

Rasmussen, Steen *Towns and Buildings*. Harvard University Press, Cambridge, 1951

Read, Sir Herbert *Arts and Architecture*, May, 1954

Reed, Henry H., Jr., *Perspecta* (the Yale architectural journal), 1952

Russell, Bertrand "The Expanding Mental Universe," *The Saturday Evening Post*, July 18, 1959

Saarinen, Eliel *The City, Its Growth, Its Decay, Its Future*. Reinhold Publishing Corp., New York, 1943 (page this book 202)

Saarinen, Eliel *Search for Form*. Reinhold Publishing Corp., New York, 1948 (pages this book 137, 142, 178, 197, and 218)

Santayana, George *The Sense of Beauty*. Dover Publications, Inc., New York, 1955

Sert, Jose Luis and C.I.A.M *Can Our Cities Survive?* Harvard University Press, Cambridge, 1942

Severud, Fred M., "Turtles and Walnuts, Morning Glories and Grass," *Architectural Forum*, September, 1945

Sitte, Camillo *The Art of Building Cities*. Reinhold Publishing Corp., New York, 1945

Spengler, Oswald *Decline of the West*. Alfred A. Knopf, Inc., New York, 1939

Sullivan, Louis H. *Kindergarten Chats*. Wittenborn, Schultz Inc., New York, 1947

Taut, Bruno *Fundamentals of Japanese Architecture*. Kokusai Bunka Shinkokai, Tokyo, 1936

Tunnard, Christopher *Gardens in the Modern Landscape*. Charles Scribner's Sons, New York, 1948

Van Loon, Hendrik *The Story of Mankind*. Boni and Liveright, New York, 1921

White, Stanley *A Primer of Landscape Architecture*. University of Illinois, 1956

Whyte, Lancelot Law "Some Thoughts on the Design of Nature and Their Implication for Education," *Arts and Architecture*, January, 1956

Whyte, William H., Jr. *The Exploding Metropolis*. Doubleday & Company, Inc., New York, 1958

Wittkower, Rudolph *Architectural Principles in the Age of Humanism*. Warburg Institute, University of London, 1949

The World's Great Religions. Time Inc., New York, 1957

Zevi, Bruno *Architecture as Space*. The Horizon Press, Inc., New York, 1957

INDEX

237